Inside the Helmet

Inside the Helmet

Life as a Sunday Afternoon Warrior

Michael Strahan
with Jay Glazer

GOTHAM BOOKS

GOTHAM BOOKS
Published by Penguin Group (USA) Inc.
375 Hudson Street, New York, New York 10014, U.S.A.
Penguin Group (Canada), 90 Eglinton Avenue East, Suite 700, Toronto, Ontario M4P
2Y3, Canada (a division of Pearson Penguin Canada Inc.); Penguin Books Ltd, 80 Strand,
London WC2R 0RL, England; Penguin Ireland, 25 St Stephen's Green, Dublin 2, Ireland
(a division of Penguin Books Ltd); Penguin Group (Australia), 250 Camberwell Road,
Camberwell, Victoria 3124, Australia (a division of Pearson Australia Group Pty Ltd);
Penguin Books India Pvt Ltd, 11 Community Centre, Panchsheel Park, New Delhi – 110
017, India; Penguin Group (NZ), 67 Apollo Drive, Rosedale, North Shore 0632, New
Zealand (a division of Pearson New Zealand Ltd); Penguin Books (South Africa) (Pty)
Ltd, 24 Sturdee Avenue, Rosebank, Johannesburg 2196, South Africa

Penguin Books Ltd, Registered Offices: 80 Strand, London WC2R 0RL, England

Published by Gotham Books, a member of Penguin Group (USA) Inc.

First printing, October 2007
10 9 8 7 6 5 4 3 2 1

Gotham Books and the skyscraper logo are trademarks of Penguin Group (USA) Inc.

LIBRARY OF CONGRESS CATALOGING-IN-PUBLICATION DATA
has been applied for.

ISBN 978-1-592-40298-4

Printed in the United States of America
Set in Melior with Compressor Slab Serif • Designed by Sabrina Bowers

While the author has made every effort to provide accurate telephone numbers and In-
ternet addresses at the time of publication, neither the publisher nor the author as-
sumes any responsibility for errors, or for changes that occur after publication. Further,
the publisher does not have any control over and does not assume any responsibility
for author or third-party Web sites or their content.

For my parents, Gene and Louise Strahan,
and for my children, Tanita, Michael Jr.,
Isabella and Sophia

Contents

Inside the Helmet

CHAPTER ONE

Preparing for Battle

I stand on our sideline, sing a couple of bars of the national anthem, say a prayer to G-d and then scan the Indianapolis Colts sideline for my target—Colts All-World quarterback Peyton Manning. I absolutely and utterly despise playing quarterbacks like Peyton. Hate it. I stand there and stare at the man, the face of the NFL. I'm there for one reason that night. To try to knock the snot out of the face of the NFL.

I showed up to Giants Stadium two and a half hours earlier with thoughts of ruining that man's night. My eyes dart from Manning to the man I'd be facing throughout this battle, Colts right tackle Ryan Diem. The anthem continues and I stand there and eyeball Diem, the man responsible for keeping me from killing Peyton that night, looking to see if he'd sneak a peak at me. If he does, he's done.

I'm staring a hole through Diem to gauge his body language. I'm looking to see if he's nervous, looking to see if he's moving back and forth like he's too loose and confident. I'm looking to pick a visual fight. Come on, look over here. He doesn't. Most of them don't, but when they do, I flash them the gap. Shoot 'em a big ol' smile letting them know I'm about to have the time of my life embarrassing the hell out of them. Don't mistake the smile that I flash as softness because when it comes to my business, I don't take any shit.

The anthem ends and I walk over, grab an ammonia cap (smelling salts) and inhale it all in. That's right, ammonia. I'll inhale the hell out of one or two of these (most of us do) to clear my head and then I'll take my place in the middle of the field.

Between the anthem, the Sunday night crowd and Peyton getting ready to meet me at midfield, I can't take it.

I walk out for the coin toss but I pay little attention to the toss itself. I act like I care, but to be truthful, I don't care about the toss. If I said I cared, that would be a lie. I like to walk out there for the toss because it puts me that much closer to YOUR sideline and brings me closer to the guy I get to torment for the next 180 minutes.

I'm not coming out there to be your friend. I may tell those guys, "Hey, man, have a good game," but I'm trying to find my guy over there and stare him down again. Right here, at the coin toss, is where my personal matchup begins each week—at this point I can't wait for the kick.

How do I explain the feeling of those minutes between the coin toss and the moment the ball was kicked off for what was dubbed the Manning Bowl? What better game than our season opener in 2006 to describe what it's like to be out there at the start of game day.

Silence turns to bedlam, pedal to the metal, zero to 120 in one second flat. Not zero to 60—zero to 120, maybe 150.

Man, we're revving through the red zone. When the ball is kicked and the flashbulbs start popping . . . INSANITY!

If you want to know what it's like the moment before we are about to strap it up, ask a soldier what he feels the moment before he knows gunfire is about to erupt. How do you contain yourself?

The emotion of the opening kick begins to build before the coin toss, well before the kickoff team takes the field. The tension, the excitement, the nerves . . . it all builds to a crescendo.

About ten minutes before the kick, it's silence in our locker room with each man living in his own private world, searching for a welcome distraction. Or fantasizing—playing the game in his mind already—willing how the course of events over the next three hours will go.

Some pace nervously back and forth while others shake out their limbs, barely able to contain their excitement as their music blares from their iPods. Some sit on their stools with eyes closed, trying not to get overexcited, while others go through the final touches of their routine. We all have some routine we go through prior to kickoff each Sunday. Me, I have to take the same exact route in every morning, walk the same path and go to the bathroom at the same exact time.

When I get to the stadium, one of my first routines is an odd one. I actually make a ritual of reading the program while sitting on the can whether I have to use it or not, and I study the head shots of every single member of the opposing team. As I sit in that stall, I burn a hole through their roster, especially my personal opponent. I try to stare into his eyes as if I can glean some sort of late-breaking information. I know it makes absolutely no sense whatsoever, but it's what I've done for the last decade. Who am I to mess with ritual? Rituals lead to confidence, confidence plus the anticipation of violence combined with the thrill of competition, which begins to gurgle to a boil as we get closer to walking out of that locker room.

I have a pretty good analogy of what my battle feels like. It may sound funny, but the Russell Crowe movie *Gladiator* is dead-on. The battle never changes, only the combatants. Rules and venues change. Whether it's an ancient gladiator or No. 92 for the Big Blue, we go through the same damn feelings and similar rituals.

Those ancient warriors sat behind bars and made final adjustments to what little gear they had while we sit behind a steel door and concrete walls, putting tape on various parts of our bodies, hoping the tape holds us in place for the 180 minutes that will feel like eighty car accidents.

I use three different types of tape. Prewrap, hard tape and soft tape to secure my ankles, wrists and every single one of my fingers. I tape a certain way depending on where my aches and pains are, so my body parts will only move a certain way. I use about eight rolls of tape per game.

Prior to our Sundays of violence, after we make sure our tape is set, we make sure our uniforms are just the way we want them. EXACTLY as we want them, even though they'll get tugged, torn, ripped and manhandled in about twenty minutes. It's got to be just right, exact, because it provides us with the security and comfort to run out onto that field.

At this point I seek out our quarterback, young Eli. Can he possibly have any more pressure on him than this night? I say something very simple to him in our locker room.

"Young buck, go out and have some fun."

That's it, nothing more. I don't say anything to him on the sideline beforehand. So much has been made of Eli ver-

sus Peyton, I don't want to add to it. Actually, considering how the game was built up before the season, like a Super Bowl, how could I have added to it? Plus, I'm about to have my own Peyton problems, so who the hell am I to talk?

With about two minutes to go before the game, our team splits in half, with the offensive coordinator talking to the offense while our defensive coordinator, Tim Lewis, addresses our side of the ball.

Tim's favorite thing is, "Okay, guys, you've got a great opportunity to go out here and prove yourself, that you're the best defense in the league." He says that all the time. But this time he continues with something along the lines of, "We all know the game plan and if we execute, we should win this thing. Let's play together. Let's stay together. Let's communicate. Let's be eleven as one."

Then Tom Coughlin comes in the middle. We recite the Lord's Prayer first, and after the prayer, Tom gives his speech. It used to be the other way around, but sometimes when Tom gets jazzed up, he'll give us this rah-rah speech complete with curse words, bouncing up and down on his toes. Then right after, we'll recite the Lord's Prayer. In terms of blasphemy, that probably isn't the best idea. Now we make sure the prayer goes first.

When Coach gives his speech that night, I have a difficult time listening and grasping it because I'm pacing back and forth too much. Man, it's hard knowing you're about to get into a fight, like letting someone punch you in the face while you sit back and wait for it.

In his speech, Tom implores us right to the end. Protect the football! No turnovers. Every single day, in every meeting, he talks about turnovers. There is not a single day he doesn't talk about turnovers.

"Play with composure. No dumb mistakes and penalties.

Play with discipline. Play with Giant pride! Do you hear me? Play Giants football!"

Another reason it all flies past me is because, as Tom started talking, I look over at one of the stools and sitting there is a game program. That game program really pisses me off. The cover is of Peyton and Eli Manning. Why in the hell would our own organization put Peyton Manning on the cover of *our* opening night program? Whose bright idea was that?

Teams never, NEVER, put an opposing player on the cover of their own program! What was wrong with putting just Eli on the cover? Or what about Coach Coughlin or Tiki or Shockey? It was our first game with LaVar Arrington and Sam Madison, two Pro Bowl vets. Why not them? It was almost like people in our own front office were there to see Peyton, too.

I'm not just being sensitive. Maybe I'm looking for another reason to feel like someone just ran over my dog, parked, then threw it in reverse and ran over poor Lucky again. I'll deal with the program snafu after the game. I'll take that fight up with somebody after I come out of this fight. Right now we're getting ready to raise that gate, throwing us into the lion's den.

The moment Coughlin finishes his speech, we line up for the gates to open. But even when those doors open up, my teammates wait. They wait for the man who has been through these wars and fought these battles for thirteen, going on fourteen years. It's the ultimate compliment I'm given by my fellow gladiators. The men watching my back. The men I'll be fighting with today wait for me to pop a helmet off a single hook up in the air (another of my petty pregame rituals that has to be done just right), catch it, strap it up and lead the charge to battle.

How did a guy who grew up on an army base in Germany, a guy who graduated with exactly two people in his high school class, find himself in America's most glamorous city with men who wait to go to battle for him, for him to don his helmet? I can't possibly convey how it feels to be respected like that.

That is how my Sunday afternoons begin every week from September to January. This is where my battle lines are drawn.

For the last fourteen years I've spent Sundays like this. Now my goal is to bring you along for the ride. To tell you what it's really like to play inside the NFL. The pregame preparation before taking the battlefield. What truly goes into gearing up for a Sunday afternoon of smashing my body against a wall of enemy combatants. The in-game violence. How I've been able to keep myself atop this violent world for fourteen years. The characters, the adjustments and interaction between players and coaches, between players in our own locker room and players from team to team. The violence that lurks under the piles and then, of course, the recourse to such actions. What happens after the game as we start up the preparation all over again.

Thirteen years have led up to this battle against Peyton Manning and his gang. For thirteen years I've put my body through terrible things. For thirteen years I've done whatever I needed to do to get myself back to where Peyton was hoping to bring his troops this year as well—Miami and the Super Bowl. Only one of us would make it.

As we rush out of the locker room, the silence we had prior to Coach's speech is shattered by 76,000 of our closest friends, the people who pulled into the parking lot a couple of hours earlier. I'm telling you, as we walk through that tunnel we begin to transform, one by one. All the work we did all week, the pain we felt that morning, the pain we felt min-utes before begins to fade as the crowd's force makes us twitch. With each step, I forget that damn shoulder. I need to hit someone. I need it like a drug. The closer I get to the end of that tunnel, the more I transform. Bring on Caesar's gladia-tors! Bring on the lions, the swords, the spears and anything else because, for now, I am invincible. I am the hunter and not the hunted.

You remember Gladiator Crowe's character, Maximus, telling the other gladiators sent into battle to die with him, "If we stick together we live, if we don't we die." He's the first one out of that tunnel. That's exactly what it feels like to me.

This year's first Sunday nighter is even more electric, the first Sunday night game on NBC, Manning versus, well, the guy on the cover of our program. The sequel to the 1958 NFL Championship Game, Colts and Giants.

Remember those rituals I have? Well, I have one more in the tunnel, too. I go to the left side of the tunnel and bang my head lightly against the wall three times. Then I go find indi-vidual guys, guys who are integral to this game, and I give them my final two cents. I used to stand there with Jessie Armstead, when we were the last two guys waiting for intros, and say, "It'll be up to one of us to set the tempo."

On this night, as the offense is introduced, I stand in the back of the tunnel—I don't want to see the field until it's my turn. I can hardly contain myself. It's like every single person in that stadium is suddenly a family member. No matter what happened earlier in the week or the season or in your career, they're cheering you on, no matter what. They don't want Caesar's gladiators to win. They're calling upon ME to draw blood.

There's a shot of electricity. I now feel like I could run

right through that iron goalpost. I'm in the dark back here, but when I come out of the chute, it's deafening. It's like darkness, darkness, darkness . . . *BAM*, 76,000 strong, their force, their will, their cheers. . . . It send chills all through my body. At that moment, it is the best place in the world. And the only place in the world I want to be.

And that's how we get to the coin toss, where I last left off, right before the opening kick. Another sniff of ammonia and, brother, we're ready to get this party started. Isn't it amazing we don't gas ourselves out before every game? Between the Red Bull, the fans, the intensity, the insane pregame emotions and the anthem, it's amazing we don't need an IV *before* the ball is kicked.

As our young guns run onto the field for that opening kick, I come back over to our sideline and do something referred to as Roll Call. I'll call out a name, come over and head butt the teammate. Defense, let's start bashing heads!

Then I catch another glimpse of Peyton. I stare at him with respect, respect because he has the power to make me and all my teammates look bad. But he better respect me because I am here to make him look bad, too. Then I'll get pissed, frustrated really, because I know playing against him on national TV, I may not get many chances to hit the guy.

Peyton Manning's arm is in a whole different league, but it's the little things he does that people don't talk about as much that make him different from his brother, or everyone else for that matter. When I go against Peyton, the man stands there as I zero in like I'm about to kill him. At the very last second he'll either get rid of the ball or make a tiny little movement to get his butt out of my line of fire. It's not

drastic, just a subtle shift here or step there. Tom Brady does the same thing. They can sit in there while I'm thinking . . . *pay dirt, here I come* . . . BALL'S GONE! Damn!

Peyton has a clock in his head that allows him to hold the ball for a specific amount of time. His consistency is amazing. It's almost like he'll always get it off by the same time each snap. In fact, our game plan is to try not to let him feel comfortable in the pocket. We have a bunch of blitzes planned to force him to get rid of the ball quicker. The faster you come against him, the faster he'll get rid of the ball. It's all about disrupting his rhythm.

The moment before that ball is kicked, I'm thinking, we've got to win this game. Man, there is no way we'll lose. I couldn't take losing. I couldn't take hating life this early in my season. Yes, losing actually makes me hate life for the night, for the week, sometimes a little longer.

Once the opening ball is kicked off, you look at the poor souls giving up their bodies for this job, but I don't care, I just want to win. I tell myself, sacrifice whatever you need in order to prevent yourself from hating life for the next week. Put it all out there tonight, because you have plenty of time to rest after the game.

I read somewhere recently that some people simply don't have the fear gene built into them. Players are routinely asked to run downfield as fast as humanly possible after kickoffs and launch themselves into a thousand pounds of meat and muscle, with no regard for the fear gene.

Me? I'm still staring at Peyton. The whole time, I'm staring at the face of the NFL, the man who could ruin this night. Tonight, Peyton is playing for Caesar. I've faced Caesar's guys too many times and lost. I've only got one or two of these seasons left in me. I'm willing to leave whatever it takes on that field to walk off victorious.

My night will eventually be ruined by Caesar's quarterback, 26–21, but not because of his play. We'll actually keep him in check, as well as anyone could. He doesn't pick us apart. Even with our best effort against him and a solid showing by his brother Eli, I'll go home hating my life. Instead of celebrating what could be my last year, I'll be forced to sulk in anticipation of a week of righting this wrong. I'll trudge through another weekly regimen an angry, pissed-off-at-the-world man. But I'll also experience some of the day-to-day ways we players relieve the pressure through humor and outrageous behavior.

CHAPTER TWO

Practical Jokes: The Brilliance of Our Immaturity

Inside the NFL locker room, what's viewed by the outside world as stupid is often viewed on the inside as an opportunity to create wonderful locker room magic! How incredibly vile, juvenile and offensive we are behind closed doors. Welcome to the world of millionaire fifth graders.

The real world sees the violence and intensity of the NFL. But to stifle that intensity, we often look for anything remotely capable of dropping us down to grade-school level. Where else can you find a room full of people with a net worth of somewhere between $100 and $200 million and have guys actually pee on each other in the shower?

Wall Street? Nah. Microsoft world headquarters? Just can't see Paul Allen and Bill Gates's disciples whizzing on each other. NFL locker room? Definitely! I could fill up this entire book (maybe the next one) with the childish, mindless and sometimes brilliant practical jokes we play on each other.

We need practical jokes. It's the only way to get through a week after a loss like the one we had to Manning and the Colts that opening week. It's how we get through the pain of losing, soreness and repetition that mars our days.

We truly *live* to mess with each other, and in an NFL locker room, nothing is off-limits. White guys, black guys, big guys, small guys, thugs, nerds, rich dudes, vets, rookies, coaches and even owners are far from exempt from our juvenile hysteria. More often than not, we're just plain *mean* about it. The meaner we get, the funnier it usually seems. A quick example. The Giants strength and conditioning coach is a man named Jerry Palmieri. He was with Coach Coughlin down in Jacksonville. Jerry limped up to New York with Tom. Did I say limped? Jerry really needs a hip replacement. Poor guy is always dragging his leg around.

In training camp he's the guy who conducts bed check to see if we are in our rooms by curfew. So he drags that leg behind him from room to room to make sure we're all tucked in nice and cozy at night. To check each individual room, he has to pass through a suite that acts as the common living area—three bedrooms per suite.

The players have done two things to mess with Coach Palmieri. My personal favorite is when the guys took out all the lightbulbs in the suite and then rearranged the furniture. Jerry opened the door, flicked the switch on and off and when he decided the bulb had simply blown, he ventured into the pitch-black suite. All of a sudden we heard *BOOM! CRASH!* We all sat in our rooms and peed our pants. Can you imagine a group of fully grown men with their ears pressed tightly against a dorm-room door, trying not to laugh at a limping coach crashing into furniture? Since then Jerry always carries a flashlight.

The other cruel trap we set is when guys hide and wait

with water guns. When Jerry walks toward the dorms, they all jump out and squirt him and watch the poor bastard try to run away on that bad hip. It's cruel, yes. But so funny.

Our humor sinks much, much lower than that. The worst, most disgusting, grossest joke we've got in camp is the ol' take-a-dump-in-the-wrong-part-of-the-toilet joke. This joke is reserved for ultimate revenge on offensive linemen.

The aggressor in this case will venture into his victim's bathroom, take the top off the toilet tank and take a crap in it. It sits there in hiding and stinks up the room. Then, when the poor victim flushes his toilet, the poop flushes in with the clean water and stinks it up even worse. Think how hard it is to try to clean *that* out of there. Now, that's toilet humor.

Shaun O'Hara, our center, is part of a whole different subculture known as the Missing Link. Offensive linemen as a whole are conservative at home and off the field, but they're the sickest ones in the locker room and live to get each other with practical jokes. Their humor sometimes translates only to other offensive linemen and no one else on the team.

For instance, they could be talking to each other in the shower and all the while one guy, while talking and trying to distract his prey, is taking a leak on the other guy's leg. The victim can't feel it because the pee is the same temperature as the shower. The rest of the linemen crack up in hysterical laughter while we teammates shake our heads and run the other way. If you did that to me I would whip your ass.

You can tell a lot about a guy's normal behavior by how he reacts when he falls victim to our jokes. Inside our world, if a guy can't take a joke, we don't want him. We're all brothers, and if you can't let your brother wrap your entire car from front to back in plastic wrap, then what good are you to our little society?

Here are a few of my favorite practical jokes that I've either seen or heard about:

THE BLUE DOT MAN. The infamous Blue Dot Man has been sadistically rearing his ugly head inside the Giants locker room since before I came into the league in 1993. It remains a staple inside today's joke arsenal.

Here's how it works. Somehow we get our hands on a powder that the FBI uses to mark stolen items. They'll put this powder on money and when the perp sweats, the part of the body (usually the hands) that touches the powder turns blue. Believe me, this stuff is impossible to remove quickly and usually stays on for about three days. We don't put it just where someone can get his hands on it. We'll line a young guy's helmet with it so when he takes it off, he has a blue stain across his forehead that he simply can't wash off.

A sock is another favorite spot to hit with the blue dye. Kid gets out of practice, takes off his sock and sees his entire foot has turned blue. He panics, thinking he's got some actual medical problem, like a strange version of frostbite.

The Blue Dot Man usually strikes a stubborn or cocky rookie so, young boys, watch your attitudes. The Blue Dot Man never sleeps.

ICY HOT. Icy Hot is an analgesic gel that burns the living daylights out of you if it's put in the wrong place. We always find the wrong places.

One of the best jokes I heard was the use of Icy Hot by Colts star quarterback Peyton Manning. Believe it or not, Manning is one of the biggest practical jokers of anyone in the league. He's always looking to get either one of his linemen or someone at the Pro Bowl. One day he stole a stick of deodorant from one of his linemen's lockers, took off the cap

and put a very thin strip of Icy Hot on the deodorant, then replaced the cap and put it back in the locker. That dude must have hit the ceiling in fiery pain when he stepped out of the shower and rolled the stick across his armpits.

Manning's joke, however, pales in comparison with the one that former cornerback Mark Collins pulled on the one and only Lawrence Taylor. Collins took the muscle-penetrating gel and put it into LT's jockstrap. When that stuff kicked in, LT screamed and yelled all sorts of words I didn't hear until I was about ten years old. Wow, was that man in pain! He never even asked if he could leave practice. He just walked off the practice field to wash the stuff off. Believe me, Icy Hot does not come off easily. Legend has it that when LT got out of the shower, he found that Collins had the stuff inside LT's underwear, too. To this day I'm surprised he didn't kill him.

CHICKEN AND THE IDIOT. One of the best revenge jokes I've heard was directed at an equipment manager. From what I heard, the guy was a real ass. He'd do stupid things like charge players for extra socks and equipment, trying to make a buck off of them.

The players had finally had it, so they somehow got their hands on a live chicken and let the thing completely gorge. They let this thing eat all morning long. This chicken filled its belly. Then it ate some more. Then more. After that, they let him feast some more.

When the chicken had about all it could eat, they snuck over to the equipment guy's dorm room—this was during training camp—and threw the chicken into the room, shut the door and let it have its run of the room all day long. When the equipment manager came back from an eighteen-hour day, the chicken had pretty much crapped on every square

inch of his living quarters—on the floor, on the bed, on his clothes, in his clothes, on his papers.

That, my friends, is the way to sweet revenge. Forget suing a guy. Forget kicking a guy's butt. Just fill up a chicken and let him rage.

LAW OFFICES OF NOODLEMAN, LIPSHITZ & SCHWARTZ. The best joke I ever pulled I conducted with the help of Jay Glazer. He has a very demented mind when it comes to getting his friends who are players and coaches.

In my second year I told him a story about how earlier in the day, during practice, Jessie Armstead, fellow linebacker Marcus Buckley and a couple of other guys were joking about some bogus law that says if you're with a girl for more than twelve hours, she can take away half your wealth.

Quietly, guys started gesturing and nodding for me to turn around and look at this young cat we had on our team. Sure enough, this guy was counting on his fingers how many hours he was with this girl the night before. Out of respect, I won't reveal the name of the player.

When I recounted the tale to Glazer, he came up with the idea to "sue" the guy on behalf of some girl who'd claimed they spent the night together. So he cracks out his computer and generates a subpoena from the Law Offices of Noodleman, Lipshitz & Schwartz. Where he came up with that name, I don't know, but what a great one!

The subpoena included a claim from some girl that she had been with the aforementioned player for sixteen hours on a certain day and as a result, she was suing him for half of his net worth. The letter stated he was required to appear in Hackensack family court on such-and-such day at such-and-

such time in such-and-such courtroom with his own independent defense counsel and a list of all of his assets. It looked so real, it would have scared the hell out of me if I had gotten it. Letterhead. A seal. Unbelievably authentic-looking.

Jay gave it to me and I put it into the player's mailbox. Once he saw it, as good as it was, I couldn't let the guy go through with it. He was pretty upset. I couldn't let him go to the courthouse. Glazer has never forgiven me. He wanted the poor guy to show up in some judge's courtroom and say, "Uh, yeah, Your Honor, I'm here to proclaim that I was only with that girl for eleven hours so she shouldn't get any of my stuff." But I just couldn't let him do it.

LUCKY POWERBALL WINNER. The level of thought that goes into some jokes can border on evil genius. The more sinister, the more hilarious. The more ingenious, the more embarrassing. The Kansas City Chiefs had one back in 1998. This story was told by Tony Gonzalez, the Chiefs All-Pro tight end, and Greg Manusky, their former linebacker, who is now the defensive coordinator of the 49ers.

At the time there was a huge Powerball lottery, one of the early ones where the jackpot was so huge, even the richest people in the area were plunking down cash to take a shot. The Chiefs were slated to fly to Tokyo for the American Bowl, an annual overseas preseason game the NFL uses to promote the game internationally. The Powerball drawing was scheduled to take place while the Chiefs were in the air en route to Japan.

Manusky got one of their quarterbacks at the time, either Rich Gannon or Elvis Grbac, to get the lottery numbers of their young quarterback, Pat Barnes. Somehow they commandeered his ticket long enough to jot down his numbers without his knowing it.

Fast-forward to the flight. Manusky set his watch to go off at about the time of the drawing, then gave Barnes's numbers to their public relations director, Bob Moore. Moore got on the flight attendants' loudspeaker and, as if he'd been to a hundred acting classes, pulled off the second part of the prank with precision. Moore announced to the plane that the Powerball lottery balls had been drawn, and then he paused for everyone to get their tickets out before announcing the numbers.

Not only did Barnes and a handful of players take out their tickets, so did the team's owner, Lamar Hunt, their general manager, Carl Peterson, and most of the executives and coaches.

Moore announced the fake numbers, Barnes's numbers, as the winning ticket. And Barnes lost his mind.

Gonzalez was sitting right next to him and recounts that Barnes said something along the lines of "Whew!" and proceeded to sprint—not walk but break into a full sprint—up the aisle to where the owners were sitting. He was screaming at the top of his lungs, believing he'd just hit the jackpot!

Manusky, however, started crapping his pants because he was now afraid that Barnes would run to the front and curse out Hunt and Peterson and tell them to stick their job where the sun don't shine. He also feared that Hunt and his group, upon hearing the numbers, would rip up their own tickets, assuming they lost. Manusky thought he'd just got himself cut.

Neither happened. Barnes did go insane only to slowly calm down at the sound of laughter from those who knew what Manusky and the other quarterbacks had done. This kid went from being a backup third-string quarterback to the second wealthiest man on the plane to a third-string strap again, all within the span of thirty seconds. While the rest of the team got to laugh their asses off.

THE HELMET JOKE. This year William Joseph, our former first-round defensive tackle from the University of Miami, came to me with a Giants helmet and asked me to sign it as a favor for a friend of his. I pulled out a Sharpie, ready to swing my handwriting elegantly around one side of the helmet, only to hear him cracking up.

Willie Jo, as we call him, never plays a joke that's funny! He's corny as hell, but this cat got me to sign my own game helmet. If he hadn't started laughing, I may have run out there like a complete moron with my signature emblazoned on the side of my helmet.

THE BEST PRANKSTER I'VE EVER PLAYED WITH. The granddaddy of the ingenious joke in our 2006 locker room is, by far, Shaun O'Hara. He's truly a sick, deranged, psychotic yet unbelievably clever human being.

One day when Eli Manning was younger, he went to put his hands under the center and got the shock of his life. Manning squatted down, stuck his hands under O'Hara's butt cheeks and shockingly felt the skin of O'Hara's nuts. The guy actually cut a hole in his pants so his testicles hung out onto Eli's hands. Now, that's nasty!

The guys who are overly demented are the ones who can push a player to the brink of snapping, and O'Hara nearly got Amani Toomer to swing away this past year. The new Field-Turf surface that now lines many NFL playing fields is made up of millions of tiny little rubber pellets meshed in, millimeter by millimeter, with a grassy surface. They feel and look like pieces of ground-up tire.

Shaun gathered up a whole handful of the stuff one day, hid it in his hand behind his back and approached Toomer. Shaun proceeded to tell Amani he just had his tonsils taken out, then asked Amani if he'd ever had his tonsils taken out and asked to see. When Amani opened his mouth, O'Hara threw the whole handful of pellets down his throat.

We usually do this kind of stuff to a rookie, but Amani can get nosey and paid for his curiosity. He completely flipped out and started yelling, "I'm no rookie! Fuck that!" He was furious and wouldn't talk to Shaun for a month. Every time O'Hara tried making peace, Toomer walked away from him.

This was the only time I ever saw a practical joke lead to a fight. Amani totally flipped out. I have to be honest with you, if I was the recipient of that, I may have gotten physical, too. It was the single funniest thing I saw all year, but I don't think I'd feel too happy about having another man throw rubber pellets down my throat.

That's not to say I haven't fallen victim to our locker room's mad scientist. I was on the verge of being late for a meeting one day this past season and the last thing I felt like getting was a lecture and a fine from Coach Coughlin to put a damper on my morning. But I knew I was going to be cutting it close, so I threw my cell phone on the stool closest to the meeting room and ran into the meeting. Big mistake, Mike. Big, big mistake.

The reason I didn't take my phone into the meeting was because as ornery as Tom can get with our meeting times, his face turns the strangest shade of reddish purple when somebody makes the mistake of having their cell phone ring during his meetings. That's a capital crime and $5,000 inside our building. We aren't always using both sides of our brain. Why

I'd leave my cell phone out in full view is beyond me. But I never gave it any thought because I calmly took my seat, just happy not to get another fine.

When the meeting broke I walked back over to my phone and flipped it open and I was immediately smacked with the most horrifying picture I could have been greeted by. I would rather have taken the fine.

O'Hara had seen the phone sitting there, picked it up and decided to take a picture of his, um, how can I say this politically correctly? I got it, his frank and beans. Not only was that incredibly small piece of manhood on my phone, he had the sucker set as my screen saver! The sicker part is: O'Hara had no idea whose phone it was when he did it. He saw the phone, took it, whipped out his junk, aimed and snapped. Hell, it could have been Coach Coughlin's for all he knew.

The worse a guy messes up off the field, the more we'll mess with him. If a guy gets busted for drugs, we'll throw a bag of salt or a bag of brown grass under his chair during meetings and pretend it fell out of his pocket. I did this to a lineman in a meeting one day and a coach damn near had a heart attack. That's the only joke I've felt bad about and regret.

If a guy has something embarrassing happen that ends up being written about, we'll post it all over the locker room. It doesn't matter how bad it is. The jokes are still getting thrown my way after my ex-wife, Jean, insinuated to the *New York Post* and *New York Daily News* that I'm gay. Players from around the league killed me about that for months. Actually, they're still killing me about that.

The weekend the story "broke" that I supposedly liked dudes, I was playing golf with Bucs All-Pro cornerback Ronde Barber. Ronde stepped behind a tree when I wasn't looking, snapped a picture of his manhood with his phone and sent it to me via text message with the note, "I don't believe your denials. Meet me behind the 12th tee box. Love, Ronde."

The more embarrassing the situation, the more the boys inside the locker room and throughout the NFL will circle like vultures to rub it in.

As I've already said, the practical joke has a handful of purposes. Revenge, boredom, justice . . . the joke takes on several faces. While on the surface our plots and unsuspected targeting may seem cruel, these jokes serve as our greatest weapon in fighting the monotony. Every single day we hear the same garbage from the same people and look at the same faces over and over and over. We see each other more than we see our own families.

So if we take some rookie's pants, tie them in knots and throw them in the ice tub, it breaks up the day. So what if we sneak into some guy's room in the middle of the night and throw water all over him in his sleep? It means, "Hello, my friend, you're special today." What better way to break up the monotony of training camp meetings than sticking a fire extinguisher nozzle under a teammate's dorm-room door and releasing the entire contents of fire retardation foam into his room?

There is but ONE person who has protection from our childish pranks. Just one. The head coach. You don't want to risk his having a bad sense of humor. Practical jokes are used in our personal world for justice. You don't always need to use violence to get a guy back. Just hit him with a horrible joke. Instead of two guys fighting over something, we can get our point across without totally insulting anyone. If you humiliate in good fun, we're apt to forgive and forget. If

you humiliate with bad intentions, guys will hold on to that grudge forever.

No matter how much we joke and fool around on the field and off, sometimes it takes sheer physical force to get through yet another week. Oftentimes that involves violence and rage against our own fellow teammates and NFL brothers.

CHAPTER THREE

Footbrawling

October 18, 2006, flipping through my radio dials

I sped along Route 3 on my way to work, flipping through the radio dials searching for the perfect song to fuel the lousy mood I was in this morning. I was looking for something to push me into the mood to practice. To help me drag my bones through yet another day of film and meetings and whatever monotonous routine I was in no mood to participate in. I *wanted* to be pissed off today. Different moods help you trudge through the monotony and, at times, pain. Today I wanted anger. I needed a little pep in my step.

As I flipped the remote dial on my car stereo, something changed my mood in a heartbeat. Something immediately smacked me across the face. Today Tiki Barber would provide all the soap opera I needed to change things around here. During my short jaunt into work that morning, I heard radio reports that Tiki had finally revealed what many of his close friends and teammates had long known—Tiki was retiring at season's end. I had known for quite some time that

Barber was heading into his final season. Actually, it was no secret inside our locker room, either. He wasn't very discreet about it among his friends. Barber had grown sick of the business side of football.

Hearing the news took me down memory lane, and not among the best of memories, either. It got me thinking about the only time I ever threatened to whip a teammate's ass off the field, about wanting to beat the shit out of lovable little Tiki.

Tiki was the only player I ever threatened to hurt off the field, outside our locker room, outside of football. And he was the only person who sent me over the edge of what is and what isn't acceptable.

It happened in late March 2002 after I came out and stated that due to my contract, I believed my tenure in the Big Apple was over. I was convinced that I was a goner, that the team that had always taken care of me financially didn't want my services anymore. I blasted them, trying to make a strong case for why I should get paid more. I expected backlash from the organization, but I never expected it from one of my closest teammates.

I turned to the dreaded back page of the *New York Post* only to see the headline "Greediest Giant," quoting Tiki, who had blasted me for being greedy.

Fights are rarely, very rarely, personal in the NFL. But Tiki had made this one personal, as if he had been brainwashed by management. We're great friends now and he's the best running back I've ever been around. But my reaction? Thank the Lord that Tiki was not in the same room when the shock of that newspaper story sank in. I could have claimed temporary insanity and gotten my gap-toothed ass locked up for assault and battery for whipping the hell out of our best offensive weapon. The morning his quotes hit the back page of the *Post*, I called our star running back on the phone and left a very calm message, so he would call me back.

When he called back, the first words out of my mouth were, "What the fuck were you thinking?!"

He responded as if management had a hand in his back, sitting him on their knee and throwing their collective voices, "Well, Michael, I just think it's a lot of money and you should think about the team."

That got me even more furious, so I took it to a level that is considered completely unacceptable off the field. "Mind your damn business!" I screamed. "And let me tell you something. If I ever see you outside or if I get you alone, I'm going to beat the shit out of you! You better never let me get you alone! I AM GOING TO BEAT YOUR ASS!"

Could I have been any clearer? We had two taboos working here. Number one, you never, ever fight off the field. Number two, you never, ever talk about another man's business situation, especially to the press.

Ironically, Tiki's retirement had as much to do with the business side of football as anything. He'd soured on the business end of our profession. Later he said it had to do with Coach Coughlin and the daily grind on his body. I'm sure that played a part, but I'm also sure that the business part of the NFL, as in salary negotiations, is what made the physical grind unbearable. When you're as great a player as Tiki is, you want to be rewarded for it, not put through the ringer by the team every time you bring up your market value.

Yet it happens. Tiki had gone to Giants general manager Ernie Accorsi for years for a new deal—a deal that would have paid him like a perennial Pro Bowler. Every year Barber asked and every year the Giants would draft someone to replace him in the backfield, barely budging on his requests.

I believe what pushed him over the edge was when Accorsi told Tiki he'd give him a small bump in pay, but he'd have to return it if he didn't produce like an absolute stud. Ernie got him on this not once but for two years and, in my opinion, Barber got fed up with putting his body through the pain and battering and not getting enough financial appreciation in return.

I knew he had told some people he seriously considered pulling a Barry Sanders and retiring the night before camp. But ultimately he felt we were too close to winning the Super Bowl. If we had sucked on paper going into the season, I believe he would have retired.

I find it interesting that Tiki retired over the same problem I had five years prior. My contract problem was so ugly, the Giants actually shopped me around. They called Dan Reeves in Atlanta and John Fox in North Carolina, the Vikings and a handful of other teams, while vehemently denying making such overtures. Business is business, though, so I never made it a personal issue.

Tiki was another story. He made it personal for what he thought was the good of the team. Here's what it got him. Sour, that they never treated him fairly, and bitter, that they never did him right by paying him comparably to the rest of the league. I wonder, would he have tried to kick my ass if I had ripped his deal? Nah, I don't believe he would have stooped that low.

After I called Tiki out, we didn't talk or look at each other for months. Football is a funny world. No matter how much you may despise another man or resent somebody taking your job, you learn to put it aside for the common cause of a victorious Sunday. Any harm you wish on a teammate ends up hurting you as well. I also realized that no matter what

Tiki said, I was going to get paid according to how well I played and not his opinion.

Tiki and I ended up making up during a preseason game for WCBS-TV. Actually, it was orchestrated by Jay Glazer. He was the sideline reporter for the game and told the two of us to bury the hatchet. So if we were doing that, we might as well do it live on TV. To Tiki's credit, he came clean, apologized and admitted he had stepped on a subject that was none of his business.

As we approached each other for the interview, the entire stands in the section near where we were doing the interview stood up as if they were watching a prelude to a fight. We hadn't been seen together up to that point. I think they believed I was going to kill him. Had they caught us together three months earlier, they might have been right.

And that was the closest I ever came to honestly seeking out someone off the football field and beating him down. On the field? It's a completely different story.

Fights are a part of our landscape. We live, we breathe, we practice, we play and we fight. Everything in our professional lives is predicated on violence and aggression, so of course when pushed, we'll snap in the heat of battle. But the other aspect you have at work here is a brotherhood. All these guys locked together like we're on some sequestered reality show. We bond like brothers. So what do brothers do? They fight! Some worse than others.

Unfortunately, I was involved in the worst football fight I've ever seen. It was during a mini-camp practice in the mid-1990s under Dan Reeves. I remember it like it was yesterday.

Our right tackle Scott Gragg, fresh off another altercation two plays earlier, took his bearlike mitts connected to his humungous 6 foot 8, 340-pound frame and tried to take his frustration out on me. He was going after my ribs, face, stomach, whatever would cause me to crumble. This man was much bigger than me. Actually, that's an understatement. Scott Gragg was the *biggest* man on our team, towering over me by four inches and taking a seventy-pound weight differential into our impromptu battle.

I quickly surveyed the odds in my head, realized I didn't like them and that's when . . . some . . . thing . . . went . . . *Cli-i-ick*!

Snap, my brain stopped working. My blood frantically raced through my body. So this is how Bill Bixby, the Hulk, must have felt before he turned green and popped out of his purple pants. (Why is he always wearing the same pants?) Anyway, back to my fight. My common sense jumped out of my skin and suddenly, I was left alone to do things I would never, ever think I was capable of.

Like what? you might ask.

I grabbed Gragg by the face mask and violently ripped his helmet off his head. Target revealed. Remember the part about all common sense fleeing my mind and body? The sensible thing in any fair fight would have been to punch this man in the face, hope to get a couple of shots in, maybe a cut, and have my street cred in the locker room step up a rung or two. But no, that would have been too sane.

Why I made the decision to do what I did next, I still haven't figured out, but I guess I had to do what I had to do. Otherwise I can't bear thinking I'm actually capable of willingly trying to kill a man. Still, I took that helmet and swung it as hard as I could in a Tomahawk chop, right at my target, Gragg's head.

THWAAAAAP! I leveled the giant Giant, connecting good enough with my weapon to get him to fall on his back. Then the blood started trickling. I never once thought, "What

have I done to this guy?" Instead of feeling bad, my next thought was, "Go over and kick this guy's ass!" So I ran and jumped on top of him and proceeded to hit him in the face over and over. My horrified teammates thankfully stopped the carnage. Otherwise I'm not sure when I would have stopped.

It never once dawned on me that I could have killed him, only that he could have whipped my ass, a fate worse than death inside the warped philosophy of an NFL locker room. It also never dawned on me that he was a teammate, a friend and someone we certainly needed on Sundays.

Reeves immediately called an end to our off-season workout because the fight spread, causing Jessie Armstead to want a piece of somebody, so he jumped on Howard Cross. It had all the makings of one huge motorcycle gang–like rumble. Reeves later said it was the worst practice fight he'd ever seen.

Should I be proud? Should I have been scared of myself? Should I be ashamed? To be honest, I think about that fight to this day. I transformed into something ugly. But the part that scares me now is that *I* didn't scare *myself* at the time. The only thing I was ashamed of was that I used a weapon first, then my fists. That's the way you think out there. I clock into work every day into a violent world. Sometimes in order to survive, you are forced to find the ugly side of your most inner self.

Sam Madison, the longtime Pro Bowl corner for the Dolphins (and my teammate last year), has a saying for all the young guys, "Find that OTHER guy." In other words, nearly every one of us has some sort of split personality living inside of us, the off-field sane version and the maniac, barbaric gladiator we MUST connect to for survival out there on the battlefield. Find that different guy on the field! Be that other

guy who is simply a coldhearted SOB. Don't feel sorry and don't look back. If on the field you're a cornered wild animal, remember, once you're off the field, you're no longer cornered.

Finding that "other guy" is usually reserved for game day. But I found my other guy that day and I let it drift into the crevices of my conscience that I could have killed Gragg, that I actually relished my skin-splitting hit as my locker-room credibility skyrocketed and other guys realized that maybe I was not to be messed with.

Yet more surprising than the brutality of the fight was the brevity of the aftermath. I went to Gragg in the locker room and apologized. He responded with a chuckle and, "You really got me with a good shot." We never talked about it ever again. Like I said before, just two brothers acting like idiots and then, la di da di da, let's go play some football, buddy.

Imagine, I just hit this man in his skull with a deadly weapon, tried to hurt him, and thirty minutes later it was nothing more than another day at the office. Still, taking fights from the field off the field is taboo. It rarely happens, but if it does, something must be really, really off.

While some people may see us as a bunch of uncontrollable violent animals, the reality is that fights play a very important role in our world. If you don't fight back, you are seen as weak and will be pushed constantly. Some coaches use fights as a motivation tool. If a good old-fashioned fight is sometimes the best Rx for a tired team, coaches will poke and prod certain guys.

Bill Parcells secretly used this ploy to perfection during the Giants' Super Bowl week when they were preparing for the Bills for Super Bowl XXV. One story involves the great John "Jumbo" Elliott and the greatest defender of all time, Lawrence Taylor. The thing about Jumbo was, if you beat him

on a pass rush in practice, you better watch your eyes, your throat, your head and your ankles or else he'll get you. I thank G-d every day I got to practice against him early on in my career, because as bad as he gave it to me during practice, Sundays were a playground.

Jumbo was just plain vindictive, which is exactly what you'd want from your lineman on game day, but not against you every day in practice. You want your tackles to piss off the defense so much that they want to spit in somebody's face after the game. Jumbo made you want to spit in his face damn near every practice. He was always slipping his fingers under my face mask into my eyes or punching me in the throat. Every time he did it, I'd wince and take the pain and then yell, "Damn it, Jumbo! Cut the shit!" He'd giggle to himself and walk away like, "What? What did I do?"

I not only had to prepare for battle on Sundays, Jumbo Elliott made me lace up and become a warrior every day of practice during my formative NFL years.

Anyway, one week Bill Parcells wanted to really, really get under Jumbo's skin. He was going to have to block Buffalo's Bruce Smith in the biggest game of Jumbo's life.

"We were exhausted from the 49ers game in the NFC Championship Game," Jumbo recalled. "We were so lethargic, completely spent, and I didn't know he did this until years later. Parcells decided to spice it up by getting us into a fight."

What Parcells failed to factor in was just how much Jumbo could lose it when he was in one of those moods. Usually you have the scout-team guys working against the first team, but Parcells asked the starters to rush Jumbo. He wanted to infuriate the big man. And infuriate him he did. Parcells asked Pepper Johnson to go at Jumbo. Then he asked Carl Banks to take a shot. And then came the great one, LT.

35

It didn't take Nostradamus to predict that those two fire-balls were headed for a fight, Super Bowl week or no Super Bowl week.

Apparently LT got past Jumbo to the quarterback, although to this day Jumbo denies it! The two started jawing and LT called him a big stupid white boy. Jumbo responded by calling LT "nothing but a speed rusher." How great is that one! I love it. Jumbo is a classic.

LT got him again on another pass rush (Jumbo denies this one, too) and then said something else to piss off the 6 foot 7½, 320-pound blocker.

That's when it happened. "It" being the unspeakable. "It" being the unthinkable. Jumbo let a sentence escape from his lips that simply should never be uttered, never spoken, never even joked about.

"Yeah, well, you're nothing but a fucking crackhead!"

Practice came to a screeching halt. Like the scene in *Animal House* when the white frat boys accidentally meander into an all-black bar.

After everyone collectively picked their jaws up off the ground, the coaches immediately stopped the 9-on-7 drill they were running and tried to diffuse the situation. But Jumbo kept after him. I think even LT was stunned. He didn't really say anything back. He was probably concerned that Jumbo had lost his mind. Nothing like a giant loss of sanity to rile the troops before a Super Bowl.

"When I'm tired and hot and pissed, I say whatever comes out of my mouth," Jumbo recalled, laughing. "But what people may not understand, that night me and LT hung out. I guess I said something that was off-limits, but it had no effect on us after that practice ended. We hung out that same night and never brought it up."

You might be surprised there aren't more violent instances. We go crazy on each other right up to the point before it reaches criminal assault. I think deep down we know it could end up hurting the team. Even the Gragg thing, I don't know if I would have reacted that way had it happened during the season as opposed to the off-season when there's plenty of time to heal.

How we are able to turn on and off that "other guy" like the flip of a switch is beyond me. How Gragg and I or LT and Jumbo can hang that same night defies logic. The guys who can't don't last long in this league. As much as fighting and violence is a part of our world, there's a time and place for it. And a line is drawn in the sand.

The one guy who really crossed that line was Bill Romanowski when he coldcocked a Raider teammate and broke his eye socket. This stunned his teammates *and* got him sued. I'm not sure why this particular violent act appalled everyone so much. Maybe it was his reputation or that he suckered this guy. Maybe it was the fact that we all thought he was juicing or that he continuously got fined for unsportsmanlike conduct.

Isn't it amazing that considering how big and strong we are, more of us don't inflict worse damage on each other? Actually, practice fights become more of a release than a personal grudge. You can almost feel it in the air when the team needs a good old-fashioned fight to break the boredom.

Sometimes we fight over the dumbest stuff imaginable. We once had a defensive lineman named Chris Maumalanga who knocked out not one but two guys—one-punch KOs—over a video game. Two of our former defensive linemen, Erik Howard and Eric Dorsey, once got into a fight in training camp over the water tube. Both grabbed the water tube to get a drink at the same time. Neither was willing to let go.

It takes a lot of provocation for a guy to fight someone inside the locker room. That's the space you try not to violate. So you need to learn to throw verbal jabs in our world. The tongue is a lot more painful than the fist.

The sharpness of the tongue can lead to meeting-room fights. While these fights are verbal, they can soon turn into physical haymakers. The problem with meeting-room fights is that the coaches are often in harm's way. If you're going to fight, you have to fight either in front of or through the coach—not exactly ideal. Just ask my teammate of last year, LaVar Arrington. He and fellow Pro Bowler Jeremiah Trotter went at it like champs when the two played for the Redskins together.

LaVar said the tension between him and Trotter had been brewing for a while. These guys used to have disagreements over whose defense it was and who was the leader of the room. In other words, it was all about ego. It came to a head one day in a meeting room.

The fuse was lit when the two of them argued about a particular call on a particular offensive play. LaVar was actually correct in this case. After it was cleared up, Trotter said something that prompted LaVar to proclaim, "I told you I was right!"

Trotter was already standing up when suddenly LaVar rushed him. *BAM.* Trotter nailed LaVar flush. LaVar fell back, hit the table and was OUT! LaVar never admitted to me that he was out. He claimed he had the wrong shoes on to fight, but both Antonio Pierce and Jessie Armstead were there and word is, my boy got KO'd.

However, it didn't end there. LaVar woke suddenly and

jumped up like someone had attached jumper cables to his pecs. The two of them started going at it again, like two pit bulls. Trotter threw LaVar off him and actually hurt the coach. As the two were wrestling, throwing each other into walls, punching, it took five Redskins to break it up. They actually left an indentation in the wall. I heard that LaVar went as far as calling some of his boys to get Trotter.

Again, that's a very rare, extreme case and while a lot of guys threaten to bring their boys into the fray, it rarely, if ever, actually occurs. I've heard guys personally claim they would bring their homies in, but it never happens. It's just emotion. If they ever did bring their boys to our fight, I think we'd all lose respect for the guy and afterward he might be booted from the team.

The most inappropriately timed fight was in the locker room before our first game back after 9/11. Arrowhead Stadium in Kansas City. It was the game where they passed around a fireman's boot to collect money from the fans to help out the rescue operation. A wonderfully humanitarian collective effort by 80,000 people. But before I got to feel the love of thousands, I was treated to the antics of two.

Our guard at the time was Glenn Parker. He once had to be separated from fighting Bruce Smith at a post–Super Bowl bash after losing to the Bills. Anyway, Parker was taping his hands and rolling little balls of tape, throwing them into the trash. Keith Hamilton's locker was next to the trash bin. Parker accidentally hit him. And Hamilton, aka Hammer, asked him to stop.

Parker wound up another ball, tossed it at Hammer. Suddenly it was *Tuesday Night Fights*. Except it was Sunday. Hammer walked over, told Parker to stand up like a man. As soon as Parker stood up, *WHAM!* Hammer went nuts. He completely lost it. Howard Cross jumped in to break it up, yelling, "Hammer, stop. You're going to kill him!" Parker to this day insists he never got hit, but later in the game he had to leave the field with a concussion. We all secretly knew the concussion came from the fight, not from the game.

To put it bluntly, our locker rooms have a prison mentality. When a guy gets sent up the river, the first thing he needs to do is knock out someone who challenges him. Same thing in our world. You have to stand up for yourself, especially whenever somebody does something to disrespect you in front of everyone else. Once Hammer issued his warning, in our eyes he had no choice but to follow through.

The greatest fight I've ever seen took place on Jeremy Shockey's first-ever official day as a signed, sealed and delivered New York Giant. Allow me to set the stage. We were in our cafeteria at the University at Albany when Shockey had just arrived. That first night, man, did we get our money's worth from this brash new kid.

One of the rites of passage by vets is to get the rookies to stand on a chair in the cafeteria and entertain us with a song. Rookies are also required to stand up and yell out their name, followed by school, draft pick and signing-bonus amount. We want to know how how much cash you have to take us out to dinner or buy our morning breakfast bagels and doughnuts.

While others caved to our demands, from his very first day, Shockey didn't act like a rookie. He stood up for himself. It's happened to all of us. If you don't follow the rules of tradition, there are ramifications. Even the coaches get pissed off by a kid who won't follow these unwritten rules.

Shockey was asked earlier by the group to announce his name, school, bonus etcetera. He had the audacity to tell the

group, "Later, I'm eating, I'm hungry." Later? Hell, rookie, you don't set the time line. We set the time line! Who the hell is this rookie to tell us *when* he'll stand on a chair and make a jackass of himself? The nerve of this kid. Brandon Short, aka B-Short, aka Shortfuse, took it exceptionally personally when he loudly informed Shockey, our new tight end, that his time had come and that time was now. Shockey told him again, "When I'm done eating."

In between all the bantering a few of the guys chimed in with "Ohhh, wowww! You gonna let him talk to you like that B-Short!?"

Shockey finally took center stage and stood up on a chair between quarterbacks Kerry Collins and Jesse "The Bachelor" Palmer and christened his first official day as a New York Giant in style.

"Jeremy Shockey, University of Miami, signing bonus, 4.9 million. Is that loud enough for you, B-Short!?!"

What happened next was straight out of a movie. With people like our owner, Wellington Mara, general manager Ernie Accorsi, guests of management and ownership, women, coaches and much of our locker room all sitting in the training camp cafeteria, linebacker B-Short jumped up without warning and sprinted toward Mr. First-Day-On-The-Job. You know how most fights occur: Two guys square off, they jaw at each other, start pushing and maybe some fists fly. Not this time.

B-Short didn't jog or mosey, he sprinted at Shockey while Collins and Palmer quietly got up and moved away from the table. Short never slowed down. He was striding toward Shockey like Dan Jansen going for the speed skating gold medal. It was unbelievable.

With the entire room watching in disbelief, without one

word, B-Short threw a wild haymaker at his new teammate as the two of them went crashing over the table, throwing bombs. And I mean bombs, people! The table flipped over. Food went flying everywhere.

Both men think they won. It was like the twelfth round, a split on the judges' cards, completely down the middle. That's the type of punches Short and Shockey lobbed at each other. It was like a hockey match. Huge punches. When the table and all the stuff on it went flying over, we couldn't find a break to stop it. I'd never seen anything like it in this league. I'm sure the other players and guests hadn't, either.

Can you imagine what was going on in the minds of Mara, Bob Tisch and Accorsi as they watched Short try to tear the head off their brand-new toy on his very first day on the job? That day, as ticked off as we were with this rookie's behavior, was the day Shockey gained my respect, although I couldn't admit it at the time. Shockey was no normal rookie. He soon learned that to make it in this league, you've got to fight for your rights. That was the greatest football fight in the history of football fights.

Another great fight was during walkthrough a few years back. Shaun Williams, one of the nicest guys you'll ever meet in your life, and Dhani Jones started jawing back and forth. Actually, it was more Dhani. Dhani will get on your last nerve and jump up and down on it. He loves to question EVERY-THING! We had a rule in meetings that Dhani could only ask two questions a day. Otherwise he'd ask a question every two seconds. No answer would satisfy him. He loves to debate. If every guy from Michigan loves to argue and debate, he's the most annoying of them all.

Anyway, Sean says something to Dhani during a walk-through before practice. Dhani is a philosophical fella who likes to discuss things! Shaun, well, there's nothing philosophical about him. The man is just plain tough. Shaun, aka Left Jab, is the type of guy who will swing first and apologize later. Dhani is more a guy who will walk over in a very threatening manner, pretend he might engage in an altercation, but in the end thinks a discussion is the best way to solve things.

After the two of those guys started jawing back and forth about a misunderstood defensive formation, Dhani started walking over toward Shaun in said threatening manner. I could see the look on Shaun's face. I immediately thought to myself . . . this isn't going to be pretty. Dhani thought they would just get into each other's face, only to have it broken up. In the middle of that bright idea Shaun unloaded. He unleashed those hands, *bap, bap, bap, bap.* Man, it was nice from where I was standing. I could see Dhani's head snap back. Afterward he had some abrasions. Plus his ego must have been permanently bruised.

After the fight I said to Dhani, "Next time you get in a heated discussion, you better walk up with your hands up." We never let him live that one down.

While walkthroughs are usually extremely peaceful, sidelines are a different story. On the sidelines of games we fight verbally all the time. Tempers are hot. We're hurting. Tensions are *always* running high. We get into it all the time. I love it when the media gets hold of an instance and tries to blow it up like we're a team in turmoil. Sorry, guys. It happens every single game, inside every single locker room. No scoop there.

I'll yell at my coaches all the time. It's our normal mode of communication. If I disagree with a defense, I'll yell at my defensive line coach to tell the defensive coordinator that the call will not work. Hey, I'm down in the trenches. I can feel what the offense knows is working for them and what is

giving them fits. Yelling at coaches is all part of the heat of battle.

The most humiliated I've ever been in my career involved a fight on the field amongst ourselves in front of the world. Playoffs, 1996. Phillippi Sparks was arguing with a player about an assignment when Jessie Armstead, who was clearly our team leader, told them to shut up. We called Sparks "Deuce Deuce" for his No. 22 jersey. Later it was because we suspected he had two personalities. He snapped back at Jessie to shut the fuck up!

Uh-oh, bad move.

Jessie snatched him and yoked him up. You have to understand, the Vikings are breaking their offensive huddle. They're walking to the line, yet here we are fighting each other. It was kind of like watching someone step back during a fight and punch himself in the face. After that, we collapsed. After that, we lost the game. I was completely embarrassed to be a member of the New York Giants that day.

And, of course, there's an insane fight that involved Chris Maumalanga, who I wrote about earlier, who knocked out two guys over a video game. He once fought a lineman from Iowa named Scott Davis during training camp practice. Chris hit Davis so hard in the face, his face mask actually snapped off of his helmet and cut Davis's nose, which Maumalanga also broke in the melee. He snapped that face mask right off. I don't know how many pounds of pressure it takes for that to happen, but I've never seen it before or since. Those things are made of steel; I thought they couldn't break. Unfortunately for Scott Davis, that day I was wrong.

As for my beef with Tiki, I felt lucky I never got Tiki alone on the street. Fortunately I never did the unthinkable, and fortu-

nately we were able to get past it. But, man, that one day? Had I seen him, I would have gone above and beyond what I did to Gragg. I would have violated the law. But just as sad, I would have violated our own unwritten code.

Codes, rules and laws. It's all part of the NFL. Only a few days later, I would encounter a whole new set of them in the form of Head Coach Tom Coughlin's own wacky universe of rules.

CHAPTER FOUR

The Coach and Player Relationship

October 20, four days before our Monday nighter in Dallas

The traffic getting to work on this particular day was brutal. Damn Lincoln Tunnel. Like the rest of the entire New York metropolitan area, I'm snakebitten by one of the Hudson River crossings. Late for work is never a good option for any employee in America, but for me I don't have the luxury of just walking away with a hard look from the boss. My superiors show no understanding, monetarily speaking.

Arriving late for work carries a dock in pay, starting at $500 and doubling with each violation. Freakin' Lincoln Tunnel! Plus, I *really* don't want to be late for work because it's Cowboys week. I feel a good one coming on and preparing for the Cowboys always brings excitement. It attracts more media, more attention and the old reliable plethora of Tuna stories. Love it. I'm excited to play against Drew Bledsoe because I know he's one quarterback who holds on to the ball long enough to become a nice, easy target.

There are certain quarterbacks I play against that I know

I have a better chance of sacking. I KNOW my chances are better against Bledsoe, Donovan and a young guy like Romo. Manning, Brady or Brees are harder to hone in on, though.

But it's Bledsoe week, and the last thing I want is to miss even a minute of work. Weeks like this are too much fun. I truly don't want to be late but, hey, it happens. Certain things we cannot control.

Out of my control this morning is a car that's stopped inside the tunnel. This unforeseen obstacle in my race to work forces me and about five thousand other people to collectively scream profanities at the knucklehead who forgot that cars generally run on fuel and that said fuel must be *inside* the tank.

Many of the cars stuck near the 31st Street underground pathway are carrying people who can simply explain away the stalled vehicle to their bosses. Or in many cases, the boss can jump in with a Lincoln Tunnel horror story of his own. My boss could be Al Yeganek, aka the man made famous on Seinfeld's "Soup Nazi" episode. No 'scuse for you!

You have to understand my boss, the head coach, and our history together. As big a week as Dallas week is, I just decide to cool it and not get worked up. Knowing I'm already going to be late, I stop worrying, stop rushing and just cruise on over to the stadium at my leisure. But before you throw me under the bus for being an insubordinate (one of my boss's favorite words), there's a rhyme to my rhythm here. Before passing judgment I must explain how and where it all began. Welcome to our soap opera, *As the Tom Turns*.

The first time I ever met Tom Coughlin face-to-face was his first season here, 2004, the day before his off-season program was to begin. The two of us spent the morning exchanging

words about an event I had committed to in Hawaii long before Coughlin ever took the job. This event, it so happened, fell on the same day as the inaugural meeting of Coach's off-season program.

Earlier in the day I had felt that Tom actually set me up when he had my new defensive coordinator, Tim Lewis, phone me at the ridiculous hour of eight o'clock Sunday morning to "introduce" himself. I could see eight A.M. Monday through Friday, but on a Sunday?

Both Lewis and Coughlin knew I had a prior commitment and would not be attending the first day of "voluntary" workouts. While I would certainly fulfill my commitments, I simply couldn't make it on Day One. It wouldn't be right to commit to a company or a charity and then bail out.

Considering it was eight A.M., my first thought was, Uh-oh, something bad just happened. I was wrong. Instead, something bad *was about* to happen. I was about to get bamboozled.

"Michael, how you doing?" Lewis asked. "We're looking forward to working with you. We want to put you in a better position to get you more sacks."

"That's great, Coach, but I'm not worried about the sacks. I'll get the sacks no matter what defense we're playing. I just want to know that our defense will be a great one. Whatever you need me to do, I'll do."

I was anticipating what was next. The bait for the setup.

"Michael, I can't wait to see you on Monday and . . ."

I have absolutely no idea what he said after that because, in essence, he had just moved his pawn. I was figuring out *my* next move. I've been around long enough to know a setup when I see one coming, and this was a setup, and an insulting one at that. My first-ever impression of my new coaches was that these dudes were trying to sandbag me.

"Coach, I'm not going to be able to make the first one."

"Oh?" said Lewis, not so innocently. "What are you talking about?"

"I told you guys I wasn't going to be there. I have a commitment."

"Does Coach know?"

"I assume he does."

Then came the setup.

"Hold on, Michael, actually Coach happens to be right here."

Yeah, right. As if. Wow, Coach Coughlin just happened to be walking by his office at that exact second? What a wonderful coincidence! You're a great actor, Tim. You guys really had me fooled.

Coughlin got on the phone without Lewis's "hello, my left end warrior" tone in his voice. Instead, my first-ever conversation with the third head coach of my career might as well have been in a dark room with a single light shining on my face. Let the interrogation begin.

The first thing my new coach said to me was, "Who is this appearance for? What event is it? I can't believe you won't be here for my first meeting! Michael, you need to be here! Change your flight. It's important that you're here. It's about the team."

Wow! Take a breath, sir. Nice to meet you, too, sir. I didn't want to get off on the wrong foot with this man, so I tried to pacify him by asking if I could jump in the car and come in that very afternoon to meet with him and the rest of the coaches in person. Tom reluctantly accepted my peace offering. I figured he thought it would provide him the perfect opportunity to grill me in person. Seems my assessment was accurate.

Once I got there, the first person I saw was Tim Lewis. He

walked me into Tom's office, and just as I suspected, Tom immediately began grilling me about the appearance again. So I figured I'd show a little bend. I told Tom that I would try to move my flight if possible, come in early, sit through his orientation and meeting and then take off.

At our first meeting, Tom approached me as if to say, "You've had a pretty good career, but if you listen to every single thing I say, I'll make you a real football player."

On the way home I called Jean, my wife at the time, and told her, "Enjoy this year because it will be our last in New York. This man is crazy! He's nuts! I'm not finishing up my career with this type of coach."

The whole thing began to eat away at me to the point that I called my marketing agent, Maury Gostfrand, and told him about our conversation. I'd decided I wouldn't change my flight. Why should I bend for a man who had clearly set the stage for a game? If I budged, that would send a message that he could bully me and push me around. He didn't need to start off our first meeting so aggressively. He could have asked me, not told me.

Today's player is different from years ago. Today's player is his own separate corporation subcontracted out for one single goal. Unlike yesterday's player, today's player is given so much money, we can decide to walk away at any time and hang up our cleats and not have to deal with this crap. We have the advantage of leaving on our own terms, more so than in any other era of sports.

Today's player feels empowered by free agency. Just look at Terrell Owens. He got himself out of San Francisco by complaining incessantly. Then he got himself out of a trade to Baltimore. Then he eventually moped his way out of Philly. Hell, the NFL and the union intervened to get T.O. out of a trade to the Ravens. Then it battled in his deal with the

Eagles. Of course, players are going to believe we can take matters into our own hands.

Half these guys complain in order to change cities. Daunte Culpepper did it to get out of Minnesota. When he was nearly traded to Tennessee, he told the head coach and general manager point-blank he wasn't going. Willis McGahee complained his way out of Buffalo. LaVar Arrington did the same after a bad couple of years in Washington. His former teammate Laveranues Coles complained his way out of DC. Shit, I tried the same thing earlier in my career when I thought the Giants were playing hardball on my deal. I don't think we're arrogant or overstepping the line by doing so. It's just the way it is sometimes.

Today's player has the money to be more vocal. When I first came into the league, when a coach said something, you swallowed it. But as free agency swept through and changed our game, players' attitudes changed. I had a teammate named Will Peterson who now goes by William James. Will signed a big-time deal with the Giants a few years ago and decided he would no longer take Coach Coughlin's BS. It got to the point where the two of them got into a very heated argument in the locker room that ended with Will throwing his arms out in the air, staring at Tom as if to say, "Come on, you want some of this?"

Today's player doesn't do much without knowing what kind of security he has. Will knew the salary-cap ramifications of being cut. If a guy has a cap hit that makes it impossible to cut him, what's a coach going to do to him? I'd say most of us wouldn't take it to the extreme of Will P., but when push comes to shove, we always know what's in our back pocket. Not only does today's player hold the trump card, he'll drop it on a dime. Yesterday's player had no such trump card.

Peterson ended up fracturing his vertebrae and spent about a year rehabbing before signing with the Eagles last season. But before he broke his back, the other luxury he had, which is what a lot of us rely on to give us security, is to fight for himself. If you can play, somebody will pay. Today we think, "I'll go make money somewhere else." And for the most part, we're right.

Ours is a league of egos. Owners, general managers and coaches love to believe that even if another team can't control or get the best out of a player, *they* can. They'll force themselves to believe that a kid who is unsalvageable will suddenly become a model citizen and Pro Bowl player under their tutelage. At least eight out of ten times, the team and the coach are just fooling themselves.

When I started in this league, even the malcontents learned to keep their mouths shut. Coaches back then were different, too. If a guy was an asshole, he'd not only find himself out of a job with his current team, he'd also get blackballed around the league. I think what T.O. did more than anything was to emphasize the fact that teams simply aren't listening to other teams anymore. How could a guy with that much baggage get another big contract thrown at him? The pressure to win is so much stronger, teams are now willing to take risks and gamble on players, hoping they'll change their spots. Now, instead of fearing you'll get a bad reputation in the league, the owners' failure to make our behavior affect our signings makes us unafraid of guys like Tom Coughlin.

I bet you if Adam "Pacman" Jones was cut tomorrow despite his one-year suspension by the NFL for frequent run-ins with the law, a couple of teams would still be climbing all over themselves to sign him. They all want to win so badly, they'll convince themselves he can be rehabilitated under their watchful eye.

Hate to tell you fellas, but it doesn't happen that way. We don't change that drastically. We might grow up, but we won't change that dramatically. The most you can hope for is that players will smarten up before it's too late, which does happen in this league. My good friend John Abraham, the former Jets Pro Bowler and current Atlanta Falcon, had a drinking problem. The team knew about it, yet they treaded lightly around it. He was too good a player to discipline. They were lucky he decided to grow up and sober up on his own. He realized he was screwing up his career and stopped showing up drunk to work. He quit cold turkey and threw himself into religion instead of booze.

Just look how much juice players now have. John Abraham could still go to the facility, hammered from the night before (actually from an hour before), smelling of booze, and yet he could continue as long as he didn't get arrested. You can booze as long as you produce. Your teammates will confront you before your coaches do because you can stand up to your coaches as long you know you are a good, solid player. They won't do anything to you.

As for the argument between Tom and Will, I don't recall Will getting fined, benched, suspended, nothing. It all started because Tom told us not to talk about injuries, and within minutes, Will decided to tell the media about his back injury. He didn't care about Tom's rules. He was going to protect his own reputation whether the team liked it or not. That, my friend, is the epitome of today's player.

Knowing I had a choice, and knowing Tom couldn't just up and cut me, I felt like I could push the envelope. If I was going to hate him, I had the freedom to hate him. Today's player will not hide the hate.

I began to question whether I could play even one year under this man. Prior to my meeting, several players from

Jacksonville who had played under Coughlin called me to warn me of his unusual rules and rigidness.

As players, we exchange information about coaches. Just like they scout us for free agency, we scout *them* for free agency. We compare notes. When a coach moves on to another team, players will usually call somebody who has previously worked with the new man.

When John Fox moved from our defensive coordinator to head coach at Carolina, the leaders in their locker room called Armstead and me to get the scouting report on him. What are his strengths? His weaknesses? What pisses him off? What kind of guy is he off the field? What kind of system does he use? Have you ever had a run-in with him? What things did you love about him? What things did you hate about him? The most asked question is: Is he fair?

I initially thought Tom's reputation would end up hurting our chances in free agency, or at least force us to overpay the hell out of some guys. But one thing I learned about players during the last off-season: New York and money completely supersede anybody's bad reputation. New York is too attractive an option with too much glitz and glamour and the chance of being a star for a player to pass up. A coach's reputation has a bigger impact in other cities that don't have as many off-the-field perks as New York. Still, I thought, if ever a reputation could kill our chances in free agency, it was Tom's.

The reviews I received about my new coach were horrendous. Two thumbs, two index fingers, a couple of pinkies and two ring fingers down, way down! I had at least ten players call me about Tom. All but one had horrible reviews. I mean, some were absolutely awful. One player I talked to called him an abusive warden. One good review out of ten guys? That's not good, folks.

In my eyes Tom started off on the wrong foot with me, before saying word one. Yet I'll admit I made the mistake of viewing him with a preconceived notion of what a jerk he would be. I didn't take the mature route by making a decision based solely on my experience. In the beginning, Tom probably could have told me the sky is blue and I would have questioned him. What kind of dummy does this warden think I am?

When I called to inform Tom I could neither cancel my appearance nor change my flight, to say he was infuriated would be an understatement. Based on his reaction, I thought the man had lost his mind. He wanted the names and numbers of the people running the event so he could call them personally and cancel. This guy was one of those scary crazy guys. I figured if he could be this delusional, well, who the hell knows what he's capable of during the season. So I figured I'd better try to bend a little.

"Coach, how about this. I'll come in at six A.M. to meet with you and the other coaches, go through your strength and conditioning orientation and hear you out before you meet with the team. Then I'll fly out."

Tom agreed, but even the way he agreed was confrontational. I knew our personalities would eventually clash big-time.

Monday morning, day of our meeting, I honestly, truly and absolutely believed I was getting punk'd by Ashton Kucher. I believed that since *Punk'd* was so popular and a few other NFL stars, like Warren Sapp, Jeff Garcia and Jerome Bettis, had fallen victim, somebody had set me up, too. Seriously. My first-ever OFFICIAL meeting with the new head coach, and there was no doubt in my mind that it was all a setup. It had to be a joke. It had to be!

I walked into Coughlin's office. Sitting there on his desk was a legal pad with one single piece of yellow paper left. The rest had been ripped out. A yellow No. 2 pencil lay on top of the pad.

"Michael, this pad and pencil is for you," he said as he stared through me. "I'm going to give you the same speech I will be giving the rest of the team when we meet later. I want you to write down key points. Then I want you to take it with you on the airplane and think about these points on your trip."

Man, you MTV folks, you've got some imagination. How do you think these things up? And how did you get Coughlin to go along with it? Okay, come on out now, Ashton.

About halfway through Coughlin's speech, I started to think maybe this wasn't a setup. On those hidden camera shows, they don't let you suffer too long. We had crossed the time boundary. All of a sudden I thought to myself, "This guy is actually serious? There are no cameras. This is not a joke. Are you freakin' kidding me?"

When I finally came to grips with reality, my first thought was: "Is my twelfth season *really* going to resemble fourth-grade detention?" I couldn't pay attention because I couldn't grasp what was happening. He spouted a bunch of quotes meant to inspire me. But I was well past the inspirational stage. After he finished his speech, I went downstairs, put his sheet of paper in my locker, closed it and took off for Hawaii.

That started what would be a very, very tumultuous first year with my new head coach. In today's NFL, things are so volatile, we live in a what-have-you-done-for-me-lately society. So I raced back from Hawaii in less than a day to make sure I showed up at the second and third day of Camp

Coughlin 2004. But once I got there, I resented the man to the point where if I had been driving along and saw Tom crossing the street, I might have sped up.

From that instant, my relationship with Tom sucked. I did not want to play for him. I wanted nothing to do with the man. It was shaping up to be the most horrific time of my career. All *before* I learned about all of his rules. When I finally learned about the rules from his handbook for success . . . I'm still at a loss for words to this day.

So we still have that little matter of a Lincoln Tunnel breakdown that resulted in a fine. But to explain further what it's like to play in the NFL under a guy you view as a tyrant, let's continue to examine our history.

Individually and collectively, coaches believe that players crave structure. Ask any NFL head coach and they'll tell you: Structure and consistency are the two most important qualities in our NFL lives. To be truthful, they're dead-on in their assessment.

If you gave players the option to show up only on Sundays, half the team would take that as a license to party Monday through Saturday. We need rules, regulations and guidelines. Some guys crave them, even if they don't know it.

First of all, you can't give a young kid ten million bucks and tell him you'll see him on Sunday. Some team rules are designed to protect us from ourselves. Too much money plus too much time often equals disaster. If there's one downside to today's player in regard to the money, it's this: TOO MUCH MONEY MAKES GUYS DO CRAZY THINGS. The money makes us feel like stars, even when we're not.

In today's NFL, you can have a mediocre player flying below the radar screen. The moment he makes a boatload of cash his star power skyrockets. The money in today's game overrates players. On many teams, cornerbacks are afraid to hit somebody. But those who are decent in coverage get paid more than the captain of the defense, the middle linebacker. When a guy gets a big contract, he becomes national news and he starts thinking he's much better than he really is. Today is the era of the overrated.

While consistency and regimens are probably more necessary now than ever before, a coach has to make sure he doesn't go overboard. Consistency may be just as important, if not more important, than structure; the worst possible thing a head coach can do is to be inconsistent. From day to day, week to week or even month to month, with so many different personalities and backgrounds coming together, we need at least one focal point to bring us together. That focal point—the head coach—needs to show us consistency.

But Tom's version of structure and consistency bordered on insanity. His rules and the way he did things during his first season in New York were pretty much obsolete in all other NFL locker rooms. I could see a Vince Lombardi or Tom Landry having strict rules. But last I checked, neither of these legendary coaches worked during the free-agency era. Their players were stars, but never *financial* stars like in today's locker room. As I talk to players all over the league, I can assure you other teams do not have these same rules. Other coaches, for the most part, treat you like an adult.

Example: When we go on the road we're required to travel wearing a suit and tie. All teams are. However, every other team, once they get to the hotel, has the luxury of getting comfortable.

Tom's team? You are forbidden to leave your room or go to the lobby without wearing dress slacks, a collared shirt and nice shoes. You can't even leave your room to go to another player's room dressed in a T-shirt, shorts and flip-flops like the rest of the world. Tom's rule: a collared shirt, dress socks, and dress shoes.

You are forbidden to go to the lobby to buy a toothbrush without wearing a collared shirt and slacks. No white socks whatsoever. Violate one of these rules and you're fined! Cash out of your next paycheck. What this has to do with football, I still don't understand. Will we win because we shopped for socks at Burberry? Come on!

Every other business traveler in America gets on a plane wearing a suit, gets to the hotel and is immediately allowed to relax. Not us. We're hit with a fine. I'm not saying, "Please feel sorry for the big, sad millionaire football players." All I'm saying is, if we are adults, we should be treated like adults. If something affects our performance, fine, make up a rule. If there is no clear purpose except for gaining control over guys by using a power trip, today's player not only won't respond, he'll rebel.

One young guy who wasn't going to make our club was fined by Tom because he wore sandals. Seems Coach didn't like his style of sandals. So now he's a fashion consultant? That's a joke!

Anyway, this guy who wasn't even going to make our team anyway got fined because Tom didn't like his style. That was pretty much every penny the kid made from the Giants. What Tom didn't know was that his rules made some of the young black guys feel as if he was targeting their background and their culture. It seemed like he was taking aim at the guys with the baggy jeans and diamond chains. I agree to a point that you don't want us looking like we're a bunch of gangsters. But we're all individuals with different styles. It's part of who we are.

Some guys may have nice dress shoes that look like ten-

nis shoes. But they aren't tennis shoes! They only resemble them. They actually cost more than dress shoes. Who are you to tell these guys they're not wearing proper shoes? Today, it's unfair to fine one man based upon another man's taste in shoes and clothes.

Like the time two years ago when Eagles head coach Andy Reid told his players that they needed to wear a coat and tie on the road. He also banned wearing tennis shoes. T.O. showed up wearing a tuxedo with dress shoes that looked like tennis shoes. Now that's just T.O. being a jackass to a coach he thought was being overbearing. But compared to Tom, Andy was a picture of tolerance.

Why would Tom Coughlin enter a new environment swinging so hard? You need to understand the mind-set of today's NFL head coach, the mind-set generally accepted by every coach out there. It's easier to start hard and get nicer, while it's nearly impossible to start nice and suddenly crack the whip like a hard-ass. Unfortunately even the whip was afraid of Tom.

All the crazy rules and antics of that first off-season paled in comparison to the road that would later send Tom and me to the crash-and-burn stage, a road I never want to travel again. Tom went way past hard-ass, directly to asinine and then made a sharp right turn, passing GO, driving headlong directly to psychotic.

CHAPTER FIVE

The Head Coach and I Hug It Out

I immediately grasped how different Tom Coughlin was from Dan Reeves and Jim Fassel, my two previous head coaches, as well as Andy Reid, Tony Dungy, John Fox and my other Pro Bowl coaches. Especially once I ran into his now controversial "five-minutes-early" rule. Ah yes, the great Coughlin Clock Debate. In describing Coughlin as psychotic, I still stand by that, though not in a dangerous criminal way. More in a delusional way.

By now most of the football world knows that Coughlin believes we should all show up five minutes early to every meeting. It shows how eager we are to meet. Eager? I couldn't be more eager to have bamboo shoved under my fingernails.

We meet every day, hear the same crap, and waste hours upon hours of our lives. I shouldn't use the term *waste* because those meetings certainly once had a useful role in our lives. But for guys who've been around, it's like listening to the same old Tony Robbins instructional video over and over. Why in the hell would I want to show up five minutes early to that?

We are a conglomeration of six-, seven- and eight-figure corporations. Why treat us like sixth, seventh and eighth graders? At first, who knew Coughlin had this crazy five-minute rule? Who sets a meeting time when he really wants a meeting to start five minutes *earlier*? Here's how we found out Tom wanted us to come to his meetings five minutes early: when he immediately lowered the boom on three new players in front of the rest of the team. Here's what happened.

Each week during the preseason and regular season, we're given a test on our plays and assignments. One day cornerback Terry Cousins and linebacks Barrett Green and Carlos Emmons were sitting outside the meeting room working on their tests. While the rest of the team trickled into the meeting room, the three figured they had a few more minutes to add the finishing touches to their answers.

Apparently what ticked Coughlin off was that they didn't file in with the rest of the team, so he closed the door on them. When the unsuspecting trio opened the door, with plenty of time before the meeting was slated officially to begin, Coughlin exploded. "You three were out there messing around! You're late!" So he kicked them out of the meeting and fined them for being early but not early enough.

Everybody else sat stunned, looking at our watches and thinking, "Are you kidding me?" It was Tom's way of just trying to be a hard-ass. Why? Because he could. Same reason we stand up to the coaches in today's game—because we can. Just like that phrase "What's good for the goose is good for the gander," except what's bad for one is bad for the other.

There's nothing good about how much liberty both sides now have.

Some coaches are viewed as ballbusters, as hard-asses. But even the tough ones, they'll bust your chops for a reason. Agree or disagree, there's a clear reason. Tom didn't seem to have a clear reason and that's difficult for a player, or any person for that matter, to grasp. When Seattle's head coach Mike Holmgren rips the hell out of one of his quarterbacks, which he's been known to do, it's usually because somebody somehow screwed up something somewhere.

Plus, there's a way to do it. John Fox has the uncanny ability to call you a dummy to the degree where you damn near thank him for such sensitive and constructive criticism. You can tell he's in this thing WITH you. Tom makes you feel like he's AGAINST you.

There was no way for anyone to know or even comprehend why Coughlin wanted us to show up five minutes early for everything, or else face a fine. So if that's the case, just set the damn meeting five minutes earlier, right?

Tom started an uproar inside our locker room, an uproar unseen in years. Instead of talking about goals and game plans or certain techniques, our lives were soon consumed by complaints. Every free moment was spent talking about this crazy coach's rules. The sad thing is, it never got old. The complaints only grew louder until eventually most of the team came to me to complain. I was pretty much appointed to address Coach Coughlin with the hopes of preventing a coup before the season started.

So I met with him and told him I didn't think it was right to fine guys for showing up on time. He assured me that from now on, everyone would be accounted for and that he would let guys know when the meetings were going to start. If a guy

was there within a five-minute grace period he would let him in. In other words, he promised not to sandbag the men anymore.

Remember that sharp turn on the road past insane to completely psychotic? Here's where the road forks. Barely a week or two later, I arrived for our 7:30 meeting. When I walked up to the door at 7:26, the door was already slammed closed. Our assistant strength coach and our player programs guy, Charles Way, our former fullback, were all outside the door. I pointed at the clocks on the walls. They looked at me and shrugged.

I pointed to the clock, which like every other clock in our locker room was set five minutes fast. It read 7:27. How insane is it that Tom took time to actually have somebody move the hands on our clocks forward? I told them I'd be damned if I was going to open that door, walk in there and have him explode on me like he did to my defensive teammates. No way. Not a shot. The two coaches said they would tell Coughlin I was there on time.

Okay, brace yourselves, folks, for what transpired next. The next day I went to my locker to get dressed for practice. Sitting on my stool was a fine letter for $500. When Tom fines us, the team management writes a formal letter and puts it either in our locker or on our stool. This wasn't even funny. In my world, $500 may not seem like a lot, but in principle it's everything. This fine was against every principle. I learned that being part of a team was not supposed to be players in one group, coaches in another. We're supposed to be together as one.

On the way to the team walkthrough I asked, "Coach, can I talk to you for a minute? I got a letter on my stool for being fined, but I wasn't late."

"Yes, you were."

"Coach, I wasn't late. Two of your coaches saw me."

"Well, you were late."

"Even if I wasn't there five minutes early, you said you'd give us a grace period."

"Well, Michael, in my eyes you were still late. What do you want me to do, change my rules for you?"

"No! I don't want you to change the rules for me. But I wasn't late. If I'm late, then fine me! But I was not late! In fact, I was three minutes early!"

He kept repeating the same argument over and over again. Was I really having this conversation?

"Next time don't cut it so close."

Don't cut it so close? That started my blood boiling. But it really boiled over after our new head coach added, "You're lucky. It could have been fifteen hundred dollars."

What? I'm lucky? Did he just threaten me? That pushed me past the edge. We're all grown men, yet you want to be a jerk and chastise me, and then ask me to lay my blood down on that field for *you*?

I was pushed past my point of patience. I exploded.

"You know what? Fuck it. Fine me fifteen hundred dollars next time and if I know I'm going to be late I'll just come in here whenever I damn well feel like it. Screw it. I'll go to I-Hop, I'll run a few errands. I'll show up whenever!"

He stared at me in shock, "You can't talk to me like that!"

"Yes, I can. If you don't respect me, I won't respect you. So I'll come in whenever I feel like it. Whether I'm a second late or an hour late, I'll come in whenever I want! Just fine me the max."

I started to walk away as Tom started walking after me. The rest of the team was about thirty yards away from us. They saw us talking but didn't know what we were saying.

They noticed, however, that my demeanor had changed. My switch had flipped.

Coughlin asked again, "I don't understand. Do you want me to change my rules for you?"

At this point in our relationship, I had been coming to Tom with issues from the guys, trying to bridge the gap between the coach and the locker room. We talked about what the guys were feeling and thinking about since camp and he would just nod his head and say, "I hear you. I hear you."

When Coughlin asked me that again, I snapped.

"Coach, you're losing this whole team. Do you hear me *now*?"

That turned out to be the turning point. That day became the last day that I felt Tom Coughlin and Michael Strahan disliked each other. I found the harder I pushed back, the more respect I got from Tom. I'm not stupid. I fully realize that had I not been a six-time Pro Bowler, I couldn't have pushed back the way I did. Still, I wonder how that place would have functioned had I not pushed back that day, the day Tom and I changed toward each other, the day he started treating me with respect, somewhat listening to me and giving in a bit.

One thing about Tom. Away from football, he genuinely cares about us as people. However, because of all the football things that get in the way, his concern for us as people gets grossly overlooked. I believe that when he heard how close he was to losing his team, he decided to give in a bit. He really had no choice but to change a little.

Remember what I said, that it's easier to go from hard to easy than it is from easy to hard? There's an undefined line in each locker room as to how far is too far. Tom went too far. But I don't think he realized it until that afternoon.

Our relationship has since blossomed to the point where

I can go to him with any problem, mine or someone else's. At first it's his nature not to listen. He has to be pushed. Now he sees that he doesn't have to push me. He doesn't have to make me angry for me to play well. He expects me to be ready to play, so that helped turn our tide. I pay attention to detail, which is something Coach loves. Plus, because of our ups and downs, he also learned that I don't sulk. I just try to get it right and fight to win.

Once we stepped back from our incident, it allowed our attention to shift from focusing on our differences and arguments to trying to understand each other. Remember the reviews on Tom I received around the league? The one positive review I got from another player came from the longtime Jaguars, Bucs and Chargers receiver Keenan McCardell. He told me, "Michael, the first year you have him, you'll hate him. But the more you play for him, the more you'll understand him. The more you understand him, the more you'll like him."

I now understand the man, and Keenan is right, I do like him. He changed because he had to. He realized he couldn't do it all by himself. Now he trusts some of us to help him get his message across. He now understands he's from a whole different school of thought that today's millionaire players don't naturally comprehend. His favorite movie is *Patton* with George C. Scott, and there's a quote from the movie when Patton says something along the lines of "My enemy is scared of me. My troops are scared of me. My own dog is afraid of me." I guess Tom wanted to be just like Patton. But after our confrontation, he also realized this is a different age of football. I truly believe he understands that now. You can't scare today's player because today's player might shout back at you, or go to his agent and the media and demand a ticket out of town.

The number one thing that changed about Tom is that now I can see when we meet privately, he listens. He doesn't just blow it off. Three years ago he didn't want to hear. It was like, "You're a player and you have no right to make rules." Now he doesn't take that approach anymore.

I'm not going to say that everybody likes him. Some guys don't. The thing about Tom is that he's a decent man and can be understanding when he wants to be. Maybe he needs to show that side more. After that first year, after trying to be like Patton, now every once in a while he'll show a softer side.

I remember when Kurt Warner, our former quarterback, went up to see Tom with his kids in tow. He wanted to be honest with the man. Kurt said that once Tom saw the kids, he got on the ground and played with them like they were his own grandkids. We need to see more of *that guy*. We know he's in there, but he doesn't want us to see that side a lot. Maybe he thinks it's a sign that he's weak or something.

While he's gotten better, that doesn't mean guys still don't fear the hell out of him. One day, one of our linemen, Grey Ruegamer, flipped his truck on Route 3 in New Jersey. It was a terrible wreck that closed Route 3. Not a pretty picture. Grey was so petrified of being late for one of Coughlin's meetings and having to deal with the wrath of Tom, he had the tow truck drive him directly to the stadium. And Ruegamer wasn't some rookie, either. He'd been in the league for nine years.

Some head coaches in the NFL have gotten calls in the middle of the night and driven out somewhere to help a stranded player. Former Falcons head coach Jim Mora, Jr., has done that for guys. The entire locker room loved him for the fact that they knew he was there for them. They weren't afraid to mess up and be human.

In my opinion, the perfect head coach is that approachable, like that uncle who you always knew you could go to if you were in trouble. He'd help you out.

At first not only did we think Tom wouldn't help us, but that he'd be the first one calling the cops on us. Tom needed to get the players to buy into what he was preaching before we'd run through walls for him. That's what coaches like John Fox, Lovie Smith, Tony Dungy, Sean Payton and Bill Belichick do. Andy Reid makes you crave his approval. Jeff Fisher makes you feel like crap if you let him down.

On the other extreme, coaches like Joe Gibbs, who have that old-school style, don't often have the connection with the locker room they need today. When Pro Bowl safety Sean Taylor got hit with a DUI, Gibbs immediately punished him without waiting to find out if he was guilty or not. As it turned out, he wasn't. He was completely exonerated. So how do you think Taylor and others in that locker room looked at Gibbs at that point? Legend or no legend, today's player doesn't care about your pedigree.

Players believe in the coaches who have our best interests at heart. When coaches rip into their players, guys feel ashamed. For letting Foxie down. Ashamed for disappointing Lovie. I can't tell you how many players I speak to are forever loyal and grateful to Belichick and Parcells for not only teaching them about football, but for caring about them off the field, and for teaching them how to handle their lives. They're teachers of life lessons.

This is where today's NFL coaches make a difference, especially with young guys or guys without father figures while growing up. I liked Tom enough that I truly did not want him fired at the end of 2006. I'm sure some guys did, but I absolutely did not. We'd spent the past three years learning to respect each other.

NFL players fear the unknown. Who knows what a new guy would have done had he come in here? Who knew what kind of whip he would crack or if a new coach was a good coach or a better coach? Now that I was truly happy with my hard-ass coach, I didn't have to go through the whole get-to-know-you phase all over again.

I can't believe I'm actually writing this, but I want to end my career with Tom Coughlin. I want to learn more about him. Watch him crack that exterior even more in 2007. Then finally, I'll walk into the sunset with him as the last head coach of my career.

Before this turns into a lovefest for Tom, we still have that little matter of my tardiness on the morning of October 20, due to that stalled vehicle in the Lincoln Tunnel. Remember what I told Tom that day? That if I knew I was getting fined anyway, I would show up whenever I wanted?

For the record, I had my best game of the season that Monday night against the Cowboys. I terrorized Bledsoe like I knew I would. And then Tony Romo, after Bledsoe got benched. Obviously, missing that meeting did not affect my game. Regardless of how well I played, and despite having my best game of the season, the day after that game, I received a letter at my locker from Tom that read:

Dear Michael,

This letter is to formally notify you that you were late for a team meeting on October 20, 2006. Unexcused late reporting to any mandatory team related activity is a violation of the New York Giants 2006 Rules, Regulations and Maximum Club Discipline Schedule. For such action the Club hereby fines you $1,500.00.

Please be advised that any repeat violations may

result in increased fines and/or suspension for conduct detrimental.

> *Sincerely,*
> *Tom Coughlin*
> *Head Coach*

Later that afternoon, Mr. Sincerely, Tom Coughlin, Head Coach, sent one of his assistants over to talk to me about being late. I cut the coach off in mid-sentence, proclaiming, "Look, Coach, either he's going to fine me or lecture me, I'm not getting both."

With that I walked away. I guess it's all part of the Tom-Michael relationship now. Fine me for being three minutes early, we have a problem. Fine me for being late. If I deserve it, I'll take my medicine like a man. As a veteran, at least I'd been around long enough to know that I could play the role of diplomat.

CHAPTER SIX

Behind the Locker Room Doors

The peanut butter and jelly sandwich was just itching to bust through the gap. Just begging to launch itself through my two dearly distanced front teeth. My eyes bulged in anger, but it was the freakin' sandwich everyone will remember. Why in the hell would I ever put a sandwich in my mouth before taking a stand at my locker to berate a throng of media people, in front of cameras no less?

What would possibly possess me to stuff a half-eaten sandwich in my mouth, then come out with a verbal assault? What was I thinking?

What ticked me off so much? The now infamous incident when a reporter took quotes of mine made on the radio and tried to create a rift between me and Plaxico Burress. It was alleged that I said on my radio show that Plax is a quitter. Man, I know the man isn't a quitter. He's too good a player to be remembered as a guy who gave up on a play. What I said wasn't with the intent of implying he was a bad guy or a quitter. I simply stated that the play in question—a play in which he slowed up on a route and then made a halfhearted attempt to tackle "Pacman" Jones of the Titans after his interception of an Eli pass—was not indicative of the pride he has in being the player he is.

I don't think it bothered Plax at first. He knows how I feel about him. But when the entire thing escalated, I think Plax felt obligated to get mad and defend himself. He needed to save face in the eyes of the public. As if we needed any more controversy in this place, we just got some, courtesy of my big mouth and a really bad play.

So I sought out Plax privately: "I know you're not a quitter. If I felt you were, I'd tell you to your face."

As the two of us sat in the hot tub together before practice (with shorts on, I must stress), I told him I would never beat around the bush on something like that. He didn't say anything except, "All right!" All he kept saying was, "All right!"

The next day he went out and told the media that he told me if I had something to say, I could say it to his face. I had no problem with his saving face, but I don't remember that conversation ever actually taking place. Once again I wanted to clear the air, so I approached him again in the trainer's room. This time I told him if *he* had something to say, let's clear the air. I wanted to move past this thing. I didn't want to get into a pissing contest with him. All he said was, "No, I'm cool, I'm cool."

After few days of him avoiding me, Plax finally said, "You know what? All is good now, Michael. To be honest with you, it kind of stoked my fire."

What most people don't know about me and Plax is that he is actually one of my best friends on the team. As far as who I interact with, I go out of my way to hang with Plax,

joke with Plax and talk to him every single day before each practice. The two of us soak together (again, with shorts on) and we sit and talk about pretty much everything going on in our lives.

It hurt me that I hurt a guy like that. It upset me that a guy I truly cared about was stung. Inside our locker rooms there are only a handful of guys you get close with. A handful of others you have no idea who they are because they either just got there or are about to leave. The rest you hang with loosely. Plax was one of the guys I was tightest with.

When he first came to the team, he arrived with the reputation of being a troublemaker. Word was he was not a good teammate. One day, early on in the relationship, I walked past him and said, "What's up, Plax?" He just ignored my pleasantries and kept walking, so I burst out with, "What's the matter? You're not going to speak to me today? I'm just being nice and you can't say hello?" He finally responded with a casual, "Huh? Oh, what's up?"

I don't think anyone ever came at him like that. I'd cracked the exterior. Of all the guys in the locker room, he's one of the last ones I expected to become close to, but we ended up being that friendly. Go figure. An NFL locker room is a funny thing. Our locker room is its own wild little community consisting of an entirely unique set of social rules and norms.

Think about it. We've got fifty-three guys, and five more on the practice squad, all forced to look at each other every single day. We practice together, travel together, work together, meet together, eat together, fight together, cry together, and shower together for at least six months a year, maybe longer.

We've got big farm boys fighting alongside inner-city guys. We have Ivy Leaguers befriending those who majored in eligibility or who got the big boot from school. Different races and religions, Republicans and Democrats, even a few anarchists, all bonded together for one common cause—fighting for that beautiful, elusive ring. We become one united world under the Lombardi Trophy.

We sweat together, we stink together and we sit in big vats of ice together. Imagine sitting waist-deep in an old bucket of ice with another grown man. You know what true trust is? Trust is that he won't piss in that tub with you.

Our locker rooms are like the jungle. Instead of eating each other for survival of the fittest, you've got the lions hanging out with the antelopes and the hippos. Not only do we not eat each other, we vigorously fight for the other animals in our jungle. Sounds funny but we are absolutely *that* much different.

I grew up as an army brat. While many of these guys have grown up knowing only one kind of person, I moved a lot and lived on an army base in Germany and came across a terrific array of nationalities and beliefs.

When I sit back and think about it, 98 percent of the guys I play with, if we didn't play football together, I'd probably never find myself hanging out with. We'd have nothing in common.

What sense would it make for me to hang out with a big farm boy like our former left tackle Luke Petigout from Pennsylvania? But I worked out with him every day and actually enjoyed it.

This is where football is great. If the rest of the world could follow the lead of an NFL locker room, we wouldn't have three-fourths of the wars that plague our planet. The Middle East leaders should all be thrown together in an NFL locker room, forced to do the same things we do, and I guarantee you the Israelis and Arabs would suddenly love each

other. There may be ignorance or fear of the unknown coming into a locker room, but you leave with an incredible education in sociology.

Just look at our position dinners. Each week during the season every member of our defensive line gets together and goes out to dinner. Yes, in public. The o-line does the same thing in every locker room. The defensive backs often do the same thing. Different groups gather outside our locker rooms and hit the town in a sign of bonding. Our defensive line has had guys in trouble with the law—black guys, white guys, a big gap-toothed man with a PB&J hanging out of his mouth, braniacs, complete buffoons, we all go out to dinner and converse like we're family.

How different can we be? One big lineman from Arkansas who played with us had a head the size of a watermelon. We'd get to a nice restaurant and as we're preparing to order, this young buck would declare, "Wow, I ain't never seen no thirty-dollar steak."

We'd all stare at the kid in complete disbelief. Then he'd make it worse by proclaiming he wanted to take his wife to a nice I-talian restaurant and proceed to ask if any of us knew where the nearest Olive Garden was.

Now would I ever hang out with a man like this in real life? Hell, no, but in our world, I'd fight for him and knock out anybody I had to in order to protect this man in the line of fire. I'd fight for him like I came out of the womb with him.

The craziest thing is when you see two guys become really close who couldn't be more opposite—a talkative East Coast inner-city guy and a quiet guy from California. Happens in every locker room. Not only do these cats get close, but often their wives get close as well.

Each Halloween, Eli throws a party and pretty much the

whole team shows up. In real life, three quarters of the people in this locker room would not be invited nor would they want to attend. But in our world, not only do they (and their spouses) show up, they show up in costume, so as to follow the rules of a party thrown by some country kid from Louisiana.

Actually, at that party, Eli came up with the greatest costume of all time. It was right after our then-quarterback Jesse Palmer had finished a stint starring in *The Bachelor*. Eli dressed up in one of Jesse's suits, completely gelled his hair to look like Jesse and carried a handful of roses. He walked around all night handing people roses, voting to keep them in his harem, just like Palmer did on the show. It was hilarious.

As quiet as Eli is, that party showed us that he can drink with us, party with us and bust on us just like the best of us. He had gone through some rough times, but it's parties like these that go far in reinforcing our devotion to each other.

The most important rule inside our locker room is brotherhood! Whether you're there for a day, a week, a month or several years, we all abide by a brotherhood of rules. You're OUR brother now, and we'll fight *like* brothers and fight like crazy *for* each other.

Entering the brotherhood comes with advice. You must drop your past and accept that life is now different. Cut any dead weight that has been in your life up until the day you walk into our world. The sooner you drop those negative influences, the better off you will be. But half these guys believe you have to keep it real and don't drop the dead weight.

I've had to pull kids aside and explain to them, "Those other cats you're hanging with, you need to cut them off. Cut the cord."

Also, some guys have a difficult time hearing from their friends how money has changed them. One of the most insulting things that can be said about a guy is for his crew to tell his boys back home that he's changed, that he's big-timing them. Those are damn near fightin' words.

But now, you are part of *our* family, so don't put us in harm's way. There are far too many hangers-on and users trying to take advantage of people in our world. At times things can get hairy. I don't want to be collateral damage.

Look at what happened with Ray Lewis years ago when his homeboys allegedly stabbed a couple of other guys to death. Ray realized that he needed to get away from those sorts of guys. Now he's as much a model citizen in the NFL as you have. Sean Taylor of the Redskins had his car and house sprayed with bullets by some guy he had a long-running feud with. What if one (or more) of his teammates had been at his house that night and got shot? Get that shit away from us!

The Broncos locker room got hit hard this year when some young guys who were hanging out with talented cornerback Darrent Williams got into it with some other hot-heads. Williams was the peacemaker and paid for it with his life when he was shot and died in the lap of his teammate Javon Walker.

We don't need to hang out with anyone who keeps us from reaching our goals, much less places our lives in danger. As close as you are with your boys back home, your locker-room brotherhood must run deeper. You have to hang with people who have as much or more to lose as you do.

If you simply refuse to stop hanging out with trouble, we'll distance ourselves from you. It's our version of an intervention, a silent intervention. We won't tell you about our parties. We won't include you in all of our off-field gatherings. There's way too much at stake here for any of us to get caught up in some crossfire, or even be seen with somebody who could tarnish our names.

I am not in the Bengals locker room, so I can't explain why they have so many screwups. It's not like their head coach, Marvin Lewis, accepts it. He fines the shit out of those guys. The problem is, however, that sometimes a locker room does not police itself well enough. We all have malcontents in our locker rooms. In fact, each locker room can benefit from the attitude of a couple of ornery guys. They'll bring that attitude onto the field but drop it once they walk back into the real world. They'll lose the thug attitude when the vets simply won't have any of it.

The stuff we say inside a locker room, if somebody said the same stuff on the streets, they'd want to hurt a man over it. You might want to severely injure me in the real world for some of the garbage that comes out of my mouth in that locker room. But the real world doesn't share our camaraderie.

As a result, we have a camaraderie that allows us to bag on one another—and mercilessly. When I say nothing is off-limits, I mean *nothing* is off-limits. If a guy gets arrested or has any other embarrasing incidents, we'll bust on him. If a guy even glances over at another guy in the hot tub or shower, for the rest of that year we'll call him a DW (dick watcher, a favorite term inside our domain).

William Joseph gets killed about his clothes: "Looks like you're wearing something that should be hanging in a curtain shop, William." Tiki used to get killed about his clothes, too: "Tiki, too short on the pants AND the tie!" Some of those country bumpkins show up in the brightest damn suits that make Deion Sanders look like he shops at OshKosh B'Gosh. We'll rag on them for hours at a time.

All the ribbing relieves the stress and the pressure to win

at all costs, which in turn builds camaraderie. Without that togetherness, without that bond and chemistry, we might want to kill someone every time they did something that cost us points or a game.

If you think about all the heartbreak I've had just during my fourteen years in New York, it's amazing that only once did I actually want to strangle a teammate for something he did in a game. Without this bond, there'd be a lot more incidents than just what happened on November 27, 2005.

That was the afternoon our kicker Jay Feely had three chances to win a game in Seattle. Week Twelve of the 2005 season. We were racking up the stats against the team with the best record in their conference, on their home field, no less. We had 480 yards of offense, Tiki gained 151 yards rushing, while Shockey and Plaxico Burress had more than 100 yards receiving apiece.

Playing in Seattle is tough enough because of the crowd noise. It's probably the loudest stadium in the league. We were up by six in the third quarter, then fell behind by eight with about four minutes left. With two minutes to go, we tied the game when Amani Toomer caught an 18-yard touchdown pass and Shockey caught a pass for the two-point conversion.

Here we go, 21–21, for dominance in the conference. Feely missed a 40-yard attempt on the final play of regulation. Okay, we get another chance. First possession of overtime, he misses another one, this one from 54 yards out. Understandable. Next possession, that son-of-a-you-know-what misses a 45-yarder. Seattle got the ball back and their kicker nailed the game winner.

Those kicks could have changed the course of history as Seattle moved to 9-2 and ended up with home field advantage in the playoffs on their way to the Super Bowl.

After that game, I went into the locker room and I took my chair, picked it up and threw it around the locker room, screaming my head off. I smashed the chair and then I picked up my helmet and smashed it on the ground as well.

I was so angry, sick and tired of being a bridesmaid, never the bride. Years of sacrificing my body, finally on the right track and we lose like this? There is no worse feeling in the NFL than the feeling of being snakebitten.

I had just had enough. Tim Lewis came over to calm me down. I told him, "F that! I'm done! I'm retiring after this year! Done! When are we going to win these close games? I'm sick of it!" Was I furious! Every time I looked at Feely, I had to contain myself. You're a freakin' kicker, all we needed was one out of three!

I was so angry that I honestly considered hanging up my cleats. But what's so wonderful about our locker room is, by the next day, I felt bad for having had such strong resentment toward my brother. Playing in the NFL has a way of stopping you from throwing stones while living in a glass house. Fans get to sit at home and rip us for a job done poorly. But we don't have that luxury. As a result, we've got to be mentally strong enough to stop the insanity!

Or as the great head coach Dan Reeves used to say, when you have one finger pointing like a gun at someone, you have three others pointing right back at you.

I now know firsthand how easy it is for the fans and media to rip into a guy for screwing up, just like I started that whole brouhaha with Plaxico this year. Sitting on the sidelines injured, I reacted just like you guys—the fans—would have, and realized just how easy it is to react that way.

Did I regret those quotes? Yes, but not as much as that damn peanut butter and jelly sandwich.

When I retire, the thing I'll miss more than anything else are the ribbings inside the locker room. Other players who retire always say to me the one thing they miss the most is the camaraderie. We can never, ever reproduce how close we get inside that room out in the real world. It's not the individual guys I'll miss but that overall feeling of walking into a locker room and knowing that no matter what happened in the real world that day, I'm protected behind these walls. Nothing and nobody can hurt me inside here.

CHAPTER SEVEN

Donovan, Please Answer Your Damn Phone!

Saturday, September 16,
eve of our game against Eagles

Come on, Donovan, answer your phone. Come on, buddy!

No answer, damn!

Redial.

I don't have time for this. Come on, come on, come on, come on . . . answer your phone. Man, I just don't have time for this right now!

The preparation for a game reaches a crescendo the night before with last-minute details. The monotony of the grind finally shows signs of dying and the light at the end of the tunnel people talk about so much finally comes into view.

Saturday night is when we clear our minds, trusting in all the work we did during the week, trying to believe that the work will not be in vain, believing that within twenty-four hours, all the sweat, pain and monotony of the week will prove to be worth it.

Unfortunately Saturday night also marks the start of the

worst distractions we as players deal with on a regular basis, which is exactly why I find myself hitting redial again.

Come on, Donovan, answer your damn phone!

Yes, *that* Donovan. Donovan McNabb, the same guy I will attempt to crush the next day. It's less than eighteen hours before I have to smash Jon Runyan in the face, shove Brian Westbrook aside and try to pick Donovan up and crash my body down on his. Yet it's imperative I get hold of him.

I call his phone again. No answer. Come on, brother. I got meetings I have to go to. I've got a little more film I want to study. I don't have the patience for this right now.

I try to figure out if he's in a meeting, maybe a production meeting with the TV broadcast crew or an interview. I know he's at the team hotel, but I need to find the guy who's going to try to make my life miserable the next day.

I try fifteen minutes later, hoping, come on, come on, come on, when finally, "Hey, what's up, Strahan!"

I'm not looking to cut any game deal with him. I'm not looking for any tips on their game plan. I'm certainly not looking to give him any insight into how we plan to try to slow him down. No, this is more serious business.

"Hey, man, my friend [Leeann Tweeden, who I worked with on *The Best Damn Sports Show Period*] you got those tickets for, where are they? Their tickets aren't downstairs at your hotel. Could you make sure they're taken care of?"

"Really? Yeah, no problem, I'll get it taken care of right now. Tell them I'll come down now."

"Thanks, man. Sorry to bug you about this. See you tomorrow."

"See you tomorrow." It's as if I'll be catching up with him when we get to our cubicles or meet in the corporate cafete-

ria. I'll see you tomorrow when I try to tear your fuckin' arm off your body. But thanks for getting my friends their tickets.

The night before our first division game of the 2006 season, who would have ever guessed that Mr. Eagles, in his first home game after his divorce from Terrell Owens, and Michael Strahan, fresh from *his* divorce from Mrs. Strahan, would be worrying about a couple of tickets?

Believe it or not, it happens all the time. Tickets become the biggest nuisance an NFL player has to deal with week in and week out, aside from the game. It's an annoyance that knows no boundaries. The minute we promise someone tickets, they often hound us because it's a whole big to-do for people to make plans—especially if they have kids—to travel to a game. I understand they want to make sure they don't clear their schedule, get a ride, pay for parking, and all of a sudden, they're stranded and left to listen outside to the 78,000 who actually got in.

Pestering Donovan wasn't the worst of it for me, either. This particular game wasn't a good week for me in regard to tickets. Plus, I certainly didn't want to worry about off-field distractions once I woke up on game day.

When I wake up the morning of a game, I begin to get a little ornery. As the morning progresses, my irritation continues to grow.

It's not a normal emotional function to convince yourself each and every week to rev your body up enough to hurt another human being. Actually, a handful of human beings. I know that on any given Sunday, I could break another man's neck and end his career. I also know that during that three-hour span my livelihood, my own career could come to a very painful, screeching halt.

Do you think we just walk out there and smash our

bodies around without any mental preparation toward "clicking over"? First you've got to find that other side of you, the animal side, that buries fear deep into the recesses of your mind. Firefighters have to do the same thing before rushing in while others rush out. The fear must be extinguished before the fire can be.

In order to find that "other guy" that I talked about earlier, we begin our inner psych-up job hours before the fans ever see us. I begin my transformation hours before I leave for the stadium. I talk to people. Put on a good face, a good act. But in reality, I get angrier and angrier and angrier as the hours pass. So, you think you get road rage? I try putting myself into a frame of mind as if a thousand people just flipped me the bird, cut me off on the way to work and stole my parking spot, all while laughing in my face. Things I may find amusing the day before annoy the living daylights out of me on a Sunday morning. Even little jingles I hear on a commercial bug me. Everything bugs me. But I *want* everything to bug me. I don't need to be a happy camper.

Sunday is one big contradiction for me. It's the end of a week of game plans, films, practice, painkiller injections, anti-inflammatory meds all meeting together for three hours of controlled bedlam and violence.

The moment I leave my hotel on Sunday morning and put my headphones on, I try to transform into a different human being. I try with everything I have deep down inside of me to escape from being the nice guy who hooks up his friends with tickets. I try to isolate myself from the world on the way to the game.

The last thing I want to deal with is tickets. But despite the anger and the ornery caricature I've created for myself Sunday mornings, the very first thing we do as players when we get to the stadium is deal with tickets.

At home games, I've got my routine pretty much set. First thing I do when I get to the stadium is hit the ticket table set up in our locker room and fill out envelopes for all those I'm giving tickets to, leaving them for a Giants employee to bring to "Will Call."

When we're on the road, my routine varies. As a result, sometimes I'll screw up my tickets. Unfortunately, this particular game against the Eagles was one of those times.

I spent the morning psyching myself up to destroy the man who had left tickets for Leeann. When you play in Philly, before you ever get to hit another player, you've got to psych yourself up for a fight.

Whoever named that place the City of Brotherly Love has obviously never played there. Eagles fans wrote the book on creative and immature insults. As a distraction from the insults, I try to focus on the team introductions. I don't want to listen to their crap or commit the cardinal sin of getting into it with the fans. Instead, I turn to the men who will attempt to make me look bad today. As each player is introduced, I go over mental notes about him in my mind. Little profanity-laced scouting reports crowd my brain as my heart races, as the adrenaline and anger rise and fall with the name of each player I'll go up against that day.

Here comes Runyan, which means today will be fun. I love playing that man. I love that he knows that I know exactly what he's going to do and that there's nothing he can do about it. I love the fact that just about every game he'll piss me off and get me screaming at him about something. We have a great chess match every single game.

Here comes Brian Westbrook. That little man is annoying. One of the smartest players at any position, on any team in the NFL. He's a pain and he never makes a mistake, which means he can stick a fork in you from anywhere, anytime.

You really respect the players who get better and better each year, players who allow their teams to expand their roles. That's Brian Westbrook. Whatever you saw him do on film the previous year, throw it out the window. He'll have some new wrinkles now.

There's William "Tra" Thomas, Shane Andrews, L. J. Smi—

Oh, no! Damn! I forgot to leave my other buddy tickets! Son of a . . . man, I did, I forgot! Damn it!

My friend Dougie Lawson drove all the way up from Baltimore. I was supposed to leave two tickets for him. I flat out forgot. How in the hell could I forget to leave his tickets? I got distracted from those introductions because all I could think about was poor Dougie standing outside the stadium with the world's saddest look splashed across his face. While my eyes should be fixed on Runyan, Runyan and nothing but Runyan, my mind drifts to poor Dougie in the parking lot.

I can't tell you how many times, in the middle of a game, a player panics, "Oh, damn, I forgot to leave tickets for (insert any number of jilted names here)." It honestly distracts us from our game because instead of thinking about your assignment, you begin to think about letting down a friend or a family member. I've screwed up so many times, I have excuses down to a science. I'm sorry, I'm sorry but you know I have a few things on my mind on Sundays. Like crushing McNabb or Manning or Favre.

While I can't say I'm sorry enough, believe me, it hurts me almost as much as it hurts you. Well, that's not really true, either. I do feel bad about it, bad enough for it to creep into my mind prior to and during battle. Bad enough for me to say something out loud, sometimes in the huddle when I've realized my forgetfulness.

Sometimes I'll be looking down the line, searching for a tip from an offensive lineman, digging my hand in the dirt and focusing on which way the offensive tackle seems to be leaning, and milliseconds before I explode out of my stance . . . DAMN! I forgot to leave my boy his tickets! Damn, damn, HIKE . . . uh-oh!

Sometimes I wish we never got tickets, then it would never become an issue. Even when I'm hurt it's an issue. The next time we played the Eagles, Runyan's wife, Loretta, called me for tickets for a friend. I helped them out, but what I didn't know was, the tickets sucked. Nosebleeders. The reason you call a player on another team is to get good seats. I was so embarrassed.

Our ticket manager, John Gorman, is awesome to me. Always has been. Whenever I need tickets, he always gives me great seats. But Runyan, for some reason, I got the nosebleed seats. I actually ran down (make that "limped down") after the game to make sure I apologized to him for the lousy seats I gave his wife.

It must sound crazy to the average fan that the wife of a guy who has been made out to be my archrival would call me for tickets, and that I'd be so apologetic for not getting better seats, but this isn't a unique case.

Larry Allen is the most intimidating person I've ever come across in my life. In fact, there's something in the NFL called Allen-itis, an imaginary illness players pretend to come down with when they're scheduled to face off against this on-field killer. I'm telling you, the man is as close to Mike Tyson in his prime on the football field as anything I've ever seen.

I've had teammates who've watched Larry on film hurt four, five, six guys when suddenly a hamstring or an ankle is miraculously injured in practice. In his prime it got to the point where guys, knowing they were facing Larry and the Cowboys the next week, would have the foresight to suffer a hammy or a calf injury in the fourth quarter of the previous week! When Keith Hamilton, who Larry said was one of the toughest guys he played, had to face off against him, he'd actually tell his backups to be ready to come in.

Larry bench-presses 700 pounds without a spotter. Lodges half a can of dip at a time under his lower lip. He has the meanest face in the game. To add to the fear, he never says a word. Not a word. The most I've ever heard from him on the field is when he soup-bones somebody or body-slams one or two guys on the same play. The man doesn't talk but bellows a laugh after he hurts somebody. He's the strongest, nastiest, most effective player I have ever played in my life. If there ever was a guy you should be afraid of, it's Larry Allen.

Yet, before we play his team, he gets my parents tickets and a parking pass to the game. He's the nicest guy I've ever dealt with when it comes to tickets. I don't even have to ask him about it, he'll do it on his own. In fact, that's about the only time I've ever really heard him talk.

Big-ass monster is probably thinking to himself, "Let me invite the dude's family so they can watch me maul their poor little boy in person."

Every week, players and coaches from teams playing each other call their counterparts to bum tickets or upgrade existing seats. I do it all the time with Donovan, Roy Williams when we play Dallas, Tony Gonzalez, Marshall Faulk, Mike Irvin, you name it. If there's a game I need tickets for, I

can call another Pro Bowler I've met, ask him, and vice versa.

The things we think about on that field that have nothing to do with the game are amazing. Tickets are one thing, but we also delve into fights in the stands, women, cheerleaders.

During a game, we have more in common with the fans than most people know. You know how when you guys stand up to watch a fight in the stands? You know how when the yellow-jacketed security guards go flying over to break up a brouhaha, and the whole section stands at attention to catch a glimpse? I'll let you into a little secret here: We do the same exact thing. When those yellow jackets start running and the crowd starts roaring, we flat out crane our necks and scramble to get a full-on look at you pugilistic hooligans. We'll be in the huddle waiting for the call to get signaled in to us when we hear the cheering. The crowd begins to rise and all eyes shift from us to the idiots in the stands throwing haymakers. We don't even listen to the call, we're just hoping the offense takes a little more time so we can watch these drunken fools swing away at each other.

During one of the first games I played versus the Redskins, the crowd began to swell. I could tell a fight was brewing. One of my teammates, Thomas Randolph, our former cornerback, turns to watch the fight and I suddenly hear him blurt out, "Strahan, isn't that your brother fightin' in the stands?"

How about that! I look up and there's my brother Victor swinging away at some Redskins fans who, he later explained, were ripping apart his friend who was, shall we say, overweight.

But there I was, getting ready to roll after the Redskins'

Heath Shuler or Trent Green or whoever the hell it was and I've got to watch this? Now, who in their right mind can play while his brother is fighting in the stands? Come on, knucklehead!

Of course we have the same distraction most guys have with the women. Pretty much every game I'll hear from another player something along the lines of "Oh, man, look at the third one from the right, ten rows up."

If you're losing the game, you don't pay attention at all. But if you're winning, you start wondering. We'll all be huddled up and somebody will say something like "Check out the girls two sections down, eight rows up, two of them." At the same time, we'll all turn and stare.

Some guys will actually get the equipment guys to go and give a girl in the stands or a cheerleader a phone number or ask for her number. However, I've got to say, I've never seen a guy meet a girl in the stands and actually start a relationship.

The cheerleaders are a huge, huge distraction. They aren't there just to distract the fans, they're used as a weapon against us, too. We stare at cheerleaders sometimes. It's against the rules for a cheerleader to date a player, but it happens all the time. I'll tell you the best girls in the league, by far, are *not* the famous Dallas Cowboys cheerleaders or the famed Raiderettes. It's not even close, folks. The Washington Redskins get the prize in my book. Every single one of those girls is stunning.

It's tough when we're standing on these sidelines trying to pay attention to the position coach, but you can't take your eyes off the second girl in the third row. You find yourself trying to pay attention to adjustments, but instead you focus on the figures, if you know what I mean. Philly isn't that far behind, but nothing beats the Redskins cheerleaders. Now,

combine this with the fact that I've suddenly realized I forgot to leave my friends tickets to the game. How in the world am I expected to try to blast the man who I pestered all evening for another set of tickets?

Still, I've got to clear my mind, people. It's game day, and it's been seven days since Peyton Manning made me hate my life. Today is about vindication! On to the Battle of Philly!

CHAPTER EIGHT

Communicating on the Field

Eli dropped back and the Eagles brought the house. They brought their house, their town, their city. They brought the hopes of every last city-of-brotherly-love neighbor longing for yet another sack on our quarterback. It would have been the ninth time that Eli hit the ground behind our line of scrimmage with the ball still in his hands. Think about that for a minute . . . that's ridiculous. Eight sacks so far? Utterly ridiculous.

For three quarters of this game, we played like it was the first day any of us had ever met. It was almost like we spoke different languages for the first two-plus hours of this clash.

But on this play, every single person on our offense communicated perfectly. Everyone who was supposed to be at a certain spot, everyone who was supposed to perform a certain assignment—was perfect. Eli dropped back, planted ever so slightly before fading back again and he just let it fly. One week after losing to his brother, Eli was going for broke, baby. The pass was one of those all-your-chips-all-in kind of passes.

When the ball was released, I literally stopped breathing. I was afraid to exhale, fearing my breath would push the ball off its course. I know the entire play only took three seconds, but when we're standing on that sideline, it's so slow, you feel like you could run to the kitchen for a sandwich, stop off in the bathroom, read a magazine and still have enough time to watch the end of the play. Time . . . stands . . . completely . . . still!

Plaxico Burress did what he does best. He launched himself into the air high above Philly's corner Sheldon Brown, grabbed that little baby and yet again, there was that dead, eerie kind of silence. The only difference was, this silence was caused by sound waves suffocated inside the lungs and throats of about 70,000 stunned Eagles fans, all sitting with their jaws dropped in shock.

Touchdown Giants! We win 30–24.

I started jumping up and down like a little schoolgirl. Just minutes earlier, I was exhausted. But this feeling is why I've played for fourteen years. Feeling so much joy, feeling like I'm looking to hand out forgiveness slips to anybody who has ever wronged me, these are the times players cut through all the business and money aspects of football, remembering that underneath it all, it's still a game.

This feeling, the chances of winning each week, provides us with the closest opportunity we'll get to relive the excitement of that first innocent touchdown in Pop Warner. This feeling is as close as we'll get to riding on the shoulders as a hero during the purity of high school football. These mo-

ments, it's not about the money, who makes more than who and who doesn't think he's making enough. It's not about anything but a few minutes of that pure joy of victory.

What truly makes this win even sweeter is knowing that all those Philly fans screaming and cursing at us for the last three hours had to walk out of that stadium completely shocked and sick to their stomachs. Awesome, baby!

What made it better still was that we fought back from the most futile and effortless performance I'd been associated with in a long time. For two and a half hours that Sunday afternoon I felt like I was in the ring against a fighter who I knew I should annihilate, but every time I threw a punch, he bobbed, weaved and hit me back with a sharp jab. Every time I threw a shot, he was nowhere near where he was supposed to be. There's no way we should have been taking this kind of a beating.

My head was spinning because everything Donovan McNabb and the rest of the Eagles offense wanted to do, they had their way. If Donovan wanted to go deep, he connected at will. If their head coach, Andy Reid, felt like keeping it on the ground with Brian Westbrook, they had their way with ease. Every snap they guessed right while we guessed wrong. Man, we were on the ropes.

Frustration grew by the play. But in the NFL there's never a point where you can throw your arms up and quit. No matter how bad the beating, the commissioner wasn't going to suddenly call up the Giants and Eagles owners and say, "You know, I've seen enough, let's make a mercy ruling and give this one to Philly."

We felt snakebitten, like the whole team had a bad case of the flu. We needed a quick break to gather ourselves, lick our wounds and figure out if there was indeed an answer.

The Eagles had taken a 17–7 lead into halftime and moved to 24–7 in the third quarter, yet the score was nowhere near indicative of the beating we were taking. Games like this cause a player to feel nearly as useless as the times he's forced to stand on the sidelines on crutches. It was awful. Everything we did, we screwed up.

Less than an hour before becoming our hero that afternoon, Burress had had an argument with the offensive linemen. That doesn't go over well with all the big boys up front. Guys were apologizing to Eli because he was under pressure every single time he dropped back. He'd been sacked a bordering-on-the-bizarre eight times. Defensively, everything we put into plan, we failed to execute. It seemed hopeless.

The funny thing about professional sports is that every once in a while, you just have a bad day. It happens. Days when everything you do is wrong. When Murphy and his stupid law decides to stop by for a visit, you can't give up. You can't cancel the game. You've got to spend every lull, every break in play figuring out where it's all gone terribly wrong and how to, hopefully, make it right.

That first half our problem was lack of communication. Every form of communication that we used in a game seemed to be off-line. As much as the world sees us pounding away at each other, communication is just as important out there as the physical part of our game. The mental part and how much we all need to adjust together, see things together. That's all done through a carefully crafted network of communication tools used during every game. There are a handful of communication channels that come to life within the three hours of a Sunday battle and they're all just as important as how big we are, how much we weigh and how fast we run.

Everything is communicated, whether verbally or non-verbally, and the faster we pick it all up and understand what's being relayed, the faster we can mesh and enjoy success. The fans see the hits on every play but they may not know how much of that play was a success or failure due to the crossed lines of communication. When we don't communicate, when we lack that same-page precision, that's when we get our butts handed to us like we were earlier that afternoon.

It's imperative that we recognize the formations and what we think the play will be, and then communicate to each other what call we're running. You've heard coaches proclaim in press conferences, "We really weren't on the same page." How well we communicate through the different avenues and networks throughout a game is what makes up that so-called same page.

During a game, we communicate through so many different lines that we all need to mesh at some point. It's not just coach-player speak. We use a series of photographs and even telephones on the sidelines between each series.

But trash talk, the in-your-face, I'm-gonna-kick-your-ass kind, is also a great form of communication that we use on the other team. You want to get a response from your opponent? Lay traps and dupe a guy into moving in a certain direction in order to create a space to get your work done.

When an offense is in full swing, like the Eagles were that day, their communication puts them all on the same page and leaves us all scratching our heads. Every adjustment McNabb and his offensive weapons made seemed to be the right ones. Every time one of their coaches saw something, they successfully communicated it to Donovan and friends. Every time we thought we saw something, we all failed miserably in picking it up together.

Whenever Donovan would adjust and one of us on defense would try to recognize it, we'd not only see the wrong checks, we wouldn't physically respond, either. For example, it was up to Antonio Pierce to read Donovan and make certain adjustments, but each time he made a call, Donovan responded as if he was in Antonio's mind. I know in my case I was playing like a piece of garbage. I felt like I had been hit with a bug of some sort because every time Antonio made a call that called for me to make a certain adjustment, I literally got tired coming out of my stance, never mind hitting my new assignment.

In that game we didn't hear anything and we saw nothing. Every time we'd come to the sidelines and the coaches would point out certain calls the Eagles were using, we simply couldn't get it.

No matter how hard we listened, we were deaf that Sunday. The coaches kept going to a series of photographs of the Eagles' formations, and we still we couldn't see it.

You've seen us on television looking at photographs, but you may not know how crucial they are. These aren't snapshots from the what-we-did-on-our-summer-vacation scrapbook. These come from cameras perched at a couple of spots around the stadium. They'll show us a team's formation, players' stances and then where each man moves after his first step.

We were looking for any tip against the Eagles, anything at all that would help us better understand why they were whipping us play after play. For example, we'll look to see if a guy is leaning a certain direction on a certain play. That gives us a tip that next time he leans that way, they'll be run-

ning that same direction. The quicker we can recognize that and get on the same page, the faster we can exploit it. Then we've got to get each other to immediately communicate what one person sees, hoping that everyone else recognizes it as well. The more players see it, the less chance there is to get caught by their offense. But this afternoon, we failed to recognize those tips. Never saw them. Add that to the fact that we were physically getting whipped and that didn't provide a good combination for us.

In the week leading up to that game, we had already dissected the Eagles' entire offense to the point where, on just about any play, judging by their formation, we could narrow down what we thought their call was going to be. But when I'm out there, if I think I see them lined up in a certain formation and I'm wrong, I'll anticipate a different play from the one they actually run. I was wrong a lot that day.

The photographs are meant to cure misconceptions for us, provided we can process them in time to make the right adjustments. I know the television broadcasts show us once or twice a game looking at these photos, but they're actually waiting for us after every single series, faxed to a couple of machines that usually sit against the wall of the stands right behind our bench. Then they're ripped from the fax and run over immediately.

Especially in the case of this Eagles game, we relied on those photos constantly to give us answers. They used the no-huddle offense a lot more than we anticipated, so the photos should have been huge in helping us adjust on the fly. So why was nothing we were doing working? Why were we messing up every little thing in that game? What were we missing? Obviously, McNabb and his crew saw little tips in *their* photos and we didn't see a damn thing in ours. When we did, we failed to get enough guys on the same page.

What truly, truly saved us in this game was halftime. If there was ever a time we needed to sit on our stools and gather our senses, this was the game!

That's when halftime is great. It's a quick break we use to ratchet up the physical breakdowns. But more so, it provides us with a breath of fresh air to step back, take in what we're missing. It's the only time in a game when we can honestly buy some time to find the leak in our communication pipes and fix them.

Walking into that halftime locker room was like getting sent to the executioner's chambers. We all knew Coach Coughlin was about to rip our heads off.

We're fifteen minutes from field to field, from the moment we come off to the moment we have to go back out there. In those fifteen minutes, we've got to review what the hell just happened, find a cure for our woes and then make sure everyone gets on the same page with adjustments.

When you walk through the halftime tunnel, you hear everything. It's completely the opposite from when you're on the field. In the moments before I put my fingers in the dirt bracing to race out of my stance and disrupt somebody's day, I hear the crowd roar like I'm stuck inside a loudspeaker.

But the moment I get set at that line, I fall deaf. My hearing focuses in between the tackles. The only thing I hear are the linebackers and quarterback. I don't hear the crowd. I don't hear the cheers. I don't hear the boos. I don't even hear my coaches. The moment the play ends, that silence is shattered as the noise floods back in. Suddenly, the amplifier cranks all the way back up. Again we break the huddle. I dig my hand into that dirt and again that silence returns.

But walking into that tunnel, as depressed as I was, I heard every F-bomb and insult those Eagles fans threw at us.

They're burned indelibly into my brain. They singed my last nerve.

Once we burst through those halftime doors, everything is abbreviated and hurried. Guys immediately run to the bathroom while others line the trainer's room to get taped, retaped or something looked at. Some guys will even get an IV of saline solution to prevent dehydration. All this is done within four to five minutes. The first thing I do is grab three oranges for a little energy, just like I did at halftime as a kid at those tiny tots Pop Warner games.

Then the team splits in half, with the offense taking one side of the room and the defense occupying the other for a quick adjustment period from the coordinators. In this particular game, tempers flared and we started to bicker and get defensive. In our profession, stakes are high and tempers run loose, but it's rare that there will be an actual blowup in the locker room. We're all professionals and if we're losing, we're losing as a team.

But during this particular game, our defensive coordinator, Tim Lewis, gathered the defense and immediately began to tear into us.

"What do you want me to call?" Lewis asked. "What adjustments can I make? Everything I call, you're not running it. What do you want *me* to do, because *you're* not doing shit!"

Usually, guys will just sit there and take it. Ashamed. Embarrassed by what we showed on the field. But that wasn't the case this afternoon. We had too much talent to be playing this lousy. Something was off. We were too smart to be communicating so poorly.

One of our veteran cornerbacks, R. W. McQuarters, stepped up and barked, "Put us in man to man like we need to do and just let us play ball!"

I think Tim was stunned. I know I was. We were all stunned, but when games get this frustrating, a guy's gotta step up.

Tim actually said, "Fine, you got it. We'll do that."

Still, I was getting a little concerned that there could be more backlash, so I blurted out, "It shouldn't matter what he calls because if you run it the way it's supposed to be run, it'll work. No more excuses, no more bitching and moaning about who's running what. No more complaining about the calls in the huddle. Run the defense the way it's called!"

I may address the guys every halftime, but I never call guys out. I don't want to demoralize a guy we'll need for the next ninety minutes. If one unit isn't pulling its weight, I'll challenge those guys: "DBs, give us some coverage back there and we'll get to the damn quarterback up front. Just give us some time!" Or if our line is crapping out, I'll blurt out, "DBs, we'll step it up for you out there, so we'll make him get it out quicker."

But that afternoon, even though we were getting our asses kicked, I never lost it on the guys. I never looked like I was out of control. This week was all about encouragement, all about sticking together.

But this game, Tom wasn't so nice. He came into that Week Two halftime locker room and he completely ripped the crap out of us. Tom was utterly disgusted because of how we played in the first half at Philly.

"Two weeks in a row you come out in a game of this magnitude and play like this?" Coughlin screamed at the top of his lungs. "I don't understand it! You've got to be shitting me!"

The man was pissed, but not so bad because we only got the "You've got to be shitting me" motif. When Tom gets furious, he doesn't really MoFo you a lot, but instead he comes at you more with disbelief. He tries to make us feel ashamed of ourselves. When he gets really mad, he sways back and forth during his tirades. During the Philly game, he must have had some hope, because he wasn't swaying so badly. He didn't keep screaming at us, didn't lay into us like he would the next week. The next week against Seattle would be the closest both Coach Coughlin and I got to losing our minds. When he came into the locker room at half against Seattle, he felt obligated to add a few more expletives to his speech. Then adding that "every time Seattle touches the damn ball, they're scoring on us. If we keep going this way, they're going to put up seventy points on that scoreboard. Are we going to get embarrassed or are we going to fight back?" I think everyone in the room was on alert after that, including me.

During this half against Philly, though, he felt, despite the fact that our communication was sorely lacking, we had a chance to cure our woes. It all felt salvageable. We weren't out of the game, so he didn't sway in fury and we regathered.

We came out a little poor in the second half. Gave up another quick touchdown. However, it felt a little different. We felt that our communication lines were finally opening. Things we weren't seeing earlier in the game, both sides of the ball, we began to see. Those sight adjustments began working in our favor. The photographs all started to make some sense.

We understood what we were looking at. We could finally make the adjustments that put us a step ahead. What often happens is once we acknowledge what we're looking at, the coaches will pull out a photo and tell us that the next time we see them in this formation, we're going to run a certain play. Instead of what's called in the huddle, we jump to a completely different call.

Perfect example of getting on the same page is when one

or more of us, usually a linebacker because they stand close to the line of scrimmage with the best view, recognizes the offensive formation we've just seen in the photograph and, within the span of one second, get us all to check out of our call and adjust to the new play. Any tool to help us get on the same page will be implemented. These sight adjustments started to work for us and we started to trust our game plan one play at a time.

While the photographs help us tremendously, there is another aid we use to make adjustments. The telephone. You've all seen us talking on the phones during the game, and you've probably asked yourself, "What the hell are they talking about?"

Sometimes the coaches call, asking what we're seeing on a particular formation or what technique the opposition is using to block us. Sometimes they'll call down with specific adjustments. The coaches are all on headsets, so they can talk to each other and we often convey messages to our position coaches to convey to the coordinator in the booth. Sometimes there's nothing specific, they just want to get a firsthand feel of what's happening in the trenches. Other times they have a specific play they want us to run. Sometimes it's just one adjustment for one player, maybe a corner or the safety.

But in this case, Tim recognized that even though Philly had just scored and despite being down 24–7, we finally got on the same page. He called downstairs to get the ball rolling. He used the phone to play motivational speaker.

"Michael, call the whole defense together. Tell them I called down and we NEED to get that damn ball back. We can't let them get a first down now. They can't stop what we're doing now! Tell them, Michael. Make sure they know it!"

I relayed the message word for word. Sure enough, we

finally stopped them. Tim called down again and continued to pound away at how important it was to not so much as surrender a first down. While hoping for a comeback victory, there was no time left for us to let them move. McNabb at one point was so sure of their victory, he was joking around at the line of scrimmage. But he had awoken the sleeping Giants, pun very much intended.

If in the first three quarters nothing went our way, the last quarter was one of the most amazing comebacks I've ever been associated with thus far in my career. When we held them to our first three-and-out, it was almost as if one huge collective lightbulb began to flicker on. The next time we shut them down, the light grew steadily. The third time in a row, the bulb burned brightly and everything we communicated out there, we heard loud and clear.

I remember looking into the eyes of some of the Eagles players and they were very aware of what was happening. They were starting to slide downhill and they had no idea how to stop it. Guys started pressing. They knew we had gained momentum on both sides of the ball. They knew they were in trouble. Donovan wasn't dancing anymore.

When we held them and then scored to make it 24–14, every man on our sideline suddenly put even more pressure on himself. We knew that if we allowed even a field goal, it would kill this special feeling we suddenly had. Collectively, we now understood everything we had missed earlier. Collectively, we played with urgency on every single snap. Guys were petrified to let the guys next to them down.

As we made it to the fourth quarter, we still had a heartbeat. I remember my legs actually feeling like they were getting stronger. Instead of feeling fatigued like we'd all normally feel in the final quarter of a Sunday afternoon of battle, I started to feel like I feel on the first play of the game. Everything was heightened. My awareness. My energy level. My thought process. My response time. They all moved to DEFCON 1.

We were actually going to win this thing! For the first time all game, guys started taking care of their own assignments, before racing to help with something else. We took it up another notch after Eli hit Amani Toomer to move us to 24–21.

At that point we had no choice but to go for broke. Every time we gathered on the sideline, guys were screaming directions and everyone was alert as you might be in a playoff game. If we had given them an inch and they'd pulled this one out, I'm not sure we would have won even five games this year. We would have been completely demoralized.

After the score, 24–21, we never let up. We went for the throat and stepped on their necks. Eli and Co. seemingly moved the ball at will. They had their way with them when it counted the most. If we couldn't hear and see the same thing for the first three quarters, it was as if somebody had given us all hearing aids and glasses. With seven seconds left in regulation, we were methodical in our attack. We'd tied it up with a 35-yard Jay Feely field goal. There was nothing they could do to stop us now.

We moved in range for what two hours ago I never thought was possible. Eli dropped back and Philly brought the house. They blitzed every free man. But this time Eli saw it. They wouldn't get our young buck this time. Silence permeated the stadium.

We'd never felt so empowered. You have to understand what the scene was like afterward. We were completely battered. Like we'd been beaten in a street fight. Guys had to get IVs just to be able to walk to the bus. We were cramping. We were tired. Yet we fought with the vigor of a fighter who had just seen his opponent's knees buckle and eyes roll back.

That game was so brutal mentally and physically on everybody. But I guarantee you we wouldn't have traded that victory for an easy one on any day. We righted our wrongs, came together as a team and sent the fans of Philly home eating their own crude remarks. That was worth more than any mental and physical pain we endured.

CHAPTER NINE

Snap Goes My Foot.
Welcome to Club Medical.

November 5, Giants versus Texans

Injuries are the pitfalls of our occupation. The instant I hit that Texans tackle, all I could think was: You've got to be kidding me! My career just ended! Oh, come on, not like this. Please, not with a freakin' foot injury!

I'd made that same move a thousand times—probably more like a hundred thousand times—and I'm going out like this? I tried to sling their blocker to the outside and suddenly . . . *CRUNCH* . . . I felt multiple sensations of pain shoot through my foot. The front was numb as if it were stuck in concrete. The middle of my foot felt like somebody was wringing it out like a wet towel. All the while, there was an excruciating twisting-knife feeling in my arch.

"I BROKE MY FOOT!"

I tried to take two steps but I felt it right away. "I'm done. That's it, this is the way it all ends!" In Week Eight of my fourteenth year, this was the first time I'd let an injury question my own football mortality.

The moment I felt the snap on the bottom of my foot, the first thought was that my career was over. I honestly believed I broke my foot, and at this point in my career, I couldn't miss half the year, have surgery, and then rehabilitate all off-season to work myself all the way back. For what? To play one more season? Nope! I was done.

Then another thought crept into my head. You better not let them bring the cart out! My mom is watching and I refuse to let her see me get carted off the field.

Oh, I was in complete and utter agony! I walked off the field and up the tunnel with the swagger of a boxer who had just taken Mike Tyson's best punch and didn't budge. But the moment I got far enough up that tunnel out of camera range, I let it all hang loose. I grimaced. I moaned. I grunted. Everything I'd held in came rushing out the moment I knew my mom and the rest of the world couldn't see me anymore.

The brain is such a powerful weapon. It fools your body into doing things it doesn't want to. For the entire walk down the sideline, across the back of the end zone and into the tunnel, I walked like I was just going in to get my foot retaped. Then my brain released its intense pain impulses and I could no longer place my foot on the ground. It happened that fast.

As it turned out, the foot wasn't broken after all. Instead, I was blessed with a Lisfranc injury—an injury to the joint and ligaments between the big toe and second toe. Sometimes guys undergo season-ending surgery to repair the damage. In my case, I had to sit around and wear a gigantic boot that looked like something Frankenstein would wear to his prom, and wait for the damn thing to heal.

Fourteen years in the NFL has turned me from poster

child of strength to having hundreds of X-rays and MRIs showing tears, sprains, strains, rips, breaks and dislocations.

You want to be an NFL star, kid? You want to stand in my shoes? Let's say I came to you and offered you a million dollars to let me take a huge needle, wear down the point, make it really rusty and really dull. Then I stick it into a pit of burning coals until it's white hot and I pull that sucker out of the flames and you allow me to stab you over and over again. Take that needle and stab you in the ankles, your feet and your wrists. Not just stick it in but turn that rusty old needle and twist it when it's sunk deep into your knees or shoulders. No kidding. It's a lot like that!

This Lisfranc injury in my foot was the latest in a HUUUUUUUUUGE checklist that has left me pretty much beat up. I figure if *I'm* going to have to live with this, you guys should take a little journey down the Michael Strahan Injury Road Map to My Body.

Every week for the last few years my little buddy Jack, who is now eight, leaves me a voice mail the night before a game. It goes something like "Hey, Michael, it's Jack. Good luck against the Cowboys. Get three sacks, two tips, one interception, two fumble recoveries and one touchdown. Oh, and don't get hurt!" If he only knew!

Want to know what smashing my body into Jon Runyan, Erik Williams and Jumbo Elliott has done to me? Want to know what taking a full head of steam from Stephen Davis and Jerome Bettis and chasing the daylights out of Emmitt Smith and Barry Sanders has done? Let's start from my own personal nightmare—my lower back—and zigzag from there.

Lower back. In my opinion, the most demoralizing injury that a player can suffer. It's awful. And I blew my lower back out in practice three days after our first game against Arizona

in 2005. We won, but I didn't feel victorious for very long. I blew my lower back out so badly that I stood in the shower after the game and the pain became so unbearable I lay down on the tile right there in the shower.

It hurt so much that as I lowered myself to the ground for relief, one of our trainers, Steve Kennelly, walked in as I started to go down. He ran and grabbed a stool and dragged me over to it, naked and all, and got me set. It's weird. You don't think, "Oh, shit, I'm naked." You think, "How long is it going to last *this* time?" It's demoralizing for a 250-pound so-called great athlete to crawl to a stool in the shower, moaning like a little puppy.

I was unable to stand upright until Saturday of that week. There was no way I would play against the Saints that Monday night, the Saints first "home" game after Katrina. The chiropractor told me it was a four-to-six-week healing process. I didn't want to miss it but how could I even think of playing? I played anyway. Ahhhh, the wonders of modern medicine.

My lower back can sometimes be a disaster. The problem is that I've blown it out so many times it's rarely not stiff. I have disk problems between vertebrae L4-L5-S1 (fourth and fifth lumbar vertebrae and first in my sacroiliac joint). Isn't it amazing how a supposedly dumb jock can learn modern medical jargon by spending half his football life on a trainer's table? Trust me, I know a lot about medicine after fourteen years in the NFL.

You realize the game is taking its toll when you can't do the basic things. One low point in my career was the first time somebody had to put my socks on for me. Notice the operative word here: *first*. During the season, it's a fairly regular ritual. I never knew what frustration truly felt like until about

six years ago when I woke up one morning and tried to bend over to put on my socks. I couldn't. I sat at the edge of that bed and struggled to bend far enough to reach my toes. My lower back just wouldn't give. I struggled for a few minutes and couldn't get them on. Imagine being thirty years old and needing somebody to put your socks on for you. It's humiliating.

When I began my NFL career in 1993, never once did it creep into my mind that one day I'd have to buy shoes that I could slip on because I couldn't bend down to tie my shoelaces. It doesn't creep into the mind of a young athlete who has just gotten paid and is on top of the world. Oh, by the way, fashion designers need to make hipper-looking shoes for those of us who rely on casual slip-ons.

The pain and discomfort caused by my lower back injuries has gotten so bad that at times when I have to go to the bathroom, I'll just hold it as long as I can and sit and pray that the pain goes away. I know I'll have to go eventually but I convince myself that maybe later my back will feel a little bit better. Maybe by that time I can wipe. Sounds far-fetched, but my lower back is so bad that at times I have to postpone a trip to the toilet.

I've often thought about whether or not it's all worth it. Sure, the medical society is inventing ways to try and alleviate the pain from my road map of injuries. Maybe in ten years, science will come up with something to allow me to live a normal and comfortable life.

I've earned a great amount of money and respect in my career. Sometimes it's worth it, but other times when I wake up and can't put on my socks, I question whether there's enough money or respect in the world to legitimize that.

Fingers. I've dislocated every single one of my fingers— used to pop a handful (pun intended) a few times a year. I've also torn the ligaments in my left thumb, which required surgery. My joints and knuckles are so bad that for the last several years of my career, I've used an entire roll of tape for them every single day of practice or a game. Without tape on the digits, don't touch me. Don't come near me. Every one of my knuckles is thick with calcium deposits from injury. It's gotten so bad in the past couple of years that even shaking hands can hurt. If I held my fingers up right now, you'd see that each one starts out really skinny then curves a bit to a huge swollen middle knuckle and then curves the other way to another swollen joint in the fist. My pinky look like a clothes hanger. And most of my fingers bend in all different directions and, quite frankly, they hurt every day. I've just accepted the fact that they going to hurt for the rest of my life.

Shin. One of the oddest injuries to my body was what the docs referred to as a "bruised shin."

Sounds relatively minor. The reality? I was whacked by a cleat so badly during my fifth season, I still have an indentation in the bone. In fact, I was told the bone will never heal. It hurt so badly, but I didn't miss a play. To this day, I don't even know who gave me this lifelong physical imperfection.

Feet and ankles. As I write this chapter, I'm wearing a boot on my right foot in my second week of rehabbing the second Lisfranc injury of my career. The injuries have come fourteen years apart and it was actually much worse in my left foot during my rookie season. That rehab was appalling; the pain was ridiculous. Not only did I injure my Lisfranc in my left foot that rookie year, but I also tore all the ligaments in my ankle on that same side. The ankle injury ended my rookie year prematurely and still today has to be taped a certain way so that it won't bother me.

Knees. I've sprained my left knee twice and missed one game each time. In 2006, for some reason the pain from those sprains returned and lingered all year long. Just what I needed: a recurrence of past injuries, in case I forgot.

I also popped a bursa sac behind my right knee. The pain started after a game but didn't explode behind the kneecap until I was at a restaurant on Central Park South near the Plaza Hotel later that night. (Hey, sometimes these work injuries don't respect your schedule . . . how rude.) It felt like someone had put a balloon behind my kneecap and filled it up with acid until it burst. I had no idea what had happened. It felt like I had been shot. I had to call an ambulance to take me to the hospital. But somehow I avoided missing the next game.

Neck and shoulders. Like my fingers and lower back, my shoulders will hurt me forever. I injured both AC joints in the same season. I've had my shoulders shot with more painkilling injections than any other part of my body. I've suffered more pinched nerves in my neck than I can remember.

Elbows. The same season I sprained both AC joints in my shoulders, I hyperextended both of my elbows. The elbow injuries forced me to wear braces all year long and the pain lasted the entire season. In 1999 I had only 5.5 sacks. I had no game because I couldn't do anything out there. Why? My game is built from technique and leverage, and I couldn't so much as put a hand on a blocker and extend him out. I felt so ineffective, so incompetent that year, yet I couldn't bring myself to shut it down.

Wrist. I had surgery to remove bone chips in my right wrist. Every time I'd hit someone and try to lock him out, it was as if a match had been lit under my hand and the flame shoved inside the joint. Now I wear a brace that nobody sees and it allows my wrist to bend back only to a certain angle.

Chest. I tore my pectoral muscle in 2004 when I tried to make a tackle on Bears running back Anthony Thomas. It was the same play I'd made countless times, but this one sent me to surgery and forced me into a sling for several weeks. They bring you in, cut you open, make the repair, sew you up and then off you go to rehab. Let's get 'em back out there! In addition to my pec, I've also had a slight tear in a bicep muscle.

Tongue. I once sprained my tongue. Yeah, you read it right. It was by far my strangest injury. I'm not sure which is stranger, the fact that I sprained my tongue or why I wasn't wearing a mouthpiece in the first place.

People love to talk about the gap between my teeth and now I've got a secret to admit—I never wore a mouthpiece because I was secretly hoping that I'd get a tooth knocked out so the dentist would have to fix the gap! Yup, it's true. That was my great master plan. I can't get it fixed now because it's become my physical trademark but, hey, if Orlando Pace knocked it out, well, gee, doc, I guess you better just fix it. Just make sure you leave the gap.

The sickest medical condition that I've ever heard a guy playing through was my former teammate and longtime Pro Bowl tackle Lomas Brown. Actually, it was more of an ailment. Lomas is one of the nicest and most respected guys I've ever played with, but my former teammate played a game while trying to pass kidney stones. To make matters worse, he had a catheter placed up his you-know-what to pass it . . . during the game! When the offense came off the field, Lomas's teammates would surround him so the fans couldn't see as he'd drop his pants and try to pass the last of the stones. Then he'd strap the bag up and go back out on the field! The strange thing was he was playing at the time for the lowly Cardinals, who were waaaaay out of the play-off hunt. For his troubles, Brown won the Ed Bloch Courage

Award—an annual accolade given to a player on each team for playing through adversity. Now that's crazy!

The most disturbing injury I've witnessed was to 49ers All-Pro defensive tackle Bryant Young. I was watching from the sidelines in our Week Fourteen matchup in 1998. Nearly ten years later, I still cannot extract the sound from my mind.

Linebacker Ken Norton Jr. got thrown into his teammate, helmet first. Then the helmet hit Bryant Young's leg and the *SNAP!* of that man's leg reverberated from one end zone to the other. Compound fracture. He snapped his tibia and fibula. The sight was Theismann-esque but the sound was worse than anything you could imagine. It was as if someone snapped a pair of two-by-fours in half. Bryant came back from that injury. If it had been me, I don't know if I would have been able to get back out there. That type of injury is NOT part of our everyday game. We can deal with most things, but not the sound of bone snapping in half. Something like that can ruin a team's psyche.

I was standing near LaVar Arrington when he snapped his Achilles during our Monday nighter this past season against the Cowboys. LaVar dropped down, grabbed his ankle and rolled over a bit, but he never made a peep. I figured he had aggravated an ankle injury. The doctors and trainers tell the other players nothing. They keep us in the dark and rightfully so. It's kind of hard to be told, "Hey, guys, LaVar just snapped his Achilles, but you all keep fighting. Good luck, boys."

For guys like Lomas, Bryant, LaVar and myself, injuries are as normal as death and taxes. They are pitfalls of our profession. After your first play in the NFL you wll probably never feel 100 percent again.

Every time I see an older player I respect, I ask him how

his body is. Jim Kelly told me that one of his shoulders hurts him pretty often. Former Steelers great, linebacker Greg Lloyd said he lives with an ankle that causes him to limp. When I was guest host on *The Best Damn Sports Show Period*, the legendary Houston Oilers running back Earl Campbell was a guest. There were two steps up onto the stage and Earl needed a few guys to help him up that one-foot elevation! For twenty years Earl had been the most physically imposing running back in NFL history! It scared the shit out of me. Hey Tiki, you are smart!

Throughout my career, I have to think about today and not tomorrow, because I might not be able to convince my body to do things I ask it to do on Sundays if I always think twenty years down the road. As retirement starts to creep into my mind, I realize that my back and one of my ankles will hurt me forever.

When the cheers die down and I'm left alone in my own private world, my body will hurt for no reason. I don't want to be like Earl Campbell. I want a good quality of life as I grow older. But after fourteen years, the reality is I will live the rest of my life with some form of physical pain. I can understand why guys get hooked on Vicodin and other painkillers and I hope the same fate doesn't await me. Which is worse, a life of pain or painkillers? It may be something that I avoid now but have to wrestle with as the years go by.

Maybe the NFL should institute a ten-year rule. It might be a great idea for the league to make us get out after ten years, to protect us from ourselves. That's why I respect Tiki for getting out when he did. After ten years your body feels all those hours of contact, and the healing process becomes a day-to-day ordeal.

But Tiki is different from a lot of us. Some of us, including me, will use up our bodies, hiding our long-term prob-

lems with short-term surgeries. We'll patch ourselves together and not dwell on the long-term effects. I hope I don't limp out of the league into a retirement of pain, but to be honest, that is probably wishful thinking. Yet I'm not asking for sympathy—I'd sacrifice my life and limbs all over again for those Sunday afternoons of battle.

In the twenty-four hours after we beat the Texans that Sunday, I finally started to question whether the Lisfranc sprain was a sign from above. Was this G-d's way of telling me the time has come to stop abusing my body? The bottom line is a player must constantly remind himself that we play a physical and violent game. Injuries occur. There's nothing prophetic or special or glorious about it. It truly becomes part of who you are, and when I look back on my injuries, they are my medals from my many battles and I wear them with tremendous pride.

The Lousy Life of a Rookie

November 26, Giants versus Titans

My eyes shot from the TV down to the text message that blipped across my cell phone, then quickly back to the TV again. I wasn't sure what to do next—keep looking at the TV or the cell phone?

There is no possible way that our rookie let Vince Young go on fourth-and-10, allowing him to scramble for nineteen yards and a huge first down. Absolutely no way! He had the man wrapped up for the sack. Game was over. Signed, sealed, delivered. All the rookie had to do was keep Young in his grasp until the whistle or take him to the ground and we would have won this game.

My phone was blowing up as Osi Umenyiora and I frantically sent text messages to each other.

"What was that?"

"I don't know. I'm trying to figure it out."

Both Osi and I were injured, so this gave our rookie Mathias Kiwanuka the opportunity to step in there and show the world what our first-round pick could do. What he did was send Coach Coughlin and every living, breathing Giants fan into an irate frenzy. I sat in disbelief with a feeling of absolute helplessness as my team nursed a 21–0 lead going into the fourth and blew it. Tennessee mounted a comeback but were still down 21–14 when they took over the ball on their own 24 with 3:07 remaining. They didn't gain a single yard on the next three snaps. All our rookie needed to do was wrap up this guy and we'd have an automatic score near the two-minute warning.

As a rookie, Kiwanuka was given more of a chance to shine than Osi and I put together. He stepped up when an opportunity presented itself to change the game. What else can you ask of a rookie? But on fourth-and-10, Young dropped back, strayed a bit to his left and then—*BAM*—our first-rounder sealed the deal. I jumped off my couch readying for a celebration. That's when it happened. The unthinkable! The unimaginable! The inexcusable!

The rookie let go.

I was trying to find an excuse for him. After all these years, I knew the ramifications that lay ahead for this young-ster. Maybe he heard a whistle. Maybe he thought Young got rid of the ball.

All I could think at the time was: "Damn rookie!"

The next day, I had calmed down enough to seek out Mathias. He explained that he had gotten hit with a question-able Roughing the Passer penalty earlier in the game. He was afraid he would be flagged for the same call in the most cru-cial moment of the game.

"What you do is, don't let him go. You roll to the ground with him," I explained to the rookie. "You've got to know how to work around the rules. Just roll with him, that's the solution whenever you aren't sure. You don't slam down on him. Just drop and roll with the quarterback like you're on fire."

After discussing it with him I had calmed down further, but still not to the point where everything was happy in Mayberry. I had a birthday party scheduled that night and I was so sick over the loss I just canceled it. Nothing to celebrate. No reason to party. When you lose, you feel so incredibly sick to your stomach, you want to crawl up into the fetal position and literally hide. If you can't even face the cashier at a McDonald's drive-through window, you certainly don't want to see a gang of friends at your birthday party.

When the reality that we've actually lost creeps in, life feels terrible. It's depressing, like getting knocked out in a big boxing match on national TV after you promised your family a victory in front of your hometown fans.

That first loss against Manning and the Colts? It took me the whole week to get over it. That week was brutal.

Monday, you get your butt chewed out by the coaches. They'll rip you apart, tell you what each mistake cost the team, and then rip you apart some more during a practice period supposedly dedicated to correcting your mistakes from the previous day.

But the week after a loss, especially one in which our rookie defensive end committed such a huge brain blunder, every repetition feels harder. Every stride feels more and more tiring. Every meeting feels a month long.

After a loss, I really don't want to talk to another human being. Even though I wasn't on the field for that game, I couldn't help but blame myself. I should have just shot up the foot, taped it and gotten out there. Although's that's unrealistic, I felt if I had, this agony wouldn't have fallen on my teammates. It's awful. Terrible. Horrible. Torturous. After a loss, I feel nauseated. My insides burn. I don't feel like eating and there is not a single thing that can help me get over it, aside from a win.

The pain of losing is ten times more powerful than the joys of winning. When you win, you enjoy that one night after the game. The week is more fun, but it's still tough. After a win I still make it hard on myself. I'll replay the mistakes I made over and over in my head. In football, there's rarely pure, unalloyed joy. Players have told me, when you win a Super Bowl, it lasts for a bit but players will ask themselves, "Okay, what next?" For now I'll have to take their word for it.

However, I do know how bad a Super Bowl loss burns at your insides for the rest of the off-season. Or if you never get back, maybe it'll burn for the rest of your life. I've talked to Dan Marino about it and to this day, years and years after his retirement as the greatest passer in NFL history, he still hurts. Guys never get over a loss of a Super Bowl.

When you lose, your mind plays tricks on you. You question your own brothers, the same brothers you've bled and sweat and fought beside for weeks and months. You begin questioning yourself, "Why did I take that extra shot? How is it worth it for me to play in pain? For this crap? Why bother working my ass off if this is what it gets me?"

The next time you're at a game, watch the body language of the players on both teams. The winners, no matter how banged up they are, block out the pain and the physical injuries. After a loss, as the final whistle blows, you'll see guys immediately begin to limp. Guys who spent the past three hours racing all over the field suddenly can no longer walk without a limp. The mind is a powerful tool.

After a hard loss, we're strewn around the locker room sitting on our stools, in far too much pain to even bend down and untape our cleats. Five minutes earlier I was smashing

my body into two players weighing a combined 650 pounds, running in a frenzy after the quarterback. Only minutes after that whistle blows, I can't move a muscle, can't even bend over.

There are actually stages of grief in dealing with a loss. It's much easier when you're blown out because you can strike it up to a bad day at the office. A blowout shows the holes you have to work on. But in a game where we had it won, a game where all our rookie had to do was wrap, roll and sack, it's demoralizing. You feel like you did something bad in a previous life, that you're being punished for it now. You resent the sweat and the blood lost that week. It's bad enough to lose, but when a rookie gets fingered for the loss, it's hard to imagine the guilt that young guy must feel that week.

The frequency of the games teaches you to have a very short memory. By Tuesday, let the losses go. But really, how can we? Losses lurk in the dark recesses of our minds. But as you get older, they hurt more and more. Me, I'm on borrowed time. With no time to waste, I don't have time for losses.

When I was younger I figured I'd work harder next week. There were always plenty of chances. But as I grow older, I know that each game may be my last. Sitting in on those awful meetings becomes tougher. The light at the end of the tunnel begins to dim. Before long, forget the light. The entire tunnel fades to black. Honestly, even sitting and writing about a loss bothers me. On so many wasted weekends, the pathetic emotions of loss agitated and depressed me.

The loss with Kiwanuka was terrible for me and I wasn't even in the game. That was a hard one for Coughlin to swallow. Harder, I'm sure, for the rookie to deal with. When you're younger, you're just trying to survive. Back in the day, I'd go into hiding. Today's rookies don't have that luxury.

You're picked and signed to play immediately. There is no grace period. As tough as my life was as a rookie, nothing compares to the pressure those guys feel today. My pressure was from trying not to get beat up by the veterans in the locker room, but their pressure is to not get beat up by the press or the high expectations of the fans.

In hindsight, I didn't make it any better on this kid, since the other players in the locker room realized his gaffe was the reason I canceled my birthday party. They were right. But Kiwanuka wasn't the only reason. We had just dropped our third straight game, one behind Dallas for the division. It also marked the first time in franchise history the Giants took a 20-plus-point lead into the fourth quarter and blew it.

Things got even worse for the rookie. He got absolutely lambasted and chewed to bits by Coach Coughlin. It was the rookie's first game in front of some of his family members. Imagine your family watching you play professional football for the first time and they have to watch you pull off the mistake of the year, and then your coach beats the tar out of you in front of 70,000 people.

As if it couldn't get any worse, when our plane landed in Nashville Saturday morning, Kiwanuka received word that his truck had been stolen out of the Giants Stadium parking lot.

The next week he didn't fare any better. In a home game against the Cowboys, Mathias picked off a Tony Romo pass, heading for daylight when all of a sudden he pulled a Leon Lett and the ball popped loose for a Cowboys recovery. Another rookie mistake! Wearing slick sleeves, Mathias carried the ball wrong en route to what could have been a touchdown. After said ball popped loose, Dallas scored.

That's it; the kid was permanently snakebitten. I decided at that moment I wasn't going to stand next to him for the

rest of the year. The way things were going for him, he might get struck by lightning. I didn't need to become collateral damage.

A half-eaten piece of chicken has more rights than a rookie. We all go through something that first year, every one of us. While some guys get thrown right into the fire the first year, some get thrown in the first day. After all, nobody had a wilder first day as a rookie than Jeremy Shockey.

While most of us don't start off with as much of a bang as Jeremy's fistfight with Brandon Short I told you about earlier, what most people don't know is that I went through something just like Shockey did on *my* first day in rookie camp. I was warned before setting foot onto my first NFL practice field to fight for myself at the very first sign of someone testing me. If I failed, I'd get messed with every single day, for the rest of my NFL life. If I stood up for myself early, they'd back off.

Shockey must have received the same verbal memo I did, because it took him all of one day for someone to take a hack at him just like it took all of one day for defensive tackle Keith Hamilton to start messing with me. When I first got to the Giants, that man hated me. I came into camp a week late because of contract stuff, so Hammer wanted to make sure I knew he was the vet with a whopping one more year of service under his belt.

Our defensive line coach at the time was a country guy named Earl Leggett. The man is a legend in coaching circles, and rightfully so. He served as the Raiders defensive line coach with Howie Long and all those great Raiders teams. Earl made the old-school world seem brand-new.

Every practice we started out with those same up-downs you do on the high school football field. If you didn't do them right, Earl made the whole group do more. That first day I didn't know we needed to go down and then jump all the way back up. I thought we could just come halfway up and plop down again. Of course, Earl made us do more as a result of my first-day ignorance.

When we were done, I heard Hammer talking smack about someone. It sounded an awful lot like he was talking about, well, ignorant ol' me. Gee, how dare I not do a freakin' up-down right.

Hmmm, my chance to earn respect was about to come a lot sooner than I thought. "This motherfucker just got here and now he's got me doing extra up-downs!" Hammer proclaimed to the other linemen.

I asked him who he was talking about.

"I'm talking about you!"

That's all I needed.

"If you're gonna talk about me, do it to my face." Man, was I quick and catchy with my verbal jabs back then or what?

He charged at me and pushed me. I was holding my helmet in my hand and I took it and smacked him three times— once to the top of his head, then once on either side. A quick *bam, bam, bam.* Maybe it was this that spawned the Gragg helmet-bashing incident.

The other players quickly broke it up, but I learned two great lessons from Earl Leggett that day. First, he pulled me aside and gave me this practical advice: "Don't ever fight a man in this league using a helmet as a weapon. That only exposes your face in a fight. Guys in this league are crazy. Crazier than you, man!"

His second quip was one of wisdom. "I'd love to fight for you, but I'm too old. So make sure if you're fighting, you're fighting to put food on your table."

Yeah, Earl, I was fighting for food money. With Hammer, I wasn't sure how it would end. I didn't know what was cool

and what wasn't. But it certainly didn't help me when every time Hammer talked smack to LT, Taylor would say, "Shut up, Hammer, before I get Strahan over here."

Fights are just one of the many events that makes a rookie's life rotten. You've got hazing, rookie talent shows and no rights. In terms of hazing, the life of a rookie is soooo much easier today than it was when I started in 1993. Back then, they hazed the crap out of you. Vets treated you like garbage. They demoralized you; they didn't give a rat's ass whether you were dead or alive. Actually, they probably wished I was dead.

The year before I came in, the Giants' first-round pick was Notre Dame tight end Derek Brown. At his first-ever training camp practice, he was coming across the middle on a pass route. LT took his forearm and *WHAM!* threw it in the window of Derek Brown's face mask and actually broke his nose. Derek never recovered. He was no longer able to walk around after that like he was The Man, which he had been at one time at Notre Dame. Today we can't afford to lose a Shockey or a Brandon Jacobs or an Eli Manning or any other young high draft pick, even though B-Short might not agree.

Because of all the piss and vinegar they come in with, I look at rookies as hopeless and confused souls. But today we have to treat them differently. We can't push them to break because if they actually do crack, we lose them. With the salary cap quickly forcing vets out and youngsters in, we rely on these young cats. But that doesn't give them automatic status equal to the vets. And that included young Eli Manning.

When the Giants chose Eli we had no problem with the selection. We were ecstatic that a kid with this many accolades was tabbed to eventually take over. The operative word here is *eventually*.

When the Giants released Kerry Collins, we had a group of very unhappy veterans, and guys like me and Tiki Barber had no problem voicing our displeasure. The problem for a guy like Eli is that no veteran wants to rebuild, so when the front office puts our future in the hands of a kid who hasn't done a damn thing in the league, we resent it. While we didn't resent Eli, I'm sure we acted like we did. Some guys looked at him with resentment because Eli got a lot of glamour and love without ever throwing a pass, unlike guys who had played their asses off for years. (Some guys also get upset about the amount of money rookies make before they ever prove they can play.)

A guy like Eli will always be judged harshly by his teammates and fans until he proves himself and steps up. I'm sure his brother went through the same thing those first couple of years. But when Peyton proved that as a number one overall pick he was worth it, every veteran in that locker room loved him like the best man at their wedding.

When I came into the league, I wasn't pegged to play right away, and I certainly wasn't expected to reclaim the glory of a franchise. A number one overall pick in the draft can't usually deal with that kind of pressure. Tim Couch of the Browns, David Carr, Ki-Jana Carter, Courtney Brown all had their problems and never made an imprint on the league. One of the reasons was way too much pressure on the first pick. They all have to be like Peyton Manning—All-World. That's why I have so much respect for a guy like Peyton. Despite the fact that the entire world put insurmountable pressure on him, he surmounted anyway.

Plus, you have to remember that when one of these rookies is chosen, they're chosen to replace someone that may be a close friend of the other players. That's tough on a new kid. I'm all for fair competition, but I'm not sure I'm in the major-

ity here. A lot of guys will look at a rookie like he's a jerk, even before they meet him. It's natural. He'll face a hostile environment until he proves he can play. Then we'll welcome him with open arms. If he doesn't, we won't.

I always find it amazing how much you're willing to overlook a guy's personality flaws if he can play. He can be just short of a serial killer and you'll let him live under your own roof, provided he can help you win that ring. At the same time, if he can't start effectively for you, you'll resent the guy from the time he gets here until the day he leaves. That's what Eli faces. He will continue to face skeptisim until he becomes a star player. If he never reaches his potential, never grabs the reins of the team, he'll eventually be replaced like David Carr and Tim Couch were. He'll be ridiculed by the fans, the media and, most glaringly, by his locker room peers, past and present. Once Eli proves he can play, the jealousy and resentment will disappear. Until then, it hovers and hangs over his head as if he were a spoiled rich kid whose daddy gives him everything.

During Eli's first year as a starter, it was hard on him. He was completely shell-shocked to the point where the players actually started to feel bad for him. Eli was thrown into the fire and took a complete scorching. He was a huge topic of debate among teammates, other players in the league and the press. While we rooted for him, we weren't sure how the weekly beatings would affect him. I was shocked last year when I saw him respond the way he did under the ridiculous pressure of the Manning Bowl.

Eli never crawled into the NFL version of the fetal position like so many others would have. I give him credit for that. Yet he still needs to make the Giants perennial winners. In order to achieve total validation, he needs to make the rest of the league afraid to face him.

The worst thing a team can do for a kid like Eli is to put a franchise in his hands, the hands of a "potential." Don't cripple us by hoping a kid will soon become a star. As if we already don't hate rookies enough, putting our future into the hands of a shoulda, woulda, coulda is potentially damaging. One of the things guys were upset about during Eli's rookie year was that management seemed to be sacrificing our playoff chances by benching Kurt Warner in favor of accelerating Eli's development.

Don't get me wrong, we didn't dislike Eli personally. You can still love a guy personally and have a different opinion of him professionally. He's an extremely nice kid whom everyone does love personally. But we knew that as a rookie, until Eli stepped up he wasn't ready to lead where we wanted to go.

Twice in my career, the Giants have chosen my replacement in the first round. The first was in 1996. They took Cedric Jones as the fifth overall pick of the draft. Not only did he become the highest-profile guy on our line overnight, Dan Reeves and Mike Nolan, the defensive coordinator at the time, decided to move me from right defensive end to left.

You don't think I resented Cedric for that? Of course I did! I was upset. Who the hell is this kid? Football is a funny world, though. General managers have a saying: "Everything will work itself out." When there's a logjam at a position, "everything will work itself out." When a player or coach needs a new deal, "everything will work itself out."

Cedric ended up becoming one of the best friends I ever had in or out of this league. My moving from right defensive end to left became the greatest move of my career. I guess "everything worked itself out."

When they drafted Kiwanuka, I had absolutely no problem with him at all—at this point in my career, the team

should prepare themselves for my retirement. But why they moved this kid to strong-side linebacker, I'll never know. He's turned out to be a pretty damn good pass rusher. I'll always judge another pass rusher's games compared to mine, but this kid has what it takes to become a stud. But even though I like his game, it was still his rite of passage for me to give him the basic rookie treatment.

What most of these young guys (and the public) don't know is that a player is considered a rookie until after the third game of his second year. Some of these guys think that once they make the team in Year Two, or after the last game of Year One, they're in the clear. Nope! An unwritten rule, you don't get your varsity jacket until Week Four of your second year in the NFL, so you better not act like you're a vet.

Until then, take a backseat to everything. If you're waiting to get taped and a vet comes in, the vet takes immediate priority. If you're waiting for some equipment adjustment and a vet walks in, the vet jumps to the front. You're lower on the food chain in just about everything we do. Food line, doing our dirty work, whatever.

It starts in camp when the vets make the rookies carry our helmets and shoulder pads from practice to the locker room. That's a basic rookie responsibility. Sometimes you'll see a rookie, absolutely exhausted from a 95-degree practice, struggling with three helmets and three sets of shoulder pads.

It's your basic hazing—a completely legitimate form of status recognition that happens inside the NFL. It eventually promotes bonding, but it also shows guys how to follow rules. You've got to remember, we all come from different backgrounds. We have to get on the same page, our page. Forget your boys, forget your family, forget your college teammates. It's now about us, your new family. As bizarre as it sounds, hazing helps build a family identity. It also helps break the guys who think they are special.

Hazing has been severely hampered in recent years. Back in my early days, the vets were brutal; nothing was out of the range of genius when it came to messing with the rooks. I was told that the year before I got here, Dave Brown, our former quarterback, was stripped naked, tied up with duct tape and thrown out on the lawn of Farleigh-Dickinson University (the Giants training camp in the early 1990s).

Brown was also the target of one of the greatest all-time punishments in the history of rookiedom. It stemmed from his inability to bring in the proper doughnuts one morning. Proper doughnuts, you ask? Oh, hell, yeah! Vets are damn finicky about their Saturday morning doughnuts. Those doughnuts represent a tradition of hazing still staunchly upheld today.

Here's the deal: As a rookie, it's your responsibility—scratch that, it is your DUTY—to bring in doughnuts, bagels and juice every week for the Saturday morning walkthrough. First-rounder for the doughnuts and bagels, second-rounder for the juice. Sounds nice and childish, doesn't it?

I was in the unfortunate position of being a second-round pick, but the first pick of my year's draft, the aforementioned Dave Brown, was taken by the Giants in the supplemental draft the year before, so we lost our 1993 first-rounder. In essence Dave was our first-round pick but he was given the job the year before when he and Derek Brown split the duties. So while Dave paid for the doughnuts and bagels my year, I had to go and get it all.

Not only do you have to buy, but the food and juice has to be exactly right. My first year, LT wanted to make it hard on me. So I had to buy him prune juice. Freakin' prune juice! What human being less than eighty years old drinks prune

juice on a regular basis? The answer: someone trying to bust my chops.

Another thing: Our guys are very particular about where the doughnuts originate. The biggest faux pas a rookie can make is going to Dunkin' Donuts. DO NOT under any circumstances, I repeat, DO NOT BRING IN DUNKIN' DONUTS. We're very picky about our free breakfasts and Dunkin' Donuts will get a rookie killed.

One year Thomas Lewis, our first-round wide receiver from Indiana in 1994, failed to grasp this and not only did he bring in Dunkin' Donuts, he brought in two dozen. How do you bring in twenty-four doughnuts for fifty-three players, coaches, equipment guys and trainers? To say that didn't go over well is like saying Charles Manson is just a "little" screwed up.

Damn it, T-Lew, make us feel fancy! My teammates took the doughnuts he brought in and squeezed out all the jelly into every one of his shoes and pockets, and poured juice in his helmet and smeared it with jelly. It was evil. Hey, T-Lew knew the rules, but he tried to take the easy way out. Our head coach, Dan Reeves, had no problem with the retaliation. In fact, Reeves was as angry as we were at T-Lew's poor job at the doughnut shop. Coaches gorge on the rookie's bounty, too.

There's a proper protocol that must be followed. It wasn't. We destroyed that poor man's clothes and locker that day. But that is nothing compared to what happened to Dave Brown. One morning Brown failed to bring in suitable doughnuts, so LT (I already mentioned he's very particular about his Saturday morning breakfasts) took the box and smashed it over Dave's head. What ensued next was a food fight straight out of the cafeteria scene in *Animal House*.

Here's the great part. Dave and the official first-round pick that year, Derek Brown, had to clean it up. Why? If they hadn't brought in the wrong doughnuts in the first place, the doughnuts-over-the-head smash and the ensuing food fight wouldn't have taken place. As a result of that food fight, the vets actually hired a chef to come in and cater breakfast and charged Dave and Derek.

Me, I had to get my doughnuts from Mazur's Bakery in Lyndhurst, New Jersey. I learned real fast that those freakin' doughnuts were the most important thing I did on a Saturday morning. A few times I was actually late to meetings because I was fetching the men their goods. I'd walk in and they'd break meetings to gorge on the goodies. I would rather miss that entire day and get fined by the coach than face LT, Coach Reeves, Phil Simms, Jumbo, Bart Oates and Erik Howard without the right beverages and doughnuts.

The worst guy about fulfilling his proper duties was Tyrone Wheatley, the former Heisman hopeful from Michigan. He wouldn't come in with the doughnuts. He didn't care what we thought. As a result, it took us a long time to view him as a full-fledged teammate. You're not looked at as one of us if you don't play by our rules. It's also a good gauge for the coaches to see exactly what a guy's makeup is. Wheat was a freak about it. He didn't care what we felt about him, what the recourse was, nothing. Eventually we grew to love the guy, but it took years for that to happen.

Hazing took a major step back last decade after some morons inside the Saints locker room decided it would be a good idea to make their rookies run through a gauntlet of players hitting them with socks filled with coins. That's not a unity builder, that's assault. It's also the most ridiculous thing I've ever heard. They injured their tight end Cam Cleeland, who was sidelined with an eye injury after getting hit by a sockful of coins.

That one single incident in New Orleans completely

killed hazing. We're now forced to tame things down to a more pedestrian speed. The worst we now do is take a guy and throw him in the ice tub. During last night of camp, we'd look for any rookie, including a rookie equipment guy or trainer. We'd begin with chants, "Ice tub, ice tub, ice tub," until half the team apprehended our victim, sometimes tying him up, and we'd throw him in a tub filled with ice and water. The ice tub is our only retribution. If a guy won't get up and sing for us, ice tub. If a kid refuses to carry our pads, ice tub. It's the universal answer for everything now.

Young kids today, be glad it's just guys like Brandon Short and myself or Shaun O'Hara and Tiki you have to deal with. Be glad your first day didn't include LT, Simms, Pepper Johnson, Howard, Jumbo or William Roberts. Those guys and their whole generation took hazing to a different level.

It's real easy for a rookie to get under our skin. All a kid has to do is be himself. What I mean is, if you're trying to impress, what do you do? You work your butt off. Sounds like the correct approach, right? WRONG! In fact, it's the wrongest thing in the history of wrong! Hey, rook, we're old and beat-up. The last thing we need is for some young gun to come into camp going a million miles per hour. Leave that for the game, son.

My first year, I played with a defensive end named Mike Fox. Big, nice, quiet, strong guy. But Fox also had a great motor, which is why they drafted him in the first place. It's also what got the whole team to hate him his first couple of weeks.

Big Mike had been going full speed in practice while the old offensive linemen like Oates, Jumbo and William "Big Dog" Roberts got fed up. They chop-blocked him and then hit him over the head with a helmet. Two guys held him up in a drill and the third guy went low after his knee. They figured they'd calm him down by beating him up!

After the chop, Oates ripped Fox's helmet off and smacked him in the forehead with it. Fox's reaction scared the living crap out of everyone. After getting hit, he didn't budge. It only made him angry. The guys ended up feeling bad about it and the guilt from the hazing led to his acceptance. It took him getting chop-blocked by three teammates and hit in the face with a helmet to finally be deemed okay. Fox ended up being a hell of a player, a great guy and teammate and then signed a big free-agent deal in Carolina.

We had a kid in last year's camp who didn't know how to practice. He kept grabbing Osi Umenyiora on every play, like it was the fourth quarter of a damn playoff game. He was what we call a Practice All-Pro. This kid needed to be knocked down a notch.

The kid's name was Nayshawn something-or-other. So we decided in a meeting one night that we would slow his ass down. I didn't even know what his name was, but he pissed us off something fierce because he was, heaven forbid, practicing hard. So the next day, after every single play in practice, me and a couple of other guys made sure we ran after him and got in a cheap shot on him. Trust me, if we had to run backward ten yards to get in a hard shot or a punch, we did.

Life as a rookie also means that you buy dinner. Sometimes you pay for a limo for your respective position players. The difference between limos and dinner and doughnuts is that any rookie could be tabbed to do this, even some practice squad guy making eighty grand a year.

So, did all the torture inflicted on me change the way I treat rookies? Absolutely not. Aside from trying to help him after

the Vince Young debacle, I treated Kiwanuka like crap. I bagged on his game every chance I got. First round or no first round, you've got to earn your stripes.

It bothers me when I see kids come in, especially high picks, and they don't act the way I had to. I knew my place. The only time I would show my face was when LT made us go to his parties. Those were mandatory and all I knew to say was, "Yes, sir."

Three years ago I flat out stopped stressing over learning rookies' names. Some rookies are just bodies, nothing more, nothing less—bodies to throw to the wolves so that other bodies can stay preserved. There were a lot of rookies I've played with over the years who, if they robbed my house, I wouldn't be able to identify in a lineup. At least twenty, every single year. Their faces start to morph together. If you've seen one sacrificial lamb, you've seen them all. They all look the same until one of them does something to stand out.

There have been times during an interview in camp when a reporter will ask me about a certain rookie. I'll have absolutely no idea who they're talking about. I'll answer their questions if I can wing it, but rookies really can be that anonymous to us longtime vets.

Some rooks will come up to me and ask me, "You think they'll keep me around?" Like I'm part of management? Trust me on this one, kid, the Giants would NEVER listen to me when it comes to personnel.

Other rookies will lay this one on me: "How can I do better? What can I do to show them?"

How can I tell some kid we're just renting his body for a couple of weeks to beat up on him? Usually I'll come up with a few stock answers straight out of the Vanilla Coaching Verbiage 101 Handbook.

"Don't worry about the things you can't control."

"Focus on the things you can do better every day."

"Don't focus on whether or not you're going to get cut. Prove them wrong."

Or.

"Rookies wear down, so show them you can hang in there longer than everyone else."

One rookie defensive end came to me, crying about getting cut. To be honest with you, all I thought about was, "Have I lent this kid anything? If so, I'd better get my stuff back."

I know it sounds callous, but every year of my life I see the hopes and dreams of about thirty-five kids get completely crushed. I'll see grown men cry like *American Idol* castoffs.

You think we enjoy watching men get fired from their jobs? Do you think I like looking at a rookie and thinking, "He is working his ass off and I know he won't stay here." It's the lousy part, perhaps the worst part, of our profession. You have no choice but to be callous; otherwise it'll hurt your soul.

If I had to go through my rookie season all over again, with the hazing and stress of 1993, I'd rather give up football *not* have to live through it. There's that much stress involved.

And as much as I couldn't stand my rookie year, at least I never had the pressure of Eli. I was invisible, just the way I wanted to be.

CHAPTER ELEVEN

Violence Under the Pile and Other Things That Won't Get You Arrested

October 1, Cowboys versus Titans

Titans defensive tackle Albert Haynesworth made me sick today. He was a traitor to our brotherhood. Today I saw him take his cleat and stomp on a man's head without a helmet for protection. He was clearly trying to cause injury, not pain. He took the foot of his 330-pound body and stomped on the face of Cowboys guard Andre Gurode, a downed player whose helmet had been knocked off.

He wasn't trying to make a statement. He stomped on that man's face with absolutely no acceptable provocation. He went where none of us want to go.

This may sound strange coming from someone who used his helmet as a weapon. But what this guy and others like him never get is that our careers and jobs are based upon inflicting *pain*, not *injury*, that there's a major difference between the two. We've got a code. You never try to prevent a man from feeding his family. In my view, Albert broke that law today and the NFL should have kicked his butt out of our league. From a personal standpoint, if I were Gurode, I'd consider suing the daylights out of his cheap-shot ass.

Gutless. We're all trying to provide for our families and this knucklehead stomps on a man's head. Without a helmet! That, folks, is unacceptable, even in our world. We have rules for violence. But he violated the laws of our Sunday afternoons.

If you want to kick a guy in the face, join the Ultimate Fighting Championship. If you want to get paid to play football, keep those internal demons locked up inside your own demented mind and body.

We deal with enough garbage each and every week, we don't need a guy blatantly trying to maim a guy. What if that spike had hit Gurode's eye? What if it had hit his temple? Being permanently injured affects a man's family.

Look, I'm not saying I don't want to put my opponent out, but do it within the limits of the written and unwritten laws that govern our game. I've done some awful things. Like when I hit not one but two of my teammates in their heads with my helmet. The difference? There was provocation. I was defending myself to the best of my ability. It was either stomp or be stomped. But what Haynesworth did was comparable to taking my helmet in my fight against Scott Gragg, running up behind him while he was sitting down with his back turned to me and just clubbing him. There's a line there, a bit cloudy, I admit, but a line that we all view as unacceptable to cross.

I guess what Albert did was to help define where we draw the line, how we separate what is acceptable in our world of violence and what is taboo. Even though Haynesworth said he was retaliating for getting chop-blocked a lot, it wasn't acceptable in the eyes of anyone inside the NFL. I get chopped all the time, but you don't see me out there stomping on a guy's temple. You get him back with your play.

Guys were outraged by Albert's actions. Keyshawn Johnson wanted him kicked out of the league. John Lynch felt that suspension wasn't enough. Simeon Rice said they would have had to call the game if he were Gurode, because they wouldn't have been able to stop him from killing the guy. Brian Urlacher said if Gurode were his teammate, he would have sprinted off the sideline and lost his mind, in defense of his fallen teammate. I've never seen an incident that created so much unanimous outrage as when Haynesworth crossed that line.

If you're trying to prevent a man from earning a living, you're a loser, a punk, and you should have some sort of adult time-out—forever!

Let's go over the rules again, boys and girls. Hearing a guy scream from pain you've inflicted can be sweet, sweet music. Making a guy scream from an injury, that's a bad, bad song. Even making a guy scream by punching him under the pile, or even squeezing a guy's private parts where the refs can't see, is somewhat acceptable. Why? That *just* hurts, it doesn't cause a man to miss a game check. Therein lies the great difference: If our play were limited by pain rather than injury, none of us would make a dime.

Pain is part of the world we live in. On any given play, you're going to be put in pain. Literally, on three fourths of the snaps of a ball game, something happens that ranges from not feeling too good to being in downright agony.

You should see what happens under a pile. I mean, it is ruthless.

The best I can describe it is like a big mangled car crash—a ten-car pileup where the referees are our jaws of life.

First off, it's often claustrophobic. You don't know who is who, things are somewhat dizzying as you try to reclaim your senses. First thing I usually do is shut my eyes real tight to protect from a finger finding its way into my eye socket, intentional or unintentional. I don't know if everyone does that, but it's not a bad idea. Not too many guys will try to stick a finger in your eye. But one is enough to get me to clench those lids shut.

Then, within that same second, you shift your attention toward taking an inventory of your body to make sure nothing is snapped. Within the next half second you try to identify where you are in relation to the markers, which jerseys are laying beside you, on top of you, beneath you and across your limbs.

Within a second and a half to two seconds, your head clears and you rely on your hearing to let you know what may have happened. You listen not so much to the crowd but for little or loud signals from the other players. You often hear a scream or a shriek of some sort, and as a player, you can immediately tell if it's a shriek of a painful injury or someone's just getting the business thrown his way.

I once was on top of a pile when the Eagles running back Charlie Garner snapped his leg. It was like someone took a piece of firewood and smacked it against concrete, breaking it in half. Those are scary because the sound of a man's bone snapping stays in your mind forever. It's like a permanent mental scar and it rears its ugly head at the weirdest times. I may be at a black-tie dinner and something reminds me of it, maybe a highlight tape showing something regarding Philly, and I remember that *SNAAAAP!* Oh, man, I wish I could get some hypnosis to heal those wounds. Most of the physical pain doesn't make you shiver later in life. But those awful sounds haunt you.

And it's not just the major injuries that cause guys to bark. Trust me, we've got plenty of reasons to scream. Eye gouging, punching, grabbing crotches, digging fingers and nails into flesh, it happens all the time. Not just here and there during a game, but all the time!

Getting your manhood grabbed and squeezed under a pile is the worst thing short of injury that can happen down there. And it happens a lot more than people know. As you can imagine, it sucks. There's nothing homoerotic about it, although you tend to call a guy some very politically insensitive adjectives if he pulls that garbage. They'll do it to get you off the field for a play or two.

Now you're probably asking yourself, how could you get your nuts squeezed if you're wearing a cup? Simple answer: We don't wear them!

Hardly anybody wears cups. You boot them from your equipment checklist because they slow you down by rubbing on your inner thighs. Anything that slows you down, you shed. Guys don't wear knee pads, thigh pads and a lot of times mouthpieces, either.

We are virtually exposed. For many of us, we've got absolutely nothing protecting us from the waist down except a pair of pants and some tape on our ankles. So when you're under that pile, you'll hear a guy let out a howl. And know exactly what happened.

Sometimes you'll hear a guy screaming, "My eye!" Remember when I mentioned that I immediately shut my eyelids tight? It's because really dirty players will take their fingers under the pile and jam them under or through a face mask. Trust me, that doesn't feel too wonderful, either. Imagine some idiot bracing your head and then taking his index finger and jamming it into your eye socket.

Fat old Langston Walker from the Raiders eye-gouged me

last year. He said he didn't mean it, even though it seemed to me he didn't try to avoid it. My damn eye closed up on me. I needed Mickey from *Rocky* to cut me. Cut me, Coughlin, cut me!

I had a teammate, Brian Williams, our former center, who got a finger in his eye and it ended his career. He actually had blood pouring out of his eye socket. When you get poked in the eye, like when Walker got me two years ago, your first thought is, "Is my eye on the ground?" The pain is almost as bad as the anxiety of "that son of a bitch just poked my freakin' eye out! I'll be blinded forever."

The worst pile to be under is a fumble. There's 2,500 pounds of flesh with no warden to police the inmates. Those few seconds of seclusion are brutal. Guys will do anything under the pile to get that ball and the problem is sometimes you'll do it to your own teammates. You can't tell whose fingers you are bending back or whose ribs you are digging your nails into. We consider that "friendly fire." Sorry, my brother, I was just trying to get the ball away from every other human under that pile and into my arms.

The fumble is the golden egg. Whatever it takes. Punching a rib to jar the ball loose, bending fingers in directions they don't go, sticking your fingers in rib cartilage. Unfortunately, there's only one guy with the ball. But half the time we're unsure who it is, so there's often collateral damage. Isn't it amazing that we're willing to play a game that has so many references to war? What's wrong with us?

When you're the first guy to recover the fumble, you lay there and tighten your whole body because you know they'll dive in with their helmets to get you to give up the ball. If you see that a guy is going to beat you to it, you use your helmet to pop him away. At that moment your helmet is your

tool of choice to smash a hand, wrist, elbow or rib—anything to get that ball out of his hands.

There's a whole different level of communication under that pile as well. Sometimes, believe it or not, I'll start having little conversations with guys down there if you know it will take a while for the refs to unravel the carnage. Being forced to lay face-to-face with somebody also gives me a chance to talk a little smack. Like that one time we were in Philly playing against the Eagles and their running back Duce Staley needed a certain number of yards to get a bonus in his contract. So here we are, on the bottom of the pile, we're lying face-to-face and I said, "Tell your coach if you want that money, tell the man to run you the other way. You won't get it this way."

"Shut up, Strahan!"

"No, I'm serious, tell your coach to run the other way. Hey. I'm just trying to help you poor suckers out."

Wouldn't you know it, that son of a gun ripped off a big run . . . to my side, no less. I once told Eddie George that if he wanted to get 100 yards, he should run the other way for the rest of the game. He started laughing but looked at me like I had a good idea. I said, "No, I'm serious, tell your coach to run the other way." He said that after that, he ran 95 percent of his runs the other way.

Every player on that field has a little trick of the trade to inflict at least an annoyance of pain. A running back will kick at you or get up with a knee placed perfectly in a spot that hurts like hell. He'll innocently put his knee on your rib and accidentally put all his weight on his knee as he stands up. Hey, it's survival of the fittest out there. Any running back from Clinton Portis to Jamal Lewis to Edgerrin James may use this trick. So we'll get them back. When a back is under a pile, a defender will grab his ankle and twist that sucker

about ninety more degrees than it's willing to go naturally. Or if he's lying there, we'll "accidentally and innocently" step on his hand before he has a chance to get up.

Anything goes. But like I said, the running back can retaliate once he gets up. He can kick a guy but make it look like it was just part of the natural motion. Or he can stand up on a guy's knee or calf and put all his weight on the defender and act like, "My bad, I was just trying to stand up, I didn't see your stomach under there."

Receivers have their shots, too. Out wide, they act so innocent in their own little paradise. But in reality sometimes these cats are like snipers. The wideouts use a technique called a cut block. It's complete BS. I call it a coward's block. I don't believe it should be legal, because it allows a guy to pretty much sneak up on an unsuspecting defender, usually a defensive back, and throw his body into a guy's knee. Sometimes it feels like a man walking up to you from behind with a crowbar, whacking you behind or on the side of your knees.

Guys like the Colts' Marvin Harrison and the Steelers' Hines Ward—the guys who are seen as classy—are two of the worst snipers. They take those kinds of shots often. Players hate them on the field. Don't grin and smile in our faces, then dive at our knees when we aren't looking!

The offensive line has the high-low attack. They especially love to use this cheap shot when their opponent is talking crap. What it is, they'll have one guy post you up high and then another guy will take you out at the knees, low. That's probably the cause of more fights between linemen than anything. I'd rather a guy punch me in the mouth than high-low me. If your knee is planted, there's a very good chance this will blow out at least one ligament in your knee, if not more. In some cases this isn't called in a game. But

when something is blatant, and if the NFL recognizes the viciousness of the ploy and they flag you, they'll fine you. Sometimes a lineman will high-low or cut you if you're talking smack to one of their teammates. Linemen know how to stick together.

The Denver Broncos offensive line is the worst and most notorious for this. The players, and especially the coaches who teach those guys to play the way they do, are garbage. They intentionally go down low after your knees and ankles. There is a difference between coaching players to play hard and coaching guys to injure. They must have read the Albert Haynesworth Handbook on Game Day Etiquette.

There's a difference between a cheap-shot artist and a hard player. But Denver has blurred the line. A cheap-shot artist will go after your knees or ankles with the intent to injure for no apparent reason. A hard player is a guy who plays to the whistle or maybe one step past. He doesn't intend to hurt you, but he does have every intention of making Sunday the worst day of your week.

The worst part of what Denver does is that they view their antics as tough, like they belong to some exclusive fraternity. To me it's just pure garbage. I know I probably sound like a sour defensive lineman. You're damn right I am! We've got enough violence out there on Sunday afternoons without the Broncos offensive line or the other assholes of the league trying to shelve us for an extended period of time.

In all honesty, I keep a list of the all-time cheap-shotters. There's Runyan, Steve Wisniewski, the Raiders great Jumbo Elliott, my former teammate, Erik Williams of those great Cowboys offensive lines, Kevin Gogan, a veteran guard. Some lists may differ, but that's mine.

The first four are all from the same generation. If you beat them on anything at all, the next play you'll get a finger innocently slipped under your face mask and into your eye. Or how about a punch in the windpipe or down low in the ribs? They'll wait for a scrum and suddenly, *wham*, you've got a big old leg whipping around, kicking you in the bottom of your leg.

There's a reason why four of the five guys I've named are out of the league. For some reason, today's lineman doesn't have the same nasty streak or junkyard-dog style his predecessors possessed. The officials have certainly made it harder on them, but I also think in football, different generations have different standards. Now when a guy pulls this type of junk, the whole league hates him. Back in the day, you had better play like that if you wanted to gain a nasty reputation.

While for years I hated going against Jumbo in practice, he made going against guys like Erik Williams easier for me. After practicing with Jumbo, it wasn't a shock when one of those guys grabbed my Adam's apple in retaliation.

Now Runyan is a different kind of cheap. I hated him when he first went to the Eagles because they touted his signing as an acquisition to stop me. Stop me? For some reason that really got under my skin. But what really ticked me off about Runyan, what makes him so cheap, is his behavior around the pile.

Runyan waits innocently for a play to be about over until he blasts some poor soul distracted by the play. It's like having your friend tap a guy on the shoulder, he turns the other way and your other friend runs up and punches him in the face when he turns back around.

A defender could be standing over the pile and here comes Runyan, flying into the air to take someone out right as the whistle is blown. It's gutless, as if we need any extra push.

While the NFL eventually made a rule prohibiting such

actions, Runyan made a living for a while doing that sort of garbage to people. This year, because of his history with these types of infractions, Runyan was fined his entire game play-off share with the Eagles because he hit somebody late. That's another thing the league is cracking down on, thanks to Jon Runyan.

The ironic thing about Runyan is he won't do it to guys who have earned their stripes. He doesn't pull that on me. He has a respect for me (which he should, considering how many sacks I've gotten on him).

Take away this ploy and Runyan's Eagles offensive line is exactly the difference between cheap-shotters like Denver and guys who just play mean, nasty, hard football. Philly likes to lock me up on Runyan. Then at the last moment, their guard will shoot out and sucker me in the ribs. They'll always get somebody to throw a body part at me where it'll hurt the most, and it always comes when I'm engaged with another player. I usually end up screaming at them for half the game to leave me with Runyan one-on-one. If he's so great and he was signed to stop Michael Strahan, then let him try to stop me one-on-one. Rarely do they do it.

Playing against Runyan the last few years has gotten less exhilarating because I don't hate the guy anymore. We became friends at the Pro Bowl in 2002. Now I have to find other people to hate.

As players, we'll watch the highlights to see how our brethren take a beating. We know how bad our own hits are, but we as players love to see who else gets teed up come Sundays. The next day we'll come into the locker room and either laugh at someone or get into rants about whether something was cheap or not. When Kansas City quarterback Trent Green got lit up in the opening week this year with a horrific concussion, seeing that actually put a little lump in my throat. We weren't playing until that evening, so I got to see Robert Geathers' hit on Trent over and over and over all day long.

You gulp because it's a reminder of how brutal our chosen profession really can be. Playing with the fear or anxiety that you could get hurt often leads to getting hurt. Seeing a hit such as Green's bonds us closer together in the locker room because we know it could happen to any one of us on any Sunday. We'll debate as players whether or not something was cheap, and then talk a huge game about how we'd kick the butt of any guy who did that to us.

Which brings me right back to good old Haynesworth. Monday morning, seeing his head stomp, there wasn't a single coach or player in our locker room who didn't have an opinion on the matter. A few argued, but most agreed. Sue him. Kick his ass. Kick him out of the league. Call the police. File charges.

CHAPTER TWELVE

Chess on the Gridiron

Sunday, October 8, Redskins at Giants

When the game starts, I'm so excited to put my fingers in the dirt, I literally feel like exploding, like my head may fall off. I look at football as the unequal opportunity profession. None of us are made the same and if I'm in a battle, my job is to make it unequal, tipping the scales in my favor, in favor of the Giants.

There's a winner and loser every single snap of every single game. I'll try to set my guy up and make him believe that by the time the game's final tick counts off he'll be thinking, "Damn, I just played Michael Strahan, and he's everything they said he'd be and I don't want to see him again."

Football is actually one big game of chess, and the last thing I wanted was for the Redskins and Joe Gibbs, Mark Brunell and their buddies to start swiping at will all our pieces off the board.

Chess? You must think I'm crazy. Every snap of every play of every game, there are a handful of inside battles playing out that the fans don't know about. There could be four or five different things going on between two players on any given play. A reaction to a reaction. An adjustment to an adjustment. It really is that intricate.

Coaches play chess games against the opposite coaches. There are numerous plots and subplots that go into every single play of every single game, many of which play out under the radar. Fans might see a right tackle and me battling it out like two heavyweights punching each other silly. But for both of us, there's actually a mental checklist on every play that we run down before the snap which we then recheck as we're clashing. It's so incredibly specific and detailed, only the final action and result is what the fan usually picks up. Every little thing is accounted for as the coaches break down every minute factor and incorporate it into each and every call.

On some plays the coaches make a call that requires me to line up with my inside eye on my opponent's outside eye. Sometimes they line you up foot to foot, inside foot to his outside foot, which places me a little bit farther out on the edge. Whenever Brunell lines up for the snap, we don't just line up wherever we damn well please. Everything is controlled.

At the same time, I have to adjust based on my build and the build of the blocker in front of me. It's those details that other players sometimes fail to grasp. If my opponent has really long arms, it could lead to imperceptible yet crucial shifts in how I bring on the heat. If he's strong or weak, quick or too big to move, that all factors into a snapshot judgment of how I'll bring on the heat every Sunday afternoon.

Fans see me lining up against a guy like Jon Runyan, Flozell Adams or, in the case of the Redskins, Jon Jansen and

believe we're just slugging away at each other without a plan. Nothing could be further from the truth.

After I'm sure I'm digging in with the correct alignment, next I think about exactly where I'll place my hands on a blocker, depending on the rush that has been called or on one that I've chosen. I know if I have to go outside of my guy, I've got to put my hands somewhere where he can't cut me off and pull me back inside. All of these things have to be figured out before the ball is snapped, and that doesn't even include breaking down what our actual calls and responsibilities are on each play.

On this day I'll go against Jon Jansen, whom I personally don't care for. He played one good game against me his rookie year and lives off bragging that he beats me one-on-one, but they rarely let him take me on one-on-one. And when they do, he loses.

My war, my chess game, starts with the first pass rush of the game. Usually on the first play of a game, right off the bat I come on as strong as I can, just to get into his head. On my first rush, I'll try to smack a guy in the head, run through his chest and push him back just to let him know I can do it. On that first play, I bring out my bishop, queen, rooks and knights. I try to punch him so hard that my hands go through his chest. I want his heart on the first play.

I want him thinking, "Oh, man, is it going to be like this all day?" I want him telling his teammates and coaches, whether verbally or through body language, he's not so secure with himself today.

This sets him up for later in the game when we really *need* a sack. I may use the exact same "bull rush" (a pass rush technique that uses leverage and strength to try to power through a blocker to the quarterback) three times in a row.

On the fourth play I'll act like I'm going to bull rush him again, but instead I'll swipe his arms and rip around him.

The idea is to show one rush, like jab, jab, jab and then, when he thinks another jab is coming, *bop!*, I switch to a hook to the body that sends him buckling over, gasping for air. Move a bishop to show him one thing, but it's really just a trap for when I bring my queen out.

At this point instead of just thinking about that bull rush, he has two other things to think about. I'm trying to get him to think, "When Strahan lines up like he's going to bull rush, will he really?" Your move, maestro.

As the game progresses, I try to build my options and add to his confusion. I try to make his guesswork more and more difficult, play by play. The next play I'll act like I'm going to bull, then shift like it's a fake just to get his feet moving, and then actually bull when his body is out of position. That's the art of the pass rush.

The best in the league in defending against my head games are guys who are comfortable with their own games, guys who don't get too excited. The Seahawks' Walter Jones is the best in the biz. The man is so composed, so relaxed, he never gets fooled by your first move. If you're going to beat Walter Jones, it's going to be on either a messed-up drop by the quarterback or when your defensive backs' coverage is so great, they've given us time to try a second and third move on him.

Another top-three guy is Jon Runyan, the Eagles tackle who, despite all the sacks I've dropped on him, has evolved his game. And I respect that.

My chess match with him used to be so easy because he was so anxious to get his hands on me, he'd come out after me and expose himself. Since, he's calmed down. Now he really makes me work to beat him. Jonathan Ogden of the Ra-

vens is awesome because at 6 foot 8 he has such long arms, he's confident enough that if you beat him on your first move, he'll regroup and get a piece of you before his quarterback feels the pain of another screwup.

Flozell Adams of the Cowboys could be unstoppable if he wanted to. If he had the same fight in him as his former teammate Larry Allen did, he'd be damn near unstoppable all the time. Allen is now a guard, but when he lined up at tackle, you knew it was going to be a very painful afternoon. When Larry Allen gets his hands on you, there's a big chance he'll put you in an awful lot of pain.

The personal battles and the chess games I play on Sundays changed toward the end of the last decade. Guys like Erik Williams, Kevin Gogan, Steve Wisniewski, Jumbo Elliott, those guys made Sundays a living hell. Playing those guys wasn't a game, it was a damn street fight. Now, their type of play has become extinct. After each game, every head coach in the NFL calls the league's officiating department to complain about certain calls not made by the game's officials. If a guy gets clubbed in the face, punched in the nuts, legwhipped, anything cheap, head coaches point it out and if it's on film, the league will drop a stiff fine on the blocker. Not only do they get fined, they're threatened with suspensions and on-field penalties. As a result, players can't be as aggressive.

The last generation and generations before may have been dirty, but I respected their dirtiness because they at least made it a fun fight. It was old-school, backyard football at its finest. Now everything is about the finesse of the chess game, making it much easier for guys like me.

Now I no longer have to worry about exposing my ribs or my back when I'm setting a guy up. I can focus primarily on each blocker's strengths and weaknesses.

For example, when I go against some of the larger tackles out there, I won't even show my pass rush move until after I've taken three steps on him. Why not just try to immediately shoot around him? If some guys are immovable in their little one-yard comfort zone, I try to get them to move their feet. Once I get them to step one foot out of that box, it can be like taking candy from a baby.

The chess match continues all game long and it involves many other people. After every couple of plays in the Colts game, I asked our right defensive end Osi Umenyiora how the Colts were blocking him on his side. Were they sliding toward him? Were they leaving him one-on-one or were they using another blocker or running back to chip block him?

Depending on the other team's ploys, Osi and I will talk to the defensive tackles and I may call a certain stunt. Sometimes we'll call the stunt to disrupt the play and crush the quarterback. In other cases we call the stunt to get them to adjust out of something that could be giving us trouble. If we have success with a certain stunt, they may make a slight adjustment that in the end frees us up in the trenches. Every little thing we do has a reason.

Sounds complicated, doesn't it? But that's nothing! Nothing compares to the overall matchup between offense and defense. The best way to explain it is to go through actual scenarios that have been used by one of our opponents. Let's take a play from the offense, an actual call that one of our opponents has:

Weak Right Ride 35 Bob "Kill" Horse 3 Y Flutie X Shallow Cross.

Sounds like a different language. The problem is, coaches and their quarterback buddies around the league have hundreds of these foreign-sounding phrases in their language

books. What makes a quarterback so special is that not only does he have to memorize these calls, he has to be able to execute on the drop of a dime and sometimes adjust several times before each play concludes. They store these calls in a memory bank that gets used eighty times a game.

Here's what happens on that particular play. The "Weak Right Ride 35 Bob" part of the play signifies the initial call as a running play.

Their quarterback comes to the line of scrimmage, where he'll try to do whatever he can to see what defense we've called. He'll look at our personnel, try to figure out where the safety is, and the quarterback will usually call out some fake cadence to see where we're going to be. You may hear him call out a series of colors and numbers. Generally it's all a crock of crap. He's just waiting for us to flinch and show him our cards.

Suddenly, we shift from full-contact chess to full-contact chess *and* poker. The quarterback is like a poker player staring at the table, looking for any tip. This is why guys like Drew Brees, Manning and Brett Favre come to the line so fast. They want time to use all their little decoys to get us to tip our hand, and they're awesome at it.

Let's say on that play he sees that our safety is cheating up to where they've called the tailback to run. If that's the case, the quarterback will call out a word like "Kill" or "Scrap" and that immediately shifts the call to "Horse 3 Y Flutie X Shallow Cross," which is a passing play. Some quarterbacks like to use a certain color or a girl's name to kill the play.

Once he kills the original call, every single player on that offense has to know that the run has just been killed and they're now required to adjust to another call. They've got to keep this in mind despite the fact that I've got my hand in the dirt revving my engine to take his ass apart. Try thinking under that kind of pressure.

Wait, let's take it even further. Let's use another call in our cat and mouse game.

Full Right 40 "Kill" Pass 82 All Go.

This is a running play, a draw, and just like before, the quarterback will come to the line and maybe he'll make a fake cadence, maybe he won't. It's on us to figure it out and still get a good jump on them. If in his decoying, he thinks our safety is going to cheat up for the run and thus leave one safety back deep all alone, the call shifts to "Pass 82 All Go" which has four receivers taking off vertically downfield.

If, at the last moment, he sees that we've adjusted to his adjustment by sending a pair of linebackers on a blitz, the play gets even more complicated. Now, the quarterback and the tight end have to immediately, without ever talking to each other, know the call has just shifted to "Pass 82 All Go Y Shallow Cross." Three receivers go deep and the tight end stays in and runs a "hot" route.

Hot calls are a series of routes installed in most passing plays used to counteract blitzes. They are completely non-verbal but entail the quarterback and receivers knowing when to cut routes short, so the quarterback isn't holding the ball too long on a blitz, and when not to. That's why quarterbacks and receivers have to spend so much extra time together after practice, in the off-season and in the meeting rooms. I hate meetings for the defense, but I can understand why they meet, meet and meet some more on offense.

Think about how much there is for them to process. Within the course of three seconds, a team can switch plays three times, yet never actually yell out the play once they leave the huddle.

This is also what makes guys like Peyton, Favre, Brady and Brees so great. This is where the Dan Marinos and Troy Aikmans are better than the rest of the walking world. In addition to the physical aspect, they recognize our games and make us pay.

The guys who aren't so successful, they get stuck on one thing and lock in on receivers. Most young quarterbacks do this and can't break out of the habit until they gain some success. Poor Eli, his first year he dropped back, looked at one spot and was either throwing it there or getting annihilated. He had not learned to check off. The great quarterbacks not only see all their options and use them, they create even more options on the fly. Favre is by far the best I've gone against. He can make something out of nothing. John Elway was great because he did the same thing.

If all this is a little dizzying, how do you think we feel? As nuts as this all sounds, it gets even crazier.

All those little switch-ups and adjustments and calls to counter original calls—the defense has the same exact zaniness on our side. We also have calls that are made in the huddle and then are adjusted based on their first formation and then comes another call we must all adjust to after the offense sets, following the motions and shifts of *their* players.

Full-contact chess. Whose move is it now?

Every time the offense tries to make sight adjustments and dupe us into tipping our next move, we're simultaneously trying to dupe *them* into believing we're running a defense that we're not. You never knew contact chess could be this complicated, did you?

Just like I gave you on offense, let me give you a couple of examples of how much we've got to process *mentally and defensively* before I'm unleashed to hit anybody.

We may have one call where my assignment is to drop into coverage. It's absolutely imperative on these plays that whoever is playing quarterback thinks I'm coming after his ass. Not only do I have to be a great chess and poker player, I've got to put forth a slew of Emmy Award–winning performances, too.

The cards I've been handed by my coaches calls for me to drop into coverage, but my poker face needs to scream to the quarterback, "I'm plowing through this tackle and drilling you into the ground!" At the same time I need to look over the offense to recognize the formation in order to judge where I'm supposed to drop and who I'm supposed to cover.

If there are three receivers outside to my left, my assignment may be to drop into coverage and take the third receiver, usually the tight end or a running back who shifted to the outside.

But if somebody gets up and shifts to the backfield or motions to the other side, my entire drop back could be altered. One shift or simple motion of a player from one side of the field to the other may completely change the strength of their offense, which in effect changes where we need to make the strength of our defense. Once again we switch our assignments on that play.

The safeties, linebackers and I all need to recognize this within a second or two because we may have to switch to something completely different in the next three-tenths of a second.

If they suddenly make one more minor shift, a safety or linebacker may call a kill to the blitz and yell for us to switch back to a normal play, which calls for me to rush a certain lane.

Sometimes we'll yell "Switch," but that's done simply to dupe the offense into thinking we're checking into something

that we're not. Just as they have fake calls and cadences, so do we.

Now that I've deluged your senses with a new language, factor in yet another thing. Each time we play these games within our game, we're tired, we're hurting, the crowd is going nuts and at times we can't hear a thing. But despite the fatigue, the pain, the noise and the dupes, I have to be down in my stance, listen for every little call and be ready to adjust at all times. Fatigue or no fatigue, it simply has to be done.

Now add in something that makes each snap, each altercation, more complicated. Before I get lined up in my stance for a shot at Manning, Brunell or Favre, I have to run in my mind anywhere from three to five scenarios that could happen before and as the ball is being snapped on every single play of every single game.

Not only do we have calls, checks, fakes, decoys, adjustments, shifts and games, we have separate calls and adjustments based upon current field position. When the Redskins are pushed back inside their 10, we have certain calls. If they're between the 10 and the 20 we may have different calls. When we adjust, it has to be the correct adjustment depending what makes the most sense, given where the ball sits at that point.

Once you've accounted for these different scenarios, you try to process what formation the other team has lined up in, where the strength of that formation is, what actual players are out there and what we believe the snap count will be. Already having gotten a call from the sidelines, my teammates and I, based on all this information, have to decide within a couple of seconds what our assignments will end up being.

Throw one more complication into the mix—that's just on my side of the ball! Osi does the same thing on his side.

Our linebackers run through the same fight. Then safeties play through their own battles as well. All the little chess games, all the little poker games.

To put it as bluntly as possible, you cannot be a dummy and be a longtime successful player in the NFL. If you can't process information on the spot, in a few seconds, you will become a situational player.

Everybody can get by on talent, size and speed, but the guys who can't adapt mentally are probably going to have shorter careers. If you're a thinker, you can stay on that field longer.

It honestly took me five years before I really felt comfortable with what I was doing and seeing out there. It took me five years until I truly grasped exactly how to properly process everything on the field so I could play as if I'm not thinking first, playing second. I'm thinking constantly, but now I can think at the same time I play, both with reckless abandon.

It's comparable to how your golf swing looks right after you've taken golf lessons. Your swing is awful at the end of those lessons. You understand the lesson, but at the same time you need to work it out on the range before hitting the links.

Where it's even more challenging in this game is when we're playing against an NFL vet like Brunell. Most of the older successful quarterbacks, and Peyton Manning is the absolute best at this, have such a comfort level, they can't wait to screw with the heads of some young defensive players. The vet will use all these little hand signals, claps, waving of the arms, cupping of the ears and it's up to us to decide what's real and what's phony. Much of it is completely bogus, but how are we supposed to know when to challenge or when not to?

A lot of that comes from film work. We'll study the hell out of a guy's signals and signs and try to decipher them. That's the first part of the battle. Once we think we know when it's a fake and when he's really changing the call, we've all got to get on the same page and figure out what he's changing the play to.

Every time Mark Brunell makes a hand signal or gesture Antonio Pierce, our middle linebacker and one of the brightest guys I've ever played with, or a safety has to quickly take it in and immediately decide if it's a real check or not. If it is, within the same second it took for him to figure out that part of it, he also needs to check us into a different play to counter the Colt's new play.

Antonio Pierce is the mental leader of that huddle, plain and simple. Your middle linebacker cannot be dumb. When we get into the huddle, a safety receives signals from the coaches about the offense's personnel grouping and Pierce gets the call, relays it to us, then gives us some possible adjustments.

In this particular game Brunell would come to the line and, without ever letting on, try to find the tip to our defensive call. He knows what we're going to call and probably knows what we'll check into before we do. It's up to Pierce to recognize what he recognizes and then yell out any adjustments based upon his observations.

This is where all that film he studies comes in handy. Guys give away everything; you just have to know what you're looking for.

For example, the longtime veteran quarterback Doug Flutie used to give away the snap count by a very slight thrust of his right hip the moment he was going to get the snap. For those of us who saw this on film, we knew not to jump off the line until we saw that hip move.

By recognizing flinches and habits, tiny differences in guys' stances from play to play tips a player's hand. It gives me an instant look at your playing cards. Jeff Garcia rocks ever so slightly right before he gets the snap. Daunte Culpepper used to clap his hands right before the snap, so we knew to look for the clap and ignore his cadence.

There's one team I'd rather not name because they are on our 2007 schedule. I've discovered via film work over the years that this team's players tip so much stuff, I now know whether they are running or passing, and which side the run is going to and when the quarterback is going to run a bootleg—all tipped before the quarterback drops back. It's all detected by a series of tiny habits that would never be picked up in real time.

While some quarterbacks do things like clap before the ball gets snapped or rock back on their heels on plays they'll drop back to pass, it's not just the quarterbacks who tip their hands. It's everyone.

Some centers squeeze their free hand before the snap. You have running backs who glance over and over at a certain spot if they're getting the ball. Many receivers, when they're the target, raise their upper bodies up ever so slightly while they are running so they are in position to raise their arms to make a quick catch. Most guys have no idea they're committing any of these boo-boos.

It's the same thing poker players look for. A twitch here, a slight grimace there. Maybe a vein that pops out during tense times. A tell.

It's this film work that make guys like Bruce Smith, Warren Sapp or Ray Lewis so great. They're already more talented than most. Combine that with the fact that they've got your hand figured out and you don't even know it. I learned a lot of how to properly watch for things from Bruce and even Jessie Armstead. For many of us, it becomes an art form.

Ever notice that when I'm getting down in my stance early in a game, I'm the last one to actually get all the way down and set? I'm not just being lazy or trying to work the kinks out. I'm looking at your offensive linemen, your tight end, your backs and your quarterback to see if what I saw on film is visible. I'm looking for those little nuances tipped off by hours upon hours of film work.

I can't get into specifics because for my fifteenth season, I'll need some of those secret weapons. It's all part of my chess game. When I'm lined up to play the Redskins today, I'll already know which piece I'll move where and when depending on certain tendencies I've already seen by studying film at the stadium and at home.

When we line up against guys like Brady or Brees, I head into the game knowing most of us are already at a disadvantage. They've already found things out about us that we have no idea we're doing. And while we're tipping our hand the whole time, we're trying to figure out what makes them tick.

Usually, there's no such luck. These men don't budge. Most of their offenses are pretty disciplined and don't give up a lot.

But on this day Brunell was no match for the barrage of our chess moves. His chess master didn't put him in the greatest position to win. Every time Brunell came to the line of scrimmage, we felt they had no surprises for us. They couldn't trick us. His snap count couldn't fool us. His checks, we had all figured out. This is exactly the type of chess I look forward to playing the older I get. One old man looking to outplay another old man.

The great thing about these chess matches is that it doesn't matter which one of us corners your king. Just get a check-mate. They couldn't score on us because we literally figured out every little thing they did, whether it was an adjustment or just straight up. Plus, it was as if football just didn't make sense to them this afternoon. 19–3. Checkmate!

CHAPTER THIRTEEN

The Art of Sunday Trash-talking

Sunday, October 29, Giants versus Bucs

"**H**ey, Juran, tell your boy Simeon he plays like a little bitch!" I yelled to Bucs cornerback Juran Bolden early in our game against Tampa in Week Eight. "He doesn't do nothin' but rush the passer. Tell him to play the run like a man!"

Welcome to Trash Talk 101. This is how I started my Sunday afternoon on October 29 in the Barber Bowl, Tiki versus Ronde. I wasn't just talking trash for my own benefit. I didn't initiate a war of words to begin the game simply to entertain my teammates or fire myself up.

There's a method to my madness here. I'm not just trying to insult my Pro Bowl cohort Simeon Rice for the sake of starting trouble or insulting the guy. He's been a friend of mine, but in the game of pro football, the psychological part is just as important as the physical.

Every chance I got throughout that game, I loudly repeated

my sentiments to different Bucs players, anybody I believed would deliver my message.

I yelled it at the start of the game, I yelled it between series. I yelled it over to their sideline. "Simeon, stop playing like a little bitch!"

Okay, here's the deal. Simeon is a hell of a pass rusher, one of the best in the game. Coming after that quarterback is all he's focusing on. He can seriously disrupt the outcome of any Sunday afternoon. But if you get him to think about the run, his pass rush suffers. Simeon doesn't like to play the run because sacks are what get guys like him, Julius Peppers, Jason Taylor and me paid.

Prior to the season, Simeon said in interviews that guys like me, Peppers, Taylor and Dwight Freeney are good, but we all know we're not in his league. He boldly claimed that he is the prototypical defensive end, which pisses a man off who has the single-season sack record and many more Pro Bowls under this belt. It also pisses off every single Pro Bowl defensive end in the league.

Rice is notorious for wanting to play only against the pass. He doesn't like to get his hands dirty when it comes to the run, but the position is not one-dimensional. However, when he focuses on that one dimension of his game, I admit, he's a phenomenal pass rusher.

The strongest muscle in the human body is the tongue and today I was going to try to use my hands, feet, legs, arms, and, yes, tongue to disrupt things for the Bucs. Even the tiniest thing you can find to disrupt an opponent's rhythm comes in handy on Sundays.

My goal today was to help out Luke Petitgout, our left tackle. I wanted the message to get to Simeon that he had to prove to me that he could play both ways. I wanted him to get so ticked that he would try to stick the notion he couldn't

play the run down my throat. If he did, his pass rush would suffer.

Who else can I tell? I looked for Ronde Barber, Derrick Brooks, Ike Hilliard, Joey Galloway and Anthony Becht. I drilled it home over and over and over again.

The unfortunate part of trash-talking is the unpredictability of how the target is going to react. Would he boil over and lose his temper on the field (which would be good, too, because it could draw a 15-yard penalty)? Would he forget about Eli and just try to go after Tiki and Brandon Jacobs? Would he get caught up and talk smack back to me and thus get distracted from his game?

I got no reaction from Simeon in that game. I got nothing from him after the game or in the postgame interviews, either. I didn't hear a peep until months after the season ended.

"I want to fight your boy," Rice said when he phoned my coauthor, Jay Glazer, in February. "Mike used to be my boy. Seriously, tell him I have some guys who want to set up a boxing match with us in the Bahamas this off-season. They're looking to put on a whole card. Seriously, this is no joke. Ask him if he'll fight me. I'll whip your boy's ass!

My reaction? After a tremendous burst of laughter, I pointed Simeon to the facts.

Number one, he won't play the run. All the defensive ends who play the pass and the run think this way about Simeon. He was the one out there running his mouth how he's the prototype defensive end and we're all just pretenders. He's not even the best defensive end in his division, let alone the game. I won't take anything away from his pass rushing ability, but that's what he is. He should have his own position, pass rusher. Julius Peppers causes more fear within that division. But with that being said, Simeon's still a bona fide force.

Second, he wants to fight me? Come on, man, are we in the fifth grade? Fights are an integral part of our NFL world, but they never leave the field and reach the street. It's taboo. Warren Sapp and I engaged in a terrible war of words years back, but neither one of us ever mentioned meeting the other behind the 7-11. I guess I would have broken that code with Tiki, but, thankfully, that didn't happen.

Third, I would have whipped his ass!

It's a shame this is his reaction. Simeon is my boy. I took him out on a recruiting trip to New York when he was a free agent, and off the field I really like the guy. But he let the emotions about what we do on Sundays creep over into our everyday lives.

That, my friends, is exactly why you talk trash. It'll either fire you up or take another man out of his complete focus. Let the gums start flapping. There is an art to trash-talking. Some guys need to get themselves fired up. Others want the attention and they love making guys feel like crap. Still others say it purely to be a jackass. Me? I use it for all three, but usually to alter the way a guy is playing.

Shockey is the most talkative guy we have on our team by far. He talks trash for two reasons—to fire himself up and because everybody hates him. The whole league hates Shockey because they don't know him. Every single linebacker and safety inside the NFL really despises the guy. Often when I'm at a function and I see a defender from another team, they hit me up about Shockey. If they knew him, they'd love him. I'd take fifty-two Jeremy Shockeys on my team every day of the week and I'd guarantee we'd win as many Super Bowls as we wanted.

He's a beast but there is resentment around the league for how fired up he gets out there on the field and the notoriety he gets. When he's on the field, guys love to dig at him, so

he's learned to take the offensive. He doesn't take crap from anybody. He curses at guys, "You can't cover me, you sorry bitch!"

A few years ago in a rematch against the Eagles, he said something that shows exactly why I love the guy. In the first game that year, Philly's All-World safety Brian Dawkins knocked the crap out of our wide receiver Ike Hilliard. He caused all sorts of horrific bodily damage and put Ike out for the year.

In the rematch, Shockey was pitted against B-Dawk down in the red zone, got to the end zone, turned and physically outjumped Dawk for the rock. When the two came crumbling down for the touchdown, Shockey flicked the ball at him and said, "This one's for Ike!"

Dawk is one of the classiest headhunters we have in this league and had Shockey done the same thing to some other safeties, it would have triggered a brawl.

If Shockey can't find somebody to talk smack to, he'll just talk to himself, and sometimes I have no idea what the cat is saying. He gets so excited out there that he gets into fights with himself.

Tiki is funny in how he talks smack because he kills guys with kindness. If somebody lights him up, Tiki will smile and with all sincerity congratulate the guy for a job well done. He'll bounce his little battery-shaped body up, flip the ball to the ref and say to the defender, "Great hit," like he's proud of the guy.

He kills guys with intelligence and love. How are you going to hate a guy who blesses you after you tear him a new you-know-what?

I think one of the best things he did came in our game against the Saints, Tiki's last home game. At one point he took a run toward the Saints sideline and got tackled near their bench. When he jumped up, he turned toward their head coach, Sean Payton, our former offensive coordinator, and actually gave him instructions on how he needed to adjust one of their plays. Tiki saw their blocking scheme wasn't working with a particular run, and if Sean made one simple change, they'd get a lot of production out of it in the future.

"Little bugger was right," Payton told Glazer later that week about Tiki's adjustment.

Somewhere in the heat of battle somebody is talking trash to somebody else. Sometimes it's funny. Sometimes it's not understandable. Sometimes it's just downright cruel. It's all part of the sounds of our game, the same way hits and cheers are. Except we're usually the only ones who hear these mini-battles being played out.

The best are the guys who use it to get themselves going in a contest. Denver's All-Pro former tight end Shannon Sharpe was like that. He talked smack to anybody and everybody. It was as much a part of his game as running and catching. Simply put, Shannon Sharpe was the greatest trash talker in the history of the NFL.

The man studied your background and came up with stuff that was so funny, HBO should have given him his own one-hour special. Off the field we have hung out, but on the field, Shannon knew how to stoke my fire. He got me so fired up one game I completely lost my mind on him during the coin toss and it was preseason! I just didn't feel like listening to his mental mastery that day. He got after two of my fellow defensive linemen, Christian Peter and Keith Hamilton.

"Please, both of you guys should be in jail," barked Sharpe. "You're lucky I don't call your probation officers and get your asses locked up. I'll go make a call right now and see you two get led away."

Shannon started walking around his huddle with his hands behind his back like he had handcuffs on.

"You two are criminals," he yelled as he paced with his hands in invisible cuffs.

Hammer and Christian were infuriated and it probably didn't make it any easier on them that the rest of us were laughing our asses off. How could we not? Just shut up, guys, you're no match for the Mouth That Roared.

I'd actually talk smack to Shannon for the same reason I talked to Simeon. I wanted to get him to do something that altered his game.

"You've got all those muscles looking all big and strong, use them. Hit me. Don't bitch-block me [hit me below the knees]. Why do you lift all those damn weights if you won't use it?"

I was just trying to get him to not only block me up high but to try to come after me more. If it caused him to get mad and try to hit me before he took off running his route, it could have disrupted the timing of the entire offense.

I never talk trash without some rhyme to my reason. Jon Runyan knows this as much as anybody. During our Week Two battle in Philly this year, I was as tired in that first half as I've been for any half of football in my career. I have no idea what was wrong with me, but I was dragging ass. So I started talking trash. Runyan has this bad habit of grabbing your jersey up by the V of the collar. It's holding, plain and simple, but the refs overlook it often. When he grabs hold of your neck like that, it's impossible to get away from him. That day I simply didn't have the strength to deal with it so I started baiting him, challenging him to block me without it. That was my only hope to get anything going against him.

"Why are you always holding me like that? You have to

hold me to block me. Why are you afraid to block me like a man!?!" I screamed at him, all the while just praying I got that second wind. I was screaming at him, screaming at the refs, screaming at his teammates. I complained to anybody and everybody who would listen, hoping he'd feel like his manhood was being challenged and he'd block me straight up. At least this way I'd have a shot.

I wanted to let everyone on that field believe I was the same old Michael Strahan. It's all part of the reason for talking trash. Make them believe it by the tone of your voice.

I yell at Runyan and his teammates a lot for doing cheap stuff like not letting Runyan block me one-on-one. Every time I get on him, he has this annoying chuckle he lets out and he usually just laughs at me. I try to challenge someone's manhood so they'll grow angry and foolishly and mistakenly want to prove me wrong. Once I get you one-on-one, you're done, my brother.

It's all just part of Trash Talk 101.

I'll even talk trash to head coaches to get them to let me go solo on their tackle. In one game against the Vikings, they were doubling and tripling me on every single play. Their head coach at the time, Mike Tice, had guys starting on blocks with one player, then releasing and cracking the dickens out of me after I was engaged with the tackle. Sometimes they'd slide two guys on me and keep a running back over there, too, to get a shot in. It was pissing me off beyond belief so I started yelling right at Tice. I tried to embarrass him in front of his players, another cute trash-talking trick.

"Hey, Tice, why don't you let him block me on his own!" I yelled about their tackle. "I'll kick his ass!"

Tice barked back, "What, do you think I'm fuckin' crazy!"

A few plays after this collision, I thought my career was over.

Using experience, aggression, and leverage to teach a rookie a lesson.

Pass rushing isn't all about talent, it's about who has greater will.

Closing in on the kill.

Celebrating a sack
with the fans.

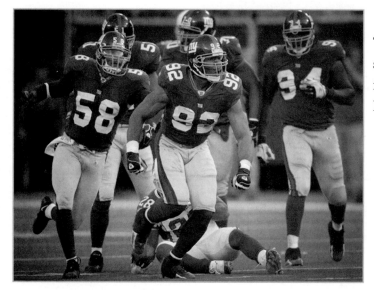

This is why I
spill my blood,
for moments
like this.

Whoever has the
best argument gets
the decision.

I'm always looking
for an advantage.

With my protégé, Osi Umenyiora.

With Jay before the game.

Taking it all in.

All is forgiven with Tiki at the Pro Bowl.

My biggest fans, Gene and Louise Strahan, at the Pro Bowl.

I've heard some wild trash-talking in my day. The great Pro Bowl defensive tackle John Randle used to accuse white guys of calling him the n-word. He would, completely out of nowhere, snap on a white guy. "What did you just call me? Did you just call me a ni@#&*! This motherfucker just called me a ni@#&*!"

Guys would want nothing to do with him. Then if a black teammate jumped in to try to diffuse a racially sensitive moment, he'd call that guy an Uncle Tom. I was just glad I wasn't on offense and that I wasn't white. Randle would make it so the white guys were horrified to go near him.

One time I heard a story in which one Pro Bowl player was supposedly hooking up with another guy's girlfriend. As the game progressed, the offensive player would come to the line of scrimmage, get in his stance and say something about the defensive player's girlfriend. Each and every play, he'd advance the story. For example, first play he'd say, "Hey, you talk to such-and-such?" A few plays later he'd talk about how fine she's looking. A few plays later maybe he'd chime in with a comment on one of her body parts. Later in the game he'd let slip how he saw her recently. Then came his revelation that he was going to see her again soon. And then . . . came the breaking point.

The offensive player walked to the line, got set and barked out the phone number of said young lady—right before the snap of the ball. And apparently it was the correct number. That was the last straw. The defensive player went berserk, absolutely nuts. In total, he was flagged for three personal foul penalties in the game and was eventually ejected. Overall, a perfect 10.0 score, showing perfect form in using trash talk to sideline an opposing team's best player. Masterful!

The only thing you don't really talk about on the field is

a guy's mother. No Yo Mamma kind of jokes permitted. Aside from this, nothing is off-limits.

Sometimes, however, it backfires on you. I once made the mistake of talking trash to the great Barry Sanders. He is the only player I've ever faced who makes the entire way we practice heading into a game completely different from normal.

To prepare for Barry the Great, we'd take a very quick wide receiver and make him play running back against us in practice. Poor guy was forced to do a drill in which three defenders tried to tackle him all at once.

We were in the game and on one particular play, Sanders came my way. I shed my block, took my shot and scored. All by myself, I took him down on my initial shot. I was so excited I started barking at him, "That's right, Barry. All day, all day! What you going to do?"

He lay there silently like he always did, because the man never said a word out there, then stood up and said to me, "I'll be back."

That was his form of talking smack, and you know what? It scared the shit out of me. I actually wanted to apologize right there on the spot. "Hey, man, I'm sorry. I didn't mean that, sir. Really, sir, can I get a mulligan on the trash-talking? Please, sir, Mr., um, Sanders, sir?"

There are certain guys you just don't talk any smack to. Barry Sanders, Larry Allen, Brett Favre, John Elway. It's not smart to do it with these guys. They'll make you pay. They're getting me back, but at the same time fifty-two other guys and coaches all suffer as this man teaches me a lesson via the scoreboard.

The fans do their part, too. Sometimes they'll engage in trash-talking with players, and the players actually get wrapped up in it. I can't tell you how many times I've got to

tell some young knucklehead to stop jawing with the fans and get his head in the game.

This year in a preseason game against the Jets, I must admit their fans got me pretty good. I don't know how they coordinated it, but a whole section started pelting me with chants of "orth-o-dontist, da, da, da, da, da! orth-o-dontist, da, da, da, da, da!" Jets fans are just as bad as Eagles fans but this chant was clever. My teammates heard it and started laughing. Some of my coaches were laughing. Hell, even I started laughing. It was great.

Another really clever guy was Cris Carter, the future Hall of Fame Vikings receiver. He never cursed, yet he used clean trash-talking to alter the way a corner covered him. Ronde Barber tells a great story about when he was younger and was assigned the task of covering him. Carter ran a route on him and then began coaching young Ronde. "Look, you're going to be good, but on this play you need to get your hips turned more."

Ronde barked at him, telling him to shut up. Carter said he was only trying to help. A few plays later, Carter ran the same route and Ronde again played it the same way. Another reception and more advice. "I told you, you need to roll your hips more this way. I'm just trying to help."

Ronde barked at him again to shut up but admitted that at this point, he started to think. Was this dude really trying to help me? Did he really like my game? I know he's a league leader and he's taken a bunch of guys under his wing. Is he really trying to teach me?

Next route, Ronde did exactly as Carter had coached him. Only this time, Carter faked it outside, saw Ronde turn his hips, and ran an inside route to burn young Ronde again. Ronde was livid, probably more so with himself. Carter ran by, this time chuckling, and added that he should only do

the other technique at certain times. Yeah, now he tells him. He had Ronde completely crossed up and never once did he utter a single curse word. It turned out to be a great lesson for Ronde.

The most clever guy in today's game is the Bengals' Chad Johnson. He boasts what he'll do to another player, but Chad is funny. Nobody in the league minds his smack, because he backs it up. It's not only harmless trash talk but creative.

Players look to see what he'll say next when he celebrates in the end zone. Terrell Owens comes across vindictive no matter how creative he is. But we look at Chad like our hilarious baby brother rather than an asshole trying to piss us off.

During our Washington game this year when our huge running back, Brandon Jacobs, was talking all type of smack to Redskins Pro Bowl safety Sean Taylor, challenging him to tackle him up high, Taylor kept going low and taking Jacobs down. Considering our young back is 265 pounds—he weighs more than I do—the more defenders try to come up high, the more people he'll plow through. Taylor looked at him like he was nuts if he thought he'd get baited in. Brandon was learning the art of trash-talking.

One time I saw my fellow Pro Bowl defensive end Osi Umenyiora actually tell a guy, "I'm going to fake inside and then use [whatever move he said] to beat you on the outside. I'm just giving you a warning, I'm going to do this to you."

Sure enough, a couple of plays later he did exactly what he said he would for a sack. Osi's trash talk put that guy in his pocket for the rest of the game. He absolutely owned the guy. It wouldn't have been as bad if Osi had gotten a sack without the talk, but now that left tackle knew that Osi could tell him what he'd do and the guy still couldn't defend it.

As bad as I can get with players, I save my best trash-

talking for the officials. I like to butter them up during television time-outs with such classics as, "Did anybody ever tell you those stripes are really slimming on you?" Or "I love the new uniforms on you guys. Really accentuates the positives."

If a guy like Runyan is holding me, I'll start in on the refs early, ask them if they're blind with all the holding they're missing. I ride those guys with the hopes that I can get a call somewhere along the lines. On a big play, I'll lose my mind. That's where diplomacy suddenly ends.

"What the hell, you don't see that? He took me to the damn ground. You don't freaking see that?"

"Next time, Michael, we'll look for it" is a usual response and one that gets me even angrier.

"Next time isn't doing no good, I need it now." Then I'll start dropping f-bombs on them. I'm ashamed to say but I do drop QUITE a few f-bombs on the refs.

We go through the same song and dance every time. They demand that I stop cursing, which prompts me to drop another f-bomb and challenge them with "What are you going to do, throw me out of the game? Do it. Come on, it'll be better than sitting out here with his BS."

I get so bad that I often end up apologizing during TV time-outs because I don't want them to have a vendetta against me later on. But it also gets the refs a little edgy and sometimes they want to ease my wrath by looking for a call that will calm me down. The hope is that whatever I say gets a desired response later on from the officials.

The worst I've ever exploded on the field came on New Year's Eve 2005 when Langston Walker of the Raiders stuck his fingers in my eye and pushed. I dropped like someone just shot me in the head. I was furious, but that fury turned to uncontrollable rage when the refs never threw a flag.

"Are you blind!" I screamed at the top of my lungs at the whole officiating crew. "What the fuck, you don't see that? Throw the flag, that'll at least give me some vindication. Right in my fucking eye. He could end my career and you don't even throw that flag? How do you miss that?"

I lit into these guys unlike any other time in my career. This dude could have ended my playing career and I can't so much as get a little hanky love? What gives? The refs didn't know how to react because I was absolutely enraged. They actually apologized to me a little later for missing it.

Tom hates when we talk trash but I'm completely in favor of it. I know fans probably sit at home and look at us as if to say, "Just shut up, and play." Trust me, if we shut up our intensity level would drop and our play would actually suffer. Wouldn't you rather see us all fired up and flying all over the field than quiet, sullen versions of guys like me and Shockey?

The funny thing is, in the real world, I really don't curse a lot. I don't have a potty mouth in normal everyday life. But on the field, it just happens. I let my mouth do the talkin' and my lips do the walkin.'

Just ask Simeon.

CHAPTER FOURTEEN

Meetings, Monotony, Playbooks and How to Sleep Through It All

Christmas Day 2006

Talk about a stocking full of coal. Today is Christmas, and you know what I got? Possible retirement. I am scheduled to fly down to Charlotte tomorrow to meet with a foot specialist, and if he tells me I need surgery to repair my Lisfranc injury aggravated in Sunday's blowout to the Saints, that's it, folks, I'm done.

I've got no yuletide cheer. I'm not spending time this Christmas worrying if I'm naughty or nice. Instead, I've been given a fifty-fifty shot that I'll have to refer to myself as an ex-player. I don't want to be an ex-player, I still want to be a current NFL player fighting for the Lombardi Trophy. While much of America is in church today praying and figuring out ways to become a better person, I'm looking at my life and my career, knowing that any chance to win that elusive ring may be over after one short doctor's visit.

I'll spend my holiday weighing the pros and cons of continuing my career, and quite frankly, if they tell me they need

to knife into me again, it'll be no more. I love the game of football. I love the camaraderie and I realize that we have a high mortality rate in this career. But I just can't go through an entire off-season being stuck at the stadium rehabilitating an injury so I can thrust myself back into the monotony.

I resent that I don't have a ring in my life. How could I have played for this long and only gotten the taste of a Super Bowl once? Those weeklong parties will be around forever but here I sit, shivering at the thought of never getting to party *on the field* at the game of games.

So I'm fighting these thoughts that are attacking my mind. Whether or not I'll ever step out onto that field again is now up to a man I've barely met. His medical opinion will make my decision.

If he says, "Michael, we've got to cut you," then it'll be "Move over, Tiki, I'm about to crash your retirement party." If not, Giants fans will have another year for me to either let them down or jack them up.

A little-known fact about players. Many of us don't hang it up because our bodies give out. It's the meetings, the practice schedule, and the minutiae of the weekly grind. As you get older, that becomes much more difficult to get through.

Retirement talk is not always because of the physical aspect of the sport. Is it physically demanding? Absolutely. But that's not the primary reason successful vets hang it up. Fans think our lives are nothing but glamour. I won't lie and discount how wonderful the glamorous side is. But at the same time our work lives are filled with meetings upon meetings upon meetings. Drills upon drills upon drills. Hell, we have meetings to talk about certain drills and then drill what we saw in the meeting, only to hold another meeting after the drills are over to see exactly what we did in those drills. It's a vicious cycle. I'm stuck in one big "Who's on First" routine.

I've talked to a lot of guys who have hung it up, and many of them said to me that they knew they were done after they had no fire left to sit through the grind anymore. The older you get, the less excited you become about going to work every day. If it was about hanging out with the guys, having a practice once a day and then taking the field together on Sundays, I'd play as long as my bones, ligaments and tendons would allow.

What is our work week like? Let's take a trek together. Most fans see only Sunday. I want you to experience my Monday through Saturday. The weekly schedule is the same every week, twenty weeks of the year. Only the opponents and the injuries change. Meetings are the biggest mental negative of playing inside the NFL.

For example, if we have an hour meeting and forty minutes of the meeting is devoted to the defensive backs, I still have to sit through their instruction. Why in the world do I need to sit every day of practice and go through things that have nothing to do with my personal assignment?

My work week starts on Monday morning. Mandatory breakfast between 8:00 and 9:30 A.M. Guys who missed a game due to injury must come in at 8:30 for treatment. Anyone hurt during the game has to be in by 9:00. For the healthy, from that time until lunch at 11:00 we all have to complete a running program *and* get in a lift.

Our bodies are still hurting from the previous day's game. Fewer than eighteen hours earlier, we were banging and slamming into each other. Now we're lifting weights and putting stress on our limbs.

After the workouts, the monotony begins with a thirty-five-minute special teams meeting that starts at 11:30. *Everyone*

has to be there because Coach Coughlin wants us to see how everyone contributes to the team. All the vets who aren't on specials sit all the way in the back. Sitting in a special teams meeting is tough enough, but it's even more difficult for the vets who haven't played on special teams in years.

As meetings get started, we look for things to lighten the boredom. Targets for a laugh. A laugh equals a break in the monotony. We'll usually look for a guy on film getting lit up on a play, or we'll yell for the coach to run it back and just when the collision is approaching, we'll make engine-revving noises followed by "colorful" commentary.

At 12:05 we'll meet as a team with Tom for the first time since Sunday's game. Coach gives a quick overview and then immediately starts in on the turnovers, the stats, the big plays and things that helped us win or lose. Even when we win, he'll point out what could have beaten us. If we win, he gives out game balls. If we lose, we get grief.

It was in one of those meetings several years ago that Jim Fassel informed us he was quitting after the year was up. We came in that morning, and he shut the door and immediately informed us that he had decided to quit and had informed ownership that he'd still coach the remaining games. That was a strange meeting. He was a goner and a lame duck for the last couple of weeks. Then we met to get ready for the next opponent. It was kind of like a wife coming home saying, "Hi, honey, how was work? How was your day? Oh, by the way, I'm leaving you for the lawn boy. What would you like for dinner tonight?"

At that point a coach can't say anything derogatory. Once he's announced he's a lame duck, he's lost any semblance of mojo he may have built up. That's where the coach's Hot Seat can really hurt a team.

When we hear a coach is gone, especially if we don't like

him, we tune him out. Sometimes we'll just blatantly disregard his marching orders. But if we like the man, and we liked Fassel, it gives you a little motivation to bust your butt for a man whose job you lost.

At 12:20, Coach wraps it up. We pull out a wall to separate the meeting room into two areas, one run by the defensive coordinator and one run by the offensive staff. By Monday morning, the coaches have already watched the game, broken down what happened on each play, sorted out who screwed up where. The good plays we don't spend an awful lot of time on. The bad plays we'll watch over and over and over again. Even when we win, our work week starts with negativity.

Said negativity doesn't stop there. From 12:20 to 1:40, our defensive coordinator uses an overhead projector to put up (for everyone to see) what mental errors were made the day before. Each call from the game will have a jersey number next to it, noting what each player's mistake was. If you have two or three of those, it doesn't go over too well. If a guy keeps making mistakes over and over again, that's when the meeting room fights that I talked about in the "Footbrawlin" chapter may take center stage.

How would you feel if you were busting your ass out there and every week the same guy screws you up? We get a tad edgy. Embarrassment is a powerful tool. The first couple of times, we'll make fun of a guy's play. When that doesn't work, it can get ugly. We'll take justice into our own hands and dress down a guy we feel isn't pulling his weight. While some guys aren't the brightest off the field, put them in a football environment and they're brilliant. On the other hand, we have some guys who are brilliant off the field but are the dumbest jocks in the world when you force them to think football.

Our first film-watching session of the week, which we do right after our first meeting, is when things get really hairy for the not-so-bright ones. The coaches break down your play in front of all your peers. They point out how much of a screwup you are, how you let them down. There's a saying in the NFL, "The eye in the sky doesn't lie." If it happened out on the field, it'll be picked up on camera for all to see. That's when you hear:

"Don't get too comfortable in this town."

"You'd better rent, don't buy."

"I'll get someone else in here who can do it if you can't."

By 12:40 we'll break out of meetings with ten minutes to get out on the field to do something we call "on-the-field corrections." It's basically a walkthrough, a practice without pads. We line up into the same formations we just played and rerun the plays we messed up in the game. We have to show the coaches that we can correct our mistakes.

I never understood this, since coaches preach how important it is that we move on from our losses, to leave them in the past. What's the value in coming out onto the field and reminding us exactly how we lost the game? Still, they'll go over each and every mental error we made the previous afternoon.

If we lost the game, that correction period becomes really rough on the guys who the coaches jumped all over because of screwups. This is where the coaches collectively unleash their frustrations from Sunday. It's more than just cursing at a grown man. It's ripping the heart out of a player. It makes the rest of us uncomfortable.

This lasts nearly a half hour. Once we come back in, we're given access to the media or more treatment for those of us banged up.

Monday. Short day, 8:00 A.M. to 3:00 P.M.

Tuesday we have off. If you win on Sunday, some coaches might cancel Mondays. That's why you'll hear players chant, "Monday, Monday!" for the reward of a Monday off to go along with your Tuesday. Unfortunately our coach isn't a huge fan of Victory Monday.

Next we shift into what is by far the absolute worst day of my week. Wednesday. Terrible, awful, dreadful day. There's nothing happy about my Hump Day.

The day after the game you don't mind coming in, because your body needs to move a bit. Even if we lose, the body's joints crave a little greasing. Plus, on Monday you sometimes want to watch the film, especially if you played well. But Wednesday is awful. It's start-your-body-up day. You get to work at 6:30 in the morning for treatment. On this day, you don't want anybody touching you. Even stretching in the morning is difficult.

I'll hurt so much on Wednesdays, I'll come to work thinking there's no possible way I'll be able to practice. I'm so sore, there's no conceivable way I can move. How can I make collisions, feeling like this? Plus, the game is four days away, a million miles away on the football horizon. Three more days of this crap before I get to play?

If you aren't in by 6:30 for treatment, you're fined. Remember that special teams meeting on Monday? We get another one at 7:45 while the quarterbacks have their own meeting at the same time.

The first meeting on Wednesday lasts until 8:25 A.M., when we meet once again as a team with Tom and the coaches. This is when Tom starts going over our next opponent. He'll give us an overview of next Sunday's team and stress what they do well and what they struggle with. He'll get pretty detailed with the statistics involving turnover ratio, when they win, when they lose, starting field position, average drive after kickoff, average drive of their opponents. Then he'll go through their entire roster, accompanied by a quick highlight tape featuring their starters and other players of note.

This is also when we get our playbook for the week. After handing in the old ones on Sundays, the rookies will then hand them back out with adjustments for the coming week's game. Every single week our personnel department and coaching staff have to come up with a new 240-plus-page manuscript. Imagine working your butt off to write a novel only to have your fan base chuck it in the trash each week after a printing. The number of staff hours put into this book designed to be read for six days is preposterous.

The stress on the family lives of coaches in our league borders on dangerous. Why? Because of these damn books. Coaches spend every waking hour breaking down film, formulating a game plan, rewatching tape and formulating more plans. That's why many sleep in the office.

Writing a 246-page playbook a week is just the tip of the iceberg. They also prepare practice and meeting schedules and break down film of our upcoming opponent's past games. Some coaches will go and watch every single game our opponent played over the last year and a half. It can get that sick.

To an outsider, the playbook looks as difficult to comprehend as a book full of Chinese writing. The day I retire, I swear I'll never, ever, look at another playbook as long as I live. It's as if we're all caught in a sick, twisted, torturous Book of the Week Club where we're forced to memorize a different and yet strangely familiar novel each week of every year. And some teams coordinators might go another hundred pages or so over the basic 246. It's a grueling journal full of information based on one team we may not face again for a couple of years.

You want to know how complicated these pages are? You really want an idea of just how dumb we *aren't*? Each one of these pages would probably take the basic B-average college student months upon months to remember. For us? Six days. The very first page of our Saints playbook, for example, in preparation for Drew Brees, Reggie Bush and friends, had eighteen different headings that broke down small portions of their offense. Base defense is covered in four different defensive fronts, including zone blitzes and man blitzes. Then we'll have nickel package coverages and a totally different heading for blitzes out of those same packages. Then there will be spaces for calls out of dime packages, red zone coverage, short yardage, goal line, two-minute drills, four minutes left and being backed up inside our own five.

Sound complicated? Wait. The fun is just beginning. The pages get even more specific. It can get so complicated that even people who work around the NFL don't get it. Perfect example, the coauthor of this book. One day Tiki let Jay Glazer study our offensive playbook—just the formations. No plays, just the names of formations. Three pages with six formations per page. He studied it with Tiki, trying to learn how complicated the coveted playbook is. The next day he went back to Tiki's and out of the eighteen formations, Jay remembered five. Five! Stupid ass!

One category on one of the pages in this page-turner deals with formations out of our base defense. This one category names the defensive front we'll use in the base defense, naming the different stunts we'll use to get to the quarterback or ball carrier.

Under one category of eighteen different headings is:

Over (TUFF): NAIL/FREEZE/TEX/NUT

Under this we have four different calls. Let's take the second call: 36. Under that call we have bullet points with our assignments:

- *Mike make closed call*
- *Rob/Lee vs. all pro sets*
- *White vs. any slot sets*
- *Any C.O.S. motion changes coverage*

Even the words that seem to make sense aren't what they seem. *Mike* is not me. It's not asking Mike Strahan for the closed call. It's asking the middle linebacker or "Mike backer" for the call. "Rob" is actually the word we use for "right." *Lee* means "left."

Why we can't call it right and left instead of Rob and Lee is beyond me.

C.O.S. stands for "change of strength." Thus if the tight end shifts from left to right, that changes the strength of their formation, which changes our coverage.

The next page details nine additional calls. They have names such as:

- *Over Tuff CL Zebra*
- *Under Tuff Sam Dog 1*
- *Okie Tilt FZ*

After Glazer struggled through three lousy pages of our novel, Tiki tested him on the formations Over Tuff, Under Tuff, Okie Tilt. These didn't even include the second part, which is the actual call, stunt or blitz.

As crazy as this all sounds, let me attempt to simplify it. When the call is made, I have half a second to decipher

which part focuses on my assignment. Let's take the second call of the three:

Under Tuff Sam Dog 1

Under is a front in which I know to line up with my inside foot to the tackle's outside foot. Since it's an *Under Tuff*, I have to shift to head up on the tackle after I initially start with my inside foot to the tackle's outside foot. I start with the Under look outside his right foot to show their offense one look, but then have to shift head up. *Sam Dog 1* means the strongside linebacker is blitzing.

I know what you're thinking. What the hell is this gap-toothed freak talking about? Is your head spinning so far? Great, because after a mere two pages, we have only 244 pages to go.

The next page is a scouting report detailing tendencies, preferences, weaknesses and strengths of their running backs and offensive line. It actually details 104 runs by Deuce McAllister, including how many yards-per-carry he gained, how many runs went right, left, up the middle, off tackle or to the outside. There are additional notes about how he likes to hold the ball, which hand he prefers, how the offensive line sets on different plays and what the running back is looking at on certain plays. There are even reports on what the tackles do with their bodies to tip running plays and passing plays.

The bottom of the page will list their five favorite types of runs out of a regular look and then the actual calls out of those runs. For example, their favorite run is called a Lead and they'll run it out of I Flip, Pro I (Yo), Ace 2x2 Flip or Kings Look 2x2 Flip.

You hear about coaches getting mad at a player for not studying his playbook. Now you can understand two things—why the coach gets mad and why the player doesn't like to study it.

After a run-game overview, we flip to page 4, where Brees' game is dissected under our personnel department's microscope. It lists his strengths and tendencies, how many balls he's had batted down, where he's scrambled in past games, directions of screens, bootlegs and rollouts. We'll even scout his snap count, how it changes in different situations in the game. It'll detail when he likes to pump the ball, where he holds it and if he carries it loose or tight.

The next eleven pages has formations and plays we plan on calling against this offense. Each page has either two or four offensive formations they may use, and each formation shows a different responsibility on the play.

Let's show just one of these pages to further elaborate the level of difficulty and specifics we're dealing with *per page*. The play we're using is:

Over Tuff Closed Zebra Zone "Y"

Out of this one play they'll use four formations:

- *1 LT*
- *1 Slot RT*
- *Kings RT*
- *Kings Trips LT*

Let's take the last one, Kings Trips LT, and break it down. Within the square are boxes or circles for each offensive player, then a letter for each of us on defense. An *E* means defensive end, *S* is SAM or strongside linebacker, *FS* is free safety and so on. But one box also contains an alert in the top right corner of Lou-Lou Closed LT.

Under these formations are Tim's overall instructions and they read:

*Set the front and blitz with a Closed RT/LT call to
the TE. Closed tackle will execute a "Nail" stunt;
will loop blitz "C" to "B." We will play 4 Under and
3 deep un coverage. The SAM and SAFETY play the
flat. The Mike and Open Tackle play the hooks. (A)
to C.O.S. motion.*

*CP: Mike = Strong Hook, Open Tackle = Weak hook
away from (Roy-Lou).*

Then under these hieroglyphics we list the position and
his responsibility.

For example: Ends, To the call—Wide 9 Technique contain the rush. Away from the call my responsibility is—4
technique "Jet" to contain. Each one of us has a little rectangle with our instructions. These make hieroglyphics look
like Hooked on Phonics. You'd probably have a much easier
time deciphering ancient wall drawings than last year's call
sheet.

Finally we get a break in the monotony. The next forty
pages or so are scouting reports of each player. There is no
secret decoding, just massive amounts of film work done by
our scouts in which they break down each player and write
up reports just like you would when you're inspecting a used
car or a new house. They'll do this for every single player we
face during an entire season.

Let's take the page from my opponent in this Saints game.
It reads, "Jon Stinchcomb, 6-5.1 inches, 318 pounds, 5.07 40-
yard dash." He gets a cute little bio that goes over his medical history, what he does well mentally and where he may
have a weakness in the heat of battle.

I'll search through all of the personnel department's
scouting report on his faults for ones that may come into play
in our matchup. "Falls short in strength areas; pushed back

by straight power in pass protection; Overset vs speed and gets beat back to the inside" are among a few that catch my eye. If my foot can hold up, these will fall right into my strengths.

Page after seemingly endless page details every possible scenario the Saints have recently used. Each formation is broken down. The players on the field on each play are detailed: what their skills players did on each of these plays, which way the play went and whether there was a gadget or trick play called, whether it was a play action or straight drop. Every scenario is broken down into more detail and then those details are broken down into finer detail. And then those details are broken down even more specifically.

At times you'd think we were in a high school geometry class rather than an NFL meeting room. The next pages are lined with still photographs, pie charts, graphs, column after column after row upon row. For those kids who don't want to pay attention in geometry class, it turns out there's a use for it after all. Our pie charts break down the player grouping the Saints use on each down, every scenario, every situation of the game and where the runs and passes were aimed.

For those next 200 pages or so, we are bored to death with still photographs, pie charts, statistics, formations, calls, the exact number of times they ran every single play they've run in the last four games, every little tiny itsy-bitsy piece of information that could possibly come into play in our game.

It's painful stuff, people. Especially if we've already played against a team. I could probably write the Eagles playbook if need be. Yet twice a year I'm still supposed to read over our 250 pages of information on their team. Painful. I understand why we study it so hard. We study for an SAT-type mind game each and every week of our seasons. We study because we try to eliminate as much guesswork as pos-

sible. Whenever the Saints are in a certain situation in the game, I'll already have a full breakdown in my mind of exactly what they've done in the past. Yes, the good players in this league actually have it memorized.

Football may be a big man's game, but it's also a thinking man's game. When the Ravens middle lineback Ray Lewis was at his best, it wasn't because he was physically more gifted than every other human being in our league. It's because his recognition of exactly what a team will do out of each formation was better than most. His anticipation is scary. And that's what makes many of those University of Miami players so great. The Ed Reeds, Warren Sapps, Armsteads, Jon Vilmas of the world. They recognize things out there faster than most. You wouldn't think that Warren Sapp would be a model student, but that joker has his game down pat, better than just about any of his peers.

Can you see why I'm on my last legs and why this game catches up mentally as fast as it does physically? Plus, we haven't even gotten to the real monotony of the week yet. We're just beginning our Wednesday mornings.

After we get these playbooks, for the next two hours, we break off into meetings again. We'll start by spending time on the running game, usually just first- and second-down runs. We focus on what their tendencies are in certain formations on first and second downs.

As specific as our playbooks are, the meetings are even worse.

Man, we have meetings for everything! The moment I retire, my body will thank me, but my mind will probably want to take me on a cruise to thank me for not putting it through those Wednesday meetings anymore. Sometimes I feel like telling the coaches, "Look, I'm going home. If you find something new to talk about, call me."

The best way to think about a game plan is this: Try to take all the variables you can possibly find and condense them into which formations a team likes to run certain plays out of. Then look to see which players are on the field for each of these plays. That allows you to cut down some of the guesswork even more. Look for specific things like, on a certain play, does the receiver line up inside or outside of the hash mark?

If a guy like the Redskins Pro Bowl wide receiver Santana Moss lines up outside a hash mark and the rest of the team is in a certain formation, by all of this film work we do and all these meetings, we know he's likely to run the couple of routes we saw in our breakdowns. Then, once we factor in which personnel are on the field at the time, we can take away another possibility or two. Then, if we see their tight end lined up somewhere specific, we can narrow it down even more.

We meet and meet and meet and meet because the more players can see these variables on the field at the same time, the better our chances are in that game. This is where coaches and personnel pro guys earn their money. They're the ones who need to see these tendencies, point them out to us and then formulate a reaction based upon this information. At the same time, the coaches need to come up with game plans that somehow hide *our* own tendencies.

After we meet as a defense, we'll break out into more meetings, this time with our position coach. More details, here we come! Every Wednesday, he'll make sure we go over every single play and every formation in our game plan. Then we'll have a detailed overview regarding all of our run-blitz packages. We spend all this time just on run blitzes because later we've got a totally different meeting for pass-rush blitzes.

Why do we need to meet just for these special calls? One week we could have a blitz that's called one thing where I run one way, and then the next week have the same exact blitz with the same name, but I start to run upfield on a slightly different route.

We already know the blitzes because we've done them in the past or learned them for another game. But the coaches make us go over them again in these meetings. The next day we'll have the same exact meeting, but for blitzes designed to get to the quarterback instead of the ball carrier.

After this meeting breaks, we have about eight minutes to rush and get dressed into different clothes and get out onto the field for walkthrough. A walkthrough is a fancy term for another damn meeting, except out on the field. As if our heads aren't spinning from the two-hour-plus meeting, for the next thirty-five minutes, we have to transfer onto the field what we just had a meeting about. It's overkill. Plus, we've got to rush to get out there on time. Everything with Tom is a rush. He's scheduled things so we're constantly running to be on time.

From 10:45 to 11:10 we'll take the field for the walk-through and work on running plays and first- and second-down pass plays. Coaches hold up cue cards with the opposing team's plays and guys on the scout team line up in the formations we just saw the other team run in the meet-ing. We've seen these first in the playbooks and then on film. So now we transfer it to the field so we can recognize their offense and their tendencies before we actually practice against it later in the day.

We'll break forty-five minutes for lunch, a media session and any other issues we have to wrap up. At high noon, there is no siesta. We go right back into the meeting rooms for another thirty minutes of reviewing what we'll be practicing today and another specific area of the other team we haven't seen yet. To say it's like a broken record is to insult the music industry. And that broken record plays over and over again. There's no stopping it until Sunday. Remember, folks, up to this point, we've only gotten through one half day of game-plan meetings. At 12:30 Wednesday we finally hit the practice field. This is the only part of the week that breaks up the painful repetition of studying, film, meetings and more studying.

Special teams go out before the rest of the team. When we first come out, we do something called tank. Stretching. Why don't we just say we're stretching? Because we've got to have a different word for everything in the NFL.

After stretch, we'll work ball-security drills, then ball-scoop drills, hand drills and pretty much any other drill the coaches can come up with. Then we'll go into individual drills and here we'll work on more specific aspects of each play—getting in and out of our stance, bag drills, hand and feet drills, specific placement of hand and feet drills. That's how we warm up every single day. If after one year it's boring, imagine how boring these same drills are after *fourteen years*. But regardless of how boring it is, these drills are important. They work on details and when you're out there on the field tired, hurting, thirsty, you hope your body naturally remembers these details on its own.

Throughout practice we'll strap on the pads and actually hit each other. We'll work every scenario you could imagine. We'll do red-zone drills, two-minute drills, goal-line drills. We've got drills and a game plan for every scenario of Sunday's game.

It's quite physical, too. We don't just dillydally out there, because the coaches are watching us and critiquing. Believe it or not, the entire two-hour workout is all caught on film.

We've got members of our video department filming high atop a crane that looms over the practice field.

Why do they film our practice? Because you have coaches and personnel people who watch practice shortly after it ends, for the sole reason of scouting our own team, to see how we perform the two plays they have designed for Sunday. We do this with every single practice of our lives. Then we study more of what we did right or wrong in practice.

Let me give an example of the value there. If a coach or scout sees that every time we run a certain play from a certain formation, Eli always checks off the receivers and throws it down to Tiki in the right flat, somebody needs to catch it and hopefully throw a wrinkle into our game plan on Sunday. We'll hope a team sees the same tendencies on film and point it out to their team in *their* monotonous meetings. When we finally get to the game, we've adjusted to where we'll show the same formation and run the same play, but Tiki will act like he's running into the flat, and instead he'll take off for a fly.

We may show on defense that every time we line up a certain way, a blitzer always comes around the left end. We need to recognize this and have him act like he's going to take the same route but instead shoot an inside gap. This is where the coaches *really* earn their bread.

It's all a big chess game and much of it isn't even played on the field. It's played inside meeting rooms, played out in the film rooms. You ever play chess? It's great for thirty minutes or an hour, but could you play one single game of chess that lasts Monday, Wednesday, Thursday and Friday? We play that chess game every single week of our season.

Once practice is over, what do we do? You guessed it, we go right into more meetings. What do we do in these meetings? We watch the tape of the practice we just had. We'll very rarely get through the entire practice tape. So, often we'll come in and finish up the next morning.

The practice film allows the coaches and scouts to catch some of the glitches, correct them and make us work on those corrections the very next day in practice. There are ways to hide tendencies, and each week we try to look for them in order to make adjustments.

The coaches also look at these tapes to see who is grasping what we're trying to do that particular week. If a guy is screwing around or shows signs that he's slacking, they'll make sure they work with him more.

We have meetings in the morning to go over our game plan and the opposing team's tendencies. We then go onto the field and get a scout team to look at what we saw in those meetings, and then meet again after lunch to remind us what we just saw on the field, which reminds us what we just saw in the meetings. We then go out to practice and work on what we saw in the meeting that was based on what we saw in the walkthrough that was based on what we saw in the morning meeting. And then? We have another meeting to go over the practice we just had that was based on, well, you get the idea.

And we get to do it all over again on Thursday! Same exact schedule, but with emphasis on other areas of the game. Just like Wednesday, we show up and get to play the whole thing all over again. Same faces, same meeting rooms, same coach-speak. Life during the season is like the movie *Groundhog Day*.

We get through it, though. Some guys resort to downloading video games onto their cell phones. A lot of guys fall asleep during the films. It's hard not to. Turn out the lights,

put on a boring movie and listen to the same guy over and over and over again.

These meetings get so repetitive and boring, and this isn't an exaggeration, that sometimes when I have trouble sleeping at night, I'll try to mentally put myself back in these meetings. It's a trick I picked up years ago and while it doesn't always work, it has a pretty good success rate.

There's an art to getting through these meetings. The primary weapon we use to battle the boredom is sleep. Frankie Walker, our cornerback who this off-season signed with Green Bay, used to fall asleep during the first five minutes of those meetings. It was so bad that the coaches made him stand up in the meetings to make sure he stayed awake until the end. What did he do? He'd fall asleep standing up! It was the damnedest thing I've ever seen. How the hell do you fall asleep while standing up in front of an entire meeting room? That's a true skill. I used to get upset with habitual sleepers because I feel like we all need to sit through the torture together. Eventually I fell asleep as well.

My first year in the league, LT would come in to meetings and blatantly lay down in the front of the meeting room and go to sleep right there in front of us. Lawrence didn't care. Our former middle lineback Micheal Barrow used to rat out players who fell asleep by screaming in his best Howard Cosell imitation:

"Down goes Strahan [or whoever just fell asleep]!"

There's an art to grabbing a few midafternoon Zs. Step One. Imperative for taking a nap is wearing a hooded sweatshirt. You put the hood up so the coaches can't see your eyes. Step Two. You put your forehead in your hand at a certain angle that makes it appear that you are diligently studying, but in reality you are hiding your eyes. Step Three. Make

sure you turn a few pages every once in a while or ask a question to trick the coaches into believing you've been all ears the whole time.

But the most important factor to getting a good sleep, the absolute number one rule before letting those lids get cozy is this: Enlist a trustworthy teammate to wake you up before the meeting is over.

Sometimes when we want to get some sleeping knucklehead, we'll tell the coach to keep the lights off and we all sneak out of the room, leaving the sleeper sitting all alone. We'll either get the coach to flip the lights on or we'll let him wake up naturally in a panic once he realizes we've all moved on to the next portion of the day's agenda.

Sometimes during film sessions, a coach will fall asleep. If we notice that, the Sneak Out is a popular favorite. Once we notice a coach dozing, we've got carte blanche to mess with him. The last thing he wants to do is fire back at us, only to have us tell the head coach his employee was sleeping on the job.

When we get behind the closed doors of these meetings, it's like being in grade school all over again. We'll do anything we can to get through a meeting. We'll have "Who can stay awake the longest" contests. We'll play Tic Tac Toe. Hangman. Anything. Guys kill time with video iPods, text messaging, writing rap lyrics, doodling.

When Deion Sanders played under Jerry Glanville in Atlanta, they had a coverage called Cat. It stood for "You see that cat over there, Deion? You got that cat." That was it. Nothing special. Jerry would take the greatest cover man in the NFL, put him on your best receiver all day long and just say, "Your job this week is to follow that cat all over the field!"

One day Deion was sleeping in a meeting. A coach yelled at him to get up.

"Get up, get up, you can't sleep in these meetings."

To which Deion replied, "Why? I know what I'm doing. I got that cat!" With that, he put his head down and went back to sleep.

As bad as the Wednesdays are, and if Thursdays are an exact copy, what about Fridays? You guessed it. More meetings and more practice. While the coaches cut back on practice on Friday, the meetings are still brutal.

Saturday mornings. More meetings and another walk-through. More treatment. Saturday night, we gather at the team hotel and have more meetings. Once the season gets into full swing, players get into a rhythm that allows us to pick up game plans much faster, so it gets even more repetitive. The coaches repeat everything step by step, day by day as if it were Day One.

At this point, I ask myself, Do I really want to go through another year of these horribly boring meetings? Do I really want to deal with reading those playbooks for another year? As I arrived at the doctor's office in Charlotte the day after Christmas, I wondered whether a negative report *is* coal in my stocking. Or should I hold a piece of mistletoe over the doctor's head and kiss him for putting me out of my misery? If he tells me I need surgery, that means I've sat in my last-ever NFL meeting. I can announce my retirement sometime in February.

Even before taking X-rays or putting it under a special moving X-ray machine, the doctor feels the foot, grabs at it and within fifteen seconds declares, "You don't need surgery,

Michael. I've seen a lot of bad ones, but this thing will get better. There's a little separation of the bones, but nothing major. While you sprained it badly, hopefully by March we can just go in and inject it."

Great news . . . I think.

I must admit, I had mixed feelings about the doctor's report. I truly love football and I love being a football player. But my world is not just about being a football player, nor does my world consist only of challenging Sundays. My world is littered with too many incredibly boring Mondays, Wednesdays, Thursdays and Fridays.

CHAPTER FIFTEEN

No More Fearing Head Coaches

November 22, Tiki versus Tom

As much as I've grown to like Tom, he still has that nasty streak that got him fired in Jacksonville and landed him in New York with the reputation of a guy the players love to hate. His nasty side reared its ugly head the week before Thanksgiving, after we lost to the Jaguars on *Monday Night Football.*

After the game, Tiki again lashed out because of the coach's decision not to run the ball more. It marked the second time in less than a year that Tiki claimed we were out-coached. The first was after a play-off loss in January against Carolina. This time he said something like we abandoned the running game. I read the story and immediately thought, "Come on, Tiki, not again."

After we got spanked by Seattle in Week Three, Shockey lashed out at Tom. But I hold Tiki to a higher standard. Tiki knows better, so I figured he must have a plan.

Tiki got summoned to the principal's office just before

Thanksgiving. Wow! Fireworks, baby. He told me about his run-in and it completely blew my fracas over Clockgate.

Tiki was steamed. He sat in a meeting room and waited for Tom to walk in. Then a *Jerry Springer Show* broke out! Coughlin stormed into the room, clutching a newspaper with Tiki's quotes, and chucked the newspaper right in Tiki's face! An aggressive stream of profanities flew from Coach's mouth. Along with the cursing, Coach called Tiki a traitor and an insubordinate.

In my fourteen years I've usually experienced one "first" per year. This was definitely a first, not a regular NFL occurrence. Coughlin continued his rant about Tiki being a traitor to the team. Tiki collected his thoughts and fired back with his own expletives and demanded he listen to him and listen to him good.

Tom was stunned as Tiki explained his side. His quotes were not a shot at Tom and the coaching staff. They were taken out of context. The question centered around the Jaguars' defensive tackle tandem of John Henderson and Marcus Stroud.

Still, I believed Tiki was right, that we did abandon the run too early. I had breakfast with him the next morning over the issue and Tiki said that what got him so upset was when the game was on the line, he believed he *earned* the right to have the ball. Other teams put the ball in the hands of their stars at critical moments. Tiki earned the right to be the hero or the goat. Sometimes, coaches get too cute for their own good and they out-think themselves. Tiki was our primary weapon with the game on the line. The whole world knew the rock was going to him, so give it to him. Unleash the man the way Philly unleashes Brian Westbrook or Seattle lets Shaun Alexander loose or San Diego relies on LaDainian Tomlinson. You must live and die by your stars.

Eventually the two of them calmed down—and Tiki was not even fined! Of course, I get fined for being three minutes early to a meeting, and he doesn't draw one penny for f-ing off the coach? I told you, the man is brilliant.

The episode is an example of how player-coach relationships have developed over the years and the difficulties we players have in channeling our frustration after games.

After a loss, the coach comes in screaming and you never hear a word he says. You sit thinking to yourself, Just get the damn speech over with. Just shut up so we can go and hide under our covers. When you lose, you're so embarrassed you don't even want to be seen by the general public. It really sucks.

It's like you've worked on a huge business deal all week long, putting every free moment of your time into it, and suddenly it all falls through. You're crushed, but then your boss hauls you into a face-to-face meeting. He lambastes you, blaming you for ruining the deal. He screams at you, questions your heart, intelligence, your will and at times your manhood. And when the grilling is over, he throws you out to the journalists and radio and TV reporters, who pepper you with questions asking how you blew the deal.

Next you're on the back page of every newspaper in town making fun of your misery with some cute tabloid headline. While you realize they have a job to sell papers, you still feel they're just enjoying your misery.

Imagine if you went through that ordeal seven times a year. How about twelve or thirteen for the losing or building teams? That's why guys like Shockey and Tiki lose patience and pop off after games.

There remains a very interesting dichotomy at play here: Every Sunday, during the game, we are asked to transform ourselves into violent, bloodthirsty warriors. Thousands scream for carnage, encouraging us to knock someone's head off. Our lives have all these military connotations and war terms like *blitz, bomb, firing bullets, in the trenches.*

After the game ends, we are required to turn the aggression off completely. We don't get time to simmer down. We must will it to come to a screeching halt or else we end up saying something we'll regret like, "We were outcoached."

You take all these uppers and meds to put you into a gladiator state, slam your body against a wall of warriors with 78,000 people screaming at you, your coach is constantly criticizing you, your knees and feet feel like you'll never walk again and then you get absolutely ripped to shreds. But you better calm down in four minutes flat, because you have to tell fifty cynical journalists why we stink without actually saying so. Go!

When I lose a big game, it takes me forever to get undressed. I sit and think and replay the game in my head. Some coaches come over, win or lose, no matter what happens. Then you have other coaches who won't go near you. I prefer someone to come to me no matter what. Then, after a few minutes of sitting and staring at the ground, an equipment guy yells, "Media here in one minute."

Now I have to collect myself so I don't say something stupid. I don't have a master's degree in public relations. Instead we learn from veteran players how to bite our tongues. Some guys learn from college, but some went to small schools with fewer opportunities. I watched LT and Phil Simms for ways to handle press people.

Nobody says a word; people are afraid to break the silence. The media usually senses this, too, so they don't come in screaming questions like you see in the movies. They'll ask questions in a low tone of voice while we get changed into our suits.

However, they do try to ask questions they know will elicit the response they need. When your answer doesn't cause controversy, other guys will ask the same question in different ways to find that adversity.

In Week Three we lost to Seattle 42–30. Tom came in and downright lambasted us, and rightfully so, considering we only managed a 42–3 score by the third quarter. Yeah, we were a finely tuned machine all right.

Tom was furious. He stormed into the postgame locker room with his face redder than a tomato.

"It looked like we've never played football before!" he yelled at us. "That was embarrassing. You guys missed your assignments, you let your guy beat you, it was a disgrace . . . but I'll take the blame." I love when Coach tells us that after ripping us apart. "I'll take the blame." Gee, thanks, now we feel better.

Tom continued, "As a competitor, I don't understand how you can go out and play as bad as you played when that much is on the line."

I like Tom a lot because he treats me like a man who has had success in this league. But when a head coach today detaches himself from the troops, guys are going to push back when times are bad. When Tom rips into us, some guys don't feel ashamed. Some get mad that he's ripping into us. Some take it as creative criticism! We're all different, but we're not living in fear any longer.

Shockey fired back at the media, "We got outplayed and outcoached. Write that one down! They were in defenses that we didn't know they were going to be in. They did things we hadn't seen. You can make adjustments all you want, but when they switch things up, we can't do anything. The coaches' jobs are supposed to be to put us in the best situations to succeed."

When I first got into the league, I would not have stood up to Tom the way Shockey did or even the way I did when Coach fined me for being three minutes early to that meeting. I certainly wouldn't have told the coaches, "Fine me or lecture me, I'm not getting both." But now there is so much money involved and so much intensity, we're all living life in one big pressure-cooker red zone. Free agency has put us all in the same boat. As a result of all the financial reward for success and all the public pressure, everyone's blood pressure in the locker room has soared. It's harder on everyone to contain themselves after a game.

It used to be that a coach would explode on us and we'd feel like garbage and bite our tongues. Coach was going to be around a lot longer than we were. But now the players are feeling as much pressure as the coaches, due to the size of our contracts. At the same time, the coach is on as shaky ground as we are. So who is he to put the whole mess on us?

The landscape changed in the late 1990s. The more money we players received and the more free agency seeped in, the more freedom we felt we could wield as players.

That's not to say that players have never stood up to their coaches. The year before I got to New York, Carl Banks jacked up Ray Handley, the head coach at the time, in the halftime locker room. Guys like LT had to step in and stop him from killing the man. But that was an isolated instance.

Players used to squabble only with the front office because that was the area of the team responsible for your pay. When we had a contract issue, there was no way to get out of Dodge and thus we were stuck.

Back then a coach and a general manager were clearly two separate entities. You often felt the coach was on your side against the big bad front office. The coaches could support our resentment and jointly blame the front office if we weren't getting paid what we thought was fair market value.

But as the bidding for head coaches became intense and the salary cap skewed player values, many owners lured coaches with the caveat of being the general manager as well. Even the coaches who aren't general managers can no longer put things on the front office. The landscape has changed; coaches are now considered part of the front office.

When a player is released, it's the front office and head coach making a decision together due to salary-cap management. When a player has an issue with a contract, the head coach usually has some sort of say as well. Thus our fight has changed from player versus front office to player versus head coach/front office.

Coaches today need to treat players with more respect than they did back in the day. Why? Coaches need to win now more than ever before. In today's climate they must win now, period, end of story. There is no longer a grace period.

In the not too distant past, a head coach was allowed time to rebuild in order to get a team on track. But because of the money involved, that grace period has been cut in half, maybe more because the owners want to get an instant bang for the buck, so rebuilding isn't really an option.

It's gotten so bad that in some places it's now a job killer to select a quarterback early in the draft and let him take his lumps. You can't have a coach survive Troy Aikman going 1-15 like he did his rookie year or Peyton Manning starting 2-14 like he did his first two seasons. The money has raised expectations while severely lowering fan and front-office patience.

Players aren't dumb. They know the public's patience for coaches has waned and the money for players has grown. So we don't fear coaches like we used to.

Just look at Terrell Owens and Bill Parcells. T.O. could give a damn what Parcells thought of him. He had little regard for his head coach's fury. That must have been quite a shock to the Tuna, who has made a career of bullying players when he had to.

The players feel much more empowered now. Coaches and front offices need to talk to us to find out things about players who become free agents. They enlist us to help them recruit free agents and even put us on chaperone duties when those players visit.

Coaches come to players for help much more so than in the past. Although it's against anti-tampering rules, coaches and assistant coaches have called me many times to ask for my opinion about an assistant or head coach hitting the open market. How about that? I have some juice and my opinion matters.

Coaching jobs are so tenuous that coaches will ask us for help to get a new job when they get fired. Some ask you to put in a good word for them if their head coach gets fired.

Whenever a team struggles and has a coach it wants to fire, the owner may hire the complete opposite type of coach to replace him. Then, when that coach wears out his welcome, the owners start to yearn for how it was with the last guy. They then go and hire the complete opposite of *that* guy, pretty much the type of personality of the coach who was fired in the first place. It goes around and around.

Say a team has a player-friendly coach and when he burns out, they'll hire a real hard-ass like Tom. Then when Tom wears out his welcome they'll say they need the exact opposite and go back to a guy more like Coach Fassel. The Jets did it last year when they hired Eric Mangini because they felt they needed the complete opposite of Herm Edwards. But what was Herm? The complete opposite of Al

Groh, the man who bolted on them right before Herm took office. Groh, by the way, is a coach from the same coaching tree as Mangini, who is from the Belichick/Parcells camp.

The pressure to win is alarming. How alarming? How many fans actually know that team trainers now hand out Lipitor, blood pressure medication, to their head coaches when they first get their job because of the huge amount of stress this position carries?

After Tiki's rant, late in the season, when it looked like Tom would be fired, he fired his offensive coordinator, John Hufnagel, and moved our quarterbacks coach, Kevin Gilbride, into that role. We realized, as players, that our voices were heard and will continue to be heard. That's the way it's going to be.

It's alarming to think how much the NFL will change over the next ten years. As our contracts double over the next decade and our financial stability increases, will our respect rise or fall? Will every single locker room have a T.O.? Will they have more? Will it even be worth it to become an NFL head coach ten years from now? I know for me it wouldn't.

CHAPTER SIXTEEN

Needles, Painkillers, Anti-inflammatories and Other Ways to Hide the Pain

December 3, Cowboys at Giants

It was my favorite week of the year, Cowboys week, and I didn't want to miss another shot at Tony Romo. This week for the first time in a month my foot felt pretty decent. I was going to give it a shot today.

Our team doctors and trainers are very conservative. They made it explicit that they were staunchly opposed to my trying to play. Two hours before the game, our medical staff took me out to the Giants Stadium turf to put me through some drills. All the drills were designed to test my foot.

That first run? I felt pretty good. Oh, baby, Romo, here I come. I'm actually going to be able to pull this thing off today. Second pass wasn't bad, but not great. I can still see Romo in my sights. Unfortunately, my celebration came to an abrupt halt when they asked on the third drill to plant and cut on the sore foot. Running straight ahead was no problem, cutting was a much different story. The moment I planted I felt a stabbing pain in my arch, but I needed to put on a good show. I figured if I could just fake it long enough and make it through one or two more drills, they would clear me and I'd go into the locker room and take care of the rest with some of my favorite medicinal helpers.

My good friend Jerome Bettis once said it best. "You try to strike a deal with pain. Me and pain . . . we got a pretty good understanding." Sometimes, unfortunately, you need to bring a third party into the negotiations. That third party goes by a variety of names. I like to call it the Law Offices of Toradol, Lidocaine & Vicodin, LLC. Sometimes we also place a call to Indocin & Naprosyn and then there's this little private investigator named Prednisone.

Toradol, lidocaine and Vicodin handle the pain; Indocin and Naprosyn are anti-inflammation drugs or anti-inflams, as we call them. While most of our drugs are administered in pill form, Toradol is one injection that has gained great love inside our locker rooms. This stuff sprouted on the scene over the last five years, but it's become so popular it even has its own nickname—Vitamin T. I could shoot you with a syringe full of Vitamin T and hit you square between your legs with a crowbar and you'd probably just laugh it off. It's wild stuff, because it seems to affect you only from the neck down. You can always tell a guy is on Vitamin T because he'll have a little blood stain in his pants by his ass, or after a game in the shower you can see the guys with a Band-Aid on that area.

I can watch a game on television and sometimes spot the Vitamin T users. In Week Six of the 2006 season the Chiefs quarterback Damon Huard took a shot before the game to deal with the pain of a strained groin. How do I know? The huge blood stain on his rear end spelled T-O-R-A-D-O-L! It was probably about four inches in diameter and had some dirt rubbed on the area, too. Hey, it's a badge of honor, except it's red, sticky and we don't pin it on our lapels—we pin it where the sun don't shine. The stuff is so good that some guys now rely on it, even if they don't need it. It's become a mental crutch for some. It dulls the pain so much that even when guys don't need it, some guys doubt themselves if they march into battle without it. I don't take it unless I'm in serious pain; but there are lots of us who take the shot game in and game out. We've asked if there are serious long-term health ramifications and thus far I've never heard of any. Still, we usually only take it for games—rarely if ever before practice.

My first Toradol shot came in a game against the Falcons in 1999. Injuries forced both Keith Hamilton and me to end up sprawled out in the trainer's room in the middle of the game. The Giants were left with virtually nobody but viable backup linemen. Hammer had torn his Achilles and I felt like I'd blown out my back. We were both lying on the trainer's table and Hammer turned to me and said, "Strahan, we've got nobody left. One of us needs to get back out there." Well, who do you think that somebody he meant was? Hmmm, let me think . . . one guy's back hurts while the other has a torn tendon. You'd eat shit if the doctors told you a pile of shit will magically get you back on that field.

I told the trainers to do whatever they had to in order to get me back out on the field. To them, that meant hitting me with Toradol. The stuff takes about thirty minutes to kick in, but once it kicks in, damn, it kicks in. Next thing I knew, me and my friend Vitamin T were back out on that field for the second half of the game. Not only back on the field, but playing like nothing happened to my back in the first place!

Before there was Toradol we got shot with lidocaine— pretty much a novacaine for the body. If rubbed on the skin in gel form, it blocks the pain from your nerve endings. But when it's shot into the body, it blocks the pain from everywhere.

I've always felt that lidocaine was more dangerous than Toradol because at least with Vitamin T, if an injury worsens, we can still feel it. But with lidocaine, it completely numbs the injected area. It's reasonable to fear a lidocaine shot. If you shot some into your side for a cracked rib, and if the rib then completely broke, you wouldn't feel it. Even if a broken rib punctured a lung, you might not feel it.

Prior to a play-off game one year, they shot Bettis with a numbing agent right before the game. Well, the doc who did it hit the wrong spot—actually hit a nerve in his groin area— and Jerome's whole leg went dead. Here he was thirty minutes before game time, a play-off game no less, and the guy has drop foot because the doctor hit the wrong spot.

On a side note: We as players make mental crib sheets of each of our docs' track records for injections. If a guy is hit or miss, we'll remember that. We had one doctor who injected us with IVs (intravenous shots of saline solution to prevent dehydration or cramping) and his aim was so bad, our former star running back Rodney Hampton used to joke, "Don't get the IV from him because he'll stick you about thirty times before he gets your vein."

But again, the needles and the lidocaine fall under that "eating a pile of shit" notion most players feel. If it works to keep us out there, no matter how long it takes to get the right area for the shot, we'll do it.

At one point my shoulders were so bad I'd get lidocaine shots in the AC joints right on top of both shoulders just to be able to make it through a game. The doctors would tell me the injuries couldn't get worse so I'd tell them to shoot it. That's morally acceptable inside the NFL: If it can't get worse, just shoot it and deal with as much pain as you can.

Unfortunately, after about the third game of getting shot with that stuff, my body started to adjust to the meds. They might as well have shot me with water. At that point I still got injected because I thought it would help. Even though I realized the effects had worn off, I wouldn't dare surrender the security blanket they provided my mind. They help put my worries at ease.

While it's considered morally acceptable and even honorable to get shot in order to play, the Giants doctors never do it out in the open. Getting shot before the game requires a certain amount of discretion. You don't announce it, but you BETTER shoot that damn thing and get your ass out there. Hell, we'll get pissed at a young guy if he can play but but won't even try to shoot it. It just goes with the territory. It's part of the unwritten job description.

In fact, it is so discreet inside our locker room that if you were blind to it all, you might not even know it goes on. It's done literally in a back room. They need to keep it out of view; otherwise it will demoralize everyone in the training room.

Not every locker room is that discreet. In fact, before our Sunday night game against the Bears this past year, my old partner in crime Jessie Armstead was recalling how the Giants at least hid the shots. When he went to the Redskins, Armstead said their docs would just walk around the locker room openly and stop at each guy's lockers to drop, aim and fire.

Armstead is the greatest example of a player who used the stuff as a badge of honor. I'll never forget once when Jessie tore his ankle. Now when I say tore, I'm talking about his foot damn near flapping in the wind. The docs wanted to shut him down but he pretty much told them to shut up and shoot it with anything they can, and let him take care of the

rest. He took those shots before a game and ran out on the field and you could literally see his ankle filled with fluid and that foot flopping all over the place. The man never missed a game. He never missed a series.

Here's a guy whose hamstring once tore and rolled, his ankle once broke, and his knee was once damn near unhinged, but come game day Jessie never missed a game. For some guys like Jessie, the shots helped much more than others. Some guys take the Vitamin T or lidocaine and it still doesn't help enough. At that point it's probably a combo of the drugs and simple pain tolerance for three hours on Sundays.

Jeremy Shockey is the same way. He'll get dinged with stuff that would put out 90 percent of the league, but Shock takes whatever is necessary to take the edge off enough for him to bite the bullet and somehow suck it up for 180 minutes per week.

That's the great hypocrisy of the NFL: You want to beat a guy's ass if he's using the *wrong* stuff, like street drugs, but at the same time you want to beat a guy's ass if he's not willing to take the *legal* stuff to get himself out there with us. If you know a guy is using heroin or smoking crack or snorting coke you look at him with shame. If a guy is banged up and doesn't use the legal stuff to get himself out there, you shake your head at him with the same shame. I'm not saying the confines of our locker room is a perfect world, but it's the reality of our psychology.

What's the most painful locker-room procedure? Technically, it's not an injection. It's the process of drawing fluid from the body—usually the knee. You know how you can tell who is getting his knee drained before a game? He's the one screaming his head off in the trainer's room. Sometimes he's screaming so loud some of us just start laughing. The more he screams, the more we laugh. In some strange way it is funny. But it's not really funny. Here's how it is done. They snake a needle into the inflamed knee, which already feels like it's on fire. Then they draw out enough fluid so that the knee doesn't look like somebody shoved an ostrich egg under the kneecap. Then they send the guy's ass out there for game time. The hope is that after the game and during the ensuing week, anti-inflammatories combined with enough ice and treatment will prevent the knee from having to get drained again. But there are guys who have to get it done every week for an extended period. Every once in a while, a guy will need it more than once a week. Man, you watch them snake that probe in and suck out the fluid, but sixty minutes later, you won't even remember they did it when you've got the quarterback zeroed in your crosshairs.

In the days bracketing game day, the necessary drug of choice is Naprosyn or Indocin. You take them with food every four hours. Honestly, without them most of us couldn't practice during the week.

There is one thing that goes along with the drugs that I will truly give the team and doctors credit for and that most people have no idea about: For every guy who is on the anti-inflams, the team has someone from a medical lab come in every month to draw blood in order to monitor the levels of the stuff and make sure our kidneys and livers are still healthy.

I've never read about this anywhere and I'm surprised people have no idea this goes on. But it certainly makes it more acceptable to us. At least we believe the docs are taking care of us for the long term. If the levels are too high, they'll switch us to another med or take us off them completely. As the corporate ad goes, better living through chemistry—with a little Bill Nye the Science Guy meets American Gladiator.

When the Indocin or Naprosyn anti-inflams have a bad effect or the docs need to change them for us, sometimes they switch to a three-day cycle of prednisone. Five pills the first day, four the second and three the third takes away the swelling . . . you hope.

Vicodin is also pretty big, but *personally* that stuff scares the shit out of me. It's great for the throbbing pains, but it also acts as a depressant. It gets you soooo up, but when you come down you really feel lousy and depressed. That's why guys can easily get hooked on it. Most guys who don't take Vicodin will take the generic brand, hydrocodone, because it's mixed with acetaminophen and that takes the edge off even more. Hydrocodone got quite a bit of attention last year with the whole T.O. suicide attempt fiasco. For anyone who has never taken the generic form of Vicodin, let me explain its effects, which will clarify why I don't think T.O. tried to kill himself after taking three hydrocodone pills.

One hydrocodone pill, even for a guy who normally takes one, may make some guys loopy. Two will make you feel like the dentist turned up the nitrous gas on high, walked out of the room for thirty minutes and then returned to crack a bottle of wine with you. Three? Hell, you'll say anything on three of these suckers.

"Are you into sheep, Mr. Owens?"

"Ummm, yup."

"Do you wish you lived on Mars, Mr. Owens?"

"Umm, yeah."

"Are you depressed, Mr. Owens?"

"Umm, uh-huh."

"Did you try to kill yourself, Mr. Owens?"

"Ummm, sure, why not?"

My advice to the younger players: Go as long as you can *without* needing this stuff. After fourteen years in this game,

I need them. I need them mentally and physically. I never wanted to become dependent on them because I always looked at football as a short period in my long life. I never wanted to pay for it later on in life but, man, it's a difficult conviction to keep. It sounds great standing on my soapbox, but as I said earlier, you do whatever it takes to play.

If they ever told me that I had to get off painkillers, I'm not sure what I'd do. I'm not sure how I'd get through a week anymore. During my thirteenth year, I'd take one Indocin on Friday night, two on Saturday, and one on Sunday morning with my breakfast to dull whatever soreness I had left. The hot tubs, massages and gels can only go so far. Even though I've taken the anti-inflams I'm still a little sore. There really is nothing that will completely take away all the years of pounding.

You definitely, especially as you get older, need the pills and the shots. You need to at least believe in your mind that you're about to wage battle with the help of something that has numbed the pain somewhat. Why? Because we all know three hours later we'll have a whole new roster of bumps, bruises, scrapes, contusions, swelling and open wounds. We'll have to book a whole new appointment that'll require the services of the Law Offices of Toradol, Lydocaine & Vicodin and their associates Indocin & Naproxen. Do I have a fear of what they'll do to me for the future? Sure. But I have a stronger fear of not playing. I have a stronger fear of disappointing myself and my team. It's sad but true. That fear paralyzes the player's common sense.

Eight paragraphs ago I was harping on how football is just a small part of life as a whole, but, man, it is hard to think about long-term pain when the short-term pain of not being on the field can scare you more. The fear of not being on the field is overwhelming. It invades and corrodes the mind and the body. Think of how demented it is to say to myself, "I know this drug or that drug could be bad for me in the long run, but let me take it anyway because I'm willing to roll the dice on the future."

Sometime in my fourteenth year, I began taking the anti-inflams during the week. I figure that my body may be able to handle it for a few years since I didn't use them heavily earlier in my career. This is just another mind trick to convince myself that it's OK. Soon they were entering my bloodstream on Thursdays and soon after they showed up on Wednesdays. By the early part of 2006 I had completely erased any line between days I took the pills and days I didn't. I didn't wait until the weekend because just getting through the weekly practices became a grueling chore. Monday I felt fine. Actually, I usually felt great. For some reason my soreness set in on Tuesday. So come Tuesday night, I started taking the meds just to get through Wednesday and Thursday's practices.

I guess that's when you know the game is winding down for you. When there is no longer a line between relief and pain, the window is definitely closing. We look at it as a badge of honor, but I'd much rather not have such medals. You'll see guys at the Pro Bowl and sometimes we'll compare war wounds, but later on in life, who will be there to compare them with me? Ten years from now, my wounds won't be honorable . . . they will just suck!

Now, after fourteen years of onfield combat, during the season, I live on these pills. Sunday afternoons have now made waking up every day a pain. Every single day of my life I have to wake up to a checklist of what's working and what's not. The second I wake up, I try to figure out what hurts before I can so much as move a muscle. I run down the checklist. My knees have their good and bad days. My back

constantly hurts. Elbows? Check! Neck? Check! Ankles . . . DAMN! Not so good. I'll be calling upon some artificial help for that. Wrists? Check . . . no scratch that, they suck today, too. This is every day and sometimes what hurts one day is fine the next and vice versa.

Again, I know there could be long-term ramifications of the anti-inflams use. But how can I possibly think about the future when I can't even get out of bed in the morning without going through a five-minute checklist? It makes no sense, actually.

I don't think the human body was made for football. But when you are on the field, it feels like that is *exactly* what it was made for. When 70,000 crazed fanatics are screaming for me as I'm picking Donovan McNabb off the ground and smashing his body onto cement covered by fake grass—man, I'll take a million pills to get that feeling. But the feeling only lasts for a few seconds. The effects of those pills? Who knows?

During the games, you feel nothing aside from the initial bump here and bruise there. It could be much worse but you don't feel it, your body won't allow it. However, when that final whistle blows, your body's protection mechanism shuts down and all the pain flows in with a vengeful force. One minute earlier you're not limping but once the game ends and you can take down your guard, and the adrenaline starts to subside, then everything starts to hurt. Guys limp off the field and into the locker room and sometimes we can't even get off our stools. How crazy is that? Not five minutes before, you're running around like a lunatic launching your body into a wall of muscle and mass. Now, you can hardly walk to take a seat.

For those precious few hours of the game you legitimize the pills and needles and the pain. It makes you feel you're made for this game. The six other days of the week? You question your sanity. What the hell am I doing this for? Sometimes when it's not game day, I'll just wake up, go through my checklist and say to myself, "Don't move. Your best move right now is to not move at all. Don't talk, don't move, the pain will all just go away." It doesn't. Hasn't since halfway through my career.

On this Sunday afternoon, I tried my hardest to make the pain go away. I tried valiantly to act like I was completely healed. "Good ollllllllllll' Michael Strahan, how 'bout them Cowboys!" But I never got the chance that Sunday against Tony Romo. I couldn't act as well as I'd hoped. The medical staff shut me down. I wasn't fooling anybody, including myself. I should have just stayed in bed.

But lying in bed would only allow my mind to dwell on the next chunk of NFL reality, one of the main reasons we live through the ups and downs, and the glory and humiliation. Money!

CHAPTER SEVENTEEN

A Cautionary Tale: Women, Money and Scams

Today I'd rather sit in an eight-hour film session while little elves drill holes into the roots of my teeth than spend my off-day this way. I'd rather practice full speed against a bunch of rookies than participate in this off-field distraction.

Rather than tackling a running back today, this morning I'm tackling my finances. Rather than bury my head in my playbook, I sit in a room and bury my head in streams upon streams of receipts and financial records with my lawyers, going through a self-audit.

It was another step in buying my freedom from my ex-wife, Jean. In our divorce she asked for a ridiculous amount of money and as a result I have to account for every dime I made and spent over the less than six years we were married. On the surface, Jean and I were a great couple in love and for a short period we were. But that quickly faded. We'd get into massive arguments and the moment we were around other people, Jean would put on her Oscar-winning performances as if we were America's sweetheart couple. In reality, we grew apart. We fought much more than we loved.

Shortly before the Eagles' Super Bowl XXXIX in 2005 against the Patriots in Jacksonville, I knew our relationship was done. We'd had it with each other, and Jean was telling my friends that she was already looking to hire a divorce lawyer. She could never keep her mouth shut about our personal business and, of course, it got back to me, too.

One night I came home and when I checked one of our bank accounts, I noticed it was short by $1.6 million. Jean had funneled money out of our account. When I confronted her about it, she acted like "I did it and what are you gonna do about it." I needed to leave the house so the woman wouldn't bait me into doing something stupid. Before I left I told her, "Jean, I'm leaving and when I return, that money better be back in my account."

Not only wasn't it back in my account, she stashed another $1.7 million somewhere. To add insult to injury, she called the police and accused me of threatening her. In the state of New Jersey, they have to bring you into the police station and process you, even when it is just one person's word against another's. While I was stuck at the police station, she took the rest of the money out of that account.

That night we were over, and a woman scorned was going to bring hell to my world. Some of her last words to me were, "I made you and I will break you." Our divorce was nasty and as much as I tried to keep my business out of the news, she had reporters on speed dial. Whatever she accused me of, the reporters dutifully wrote about. Whatever she told the reporters was written as the truth.

She attacked me over and over with allegations that I'm gay, that I'm a cheater and that I'm abusive. Yet none of it

was backed up with any proof. She tried to smear my name, hoping I would cry mercy and offer to settle. What she didn't realize was how happy I was with her out of my day-to-day life. It was as if the sun had been set for years but overnight it shined again. As badly as she tried to kill me in the press, I was too happy to really care.

Now I'm sitting in this audit room because Jean was trying to take more than she was entitled to get. I argued that she was entitled to $6 million by the terms of our prenuptial agreement, which was generous on my part, and she argued she should get more than double that total, $14 million.

The money that comes from my laying my blood on that field each week is a blessing and a curse. Dealing with Jean on this issue is definitely a curse. The blessings are obvious. Just fourteen years out of college, I have nice cars, beautiful homes, fine clothes and the ability to retire in my mid-thirties and not have to work unless I choose to. This was the life I dreamed about as a kid.

As I sit in the audit room I daydream about how far I've come financially in such a relatively short span of life. Am I really worth this much? Have I actually made as much as I've calculated? How the hell did that happen?

I play for love of the game, but I also love the money. I won't be so stiff-necked and fake to pretend to you that money isn't a huge part of my life. No matter how much I love the game, I'm not valued in society solely on gridiron accolades and total number of sacks. I'm also judged by the amount of money I make. Money is status in and out of the locker room. Money now drives NFL players as much as a Super Bowl ring. If money weren't so important, you wouldn't have guys in the last year of their contracts playing as if their lives depended on it. If you're the highest-paid at your position in the league, you feel like you're the best. If you are the best and you have not become the highest-paid at your position, then you will probably look at that as a slap in the face.

If there's one guy who should be the highest-paid in the league, it's Tom Brady because of all his championship rings. Yet he took a good deal, but not the league's highest, and restructured it down the road to help other guys' deals in the Patriots get done. When it comes to money, most guys can't put their egos aside like Brady does.

You know what used to be the worst day of the season? It was the day the salary sheets sat on every guy's stool in the locker room. The sheets were provided by the NFL Players Association, our union, and they detailed what every other player in the league made and pointed out what other guys at our position made.

We got to compare notes on who made what and gauge ourselves by everybody else. Most of the day was spent grumbling and complaining that we deserved more than certain guys around the league and often guys on our own team as well. Seriously, I wish we could remain in ignorant bliss because we're overly obsessed with salaries. I'm not above it, either. There's so much money to go around, you want as much as you can get while you can get it. You want more than the next guy and you certainly want more than the guys you believe you're better than.

Those sheets made guys hate their teammates and certainly players on other teams. We *all* believe we're better than each other and worth more than everybody else. We tell it to ourselves, and our family and friends stoke those flames even higher.

"Look at what this guy is making! I'm only making what? Please! I need to get this taken care of. They need to redo my contract!"

Eventually, the league got the union to stop distributing

salary sheets during the season because it became so disruptive. That day we'd turn from being a group with one common goal to a room full of individual athletes pissed off that they aren't getting enough of the pie. The Giants have compensated me well over the last few years, so I haven't felt that compelled to complain. At least not until this off-season, when in late February I went back to the Giants to ask for a new deal and another extension.

When I signed my last deal it was with the agreement that after Year Five we would evaluate where I was going and I would be paid accordingly. Would I be retiring? Would I be a situational player? Am I still at an elite level at my position? Would the Giants even want me anymore? My salary was cut. Yet I'm still a starter and am counted on to be the team leader. As a result, I asked that my salary be increased to what I'd made the last several years of my deal.

So I had my first meeting with our new general manager, Jerry Reese, to discuss restructuring my contract to pay me more in line with my past salaries and with that of other players at my position. Some of you may think I must be greedy and self-centered for wanting to renegotiate after missing quite a few games over the last three seasons. But remember, this is a business for me, too. As a player, the sooner you realize that you're a disposable commodity, the better off you'll be. When your playing days are over, there is no coming back for another piece of the pie.

So get it while you can as often as you can and for as long as you can. This year is going to be one of my most challenging. We no longer have a lot of the veteran leadership we had in the past. No Tiki, no LaVar, no Luke! This makes my job harder because now all the responsibility of leadership falls on my shoulders.

Let's say your boss lays off several employees and he

dumps their work on your desk and tells you to handle it. Would you just smile and do your job without feeling a need to be compensated appropriately? I don't think so.

My meeting with Reese went badly. I didn't get the answers I wanted, but that didn't surprise me. Upset? Yes! Surprised? No! Jerry made it clear they had to make what they felt was the best business decision, which was to make me play for the amount that was on the contract for the upcoming season. He told me to my face that they wouldn't renegotiate my deal because I had been hurt and they "will find other leaders." That last comment pushed me over the brink. I fired back at Jerry that if they were going to find another leader, one would have already emerged in the two years I was hurt. But nobody wanted the damn job! Nobody but me wanted to play buffer between Tom and the team.

I told Jerry if I was hurt so much and they could replace my leadership, maybe they should cut me or trade me. I told him I wanted out of his locker room. I wanted out of town.

Did I really want out? Absolutely not. But I was pissed and reacted with my own venom.

Now, this is where the agent game comes into play. Negotiations can get quite nasty, which is why a player doesn't want to be present, although this time I made an exception. One side talks about how his player is the greatest and the other side tries to poke holes in the player's game. This is one reason why there's so little loyalty in sports anymore. When you hear the crap that a team will say about you in your negotiations in order to pinch a penny, of course it's going to cause bitterness. At the same time, what's a general manager supposed to do? Agree with every agent who says their client is the best? They'd be forced to overpay the whole league.

The problem is that it gets emotional, like it did for me

in late February. Agents tell players about the insults the front office hurls at us about our play and/or about our toughness. They pile on. They want to infuriate the player so they can "advise" them to hold out or force that player out of town. The agents play us against the team while the team plays us against the agents. Agents try to get a new deal because that's how they get paid. They collect 3 percent, and a new deal with new money means more in their pocket.

The business side of football has grown so much that some agents have become celebrities. Look at Drew Rosenhaus and his now infamous "Next question" routine with T.O. He became as much of the story as the client. He even got his own Burger King commercial. This quest for fame has devoured other agents. Some of the biggest agents of 1990s were larger than life. They became the story instead of their clients at times and got too big for their own good. Then they crashed back to Earth, and now they have few, if any, clients and nowhere near the power they held in their heyday.

Because so much money is involved, agents peek, pry and recruit whenever they get a chance. They'll buddy up to you when they realize you're going to be a major player. They love to hit you with that "Are you happy with your deal?" line. Hey, guys, where were *you* before I made the Pro Bowl? It's illegal under NFLPA guidelines, but it happens all the time. After my first Pro Bowl, agents emerged out of nowhere to convince me they could get me "star" money.

When it looked like I was going to be a pretty high draft pick coming out of college, one agent flew me to a big city to meet a man at a bank. They recruited me in the office of some bigwig banker who had partnered with this particular agent. I don't remember the agent's name, but I recall the banker.

Pulling out $50,000 in cash, he pushed it across the table and told me if I signed right there on the spot, I could just walk away with the cash. It was more money than I'd ever seen in my life. How could I not jump on that?

They didn't tell me it was a loan, that after I received my signing bonus, I'd get a bill for that $50,000 plus interest. If they buy us cars before we're drafted, it's all a loan. Most kids don't realize we have to pay that money back.

The agent game is so big now, bigger firms pay to send athlete clients to work out at specialized training centers to prepare for the draft. The agent spends money to fly the kid back and forth, put him up in a hotel for weeks and pay for all his meals and entertainment. That's a heck of a lot of cash for one kid, much less ten to twenty athletes. The agents hope these workouts will propel them higher in the draft, which in turn raises their signing bonus, which in turn increases the value of their 3 percent. They spend money to make money. These people find a way to do whatever it takes.

One of the great ironies of our game is, while we're all consumed with earning more money, half of the young players who come into the NFL try to convince their homeboys that money hasn't changed them.

Memo to all young players coming into the league: "You're damn right the money changes you! Know it and accept it. Your world is about to change, period!"

Without the money, we wouldn't be invited to 99 percent of the upscale events and social gatherings we attend. Financial stability is a major quest in our daily lives. Money puts you in a completely different social stratum. Do you think without money and status, I'd be invited to play golf with some of the most successful and powerful people in this country? It opens up avenues for me and my future. I welcome this change in my life.

Football gives me the ability to never have to worry about

financial security. Yet to a young player it's a grave insult if his friends think money has changed him. Often the money changes the people *around* you more than it changes *you*. It's crazy that some kids would forgo the opportunity to be rich after football in order to save face back home.

When players first come into the league, they want the nice bling, cars and clothes to bring back and show off at home. One reason players can have an issue with another player's personal conduct is because one person can make all players look irresponsible and careless when it comes to increased finances and notoriety.

This off-season, instead of going to functions and getting grilled about the New York Giants, everyone wanted to know my views on Pacman. It was sickening. We get lumped in with knuckleheads like him, as if the typical NFL locker room is filled with dozens of Pacman Joneses. Pacman should be booted from the league. He doesn't yet understand the responsibility of being in the NFL and until he does, he shouldn't be allowed in.

Another memo to the newbies in our league: Evaluate your inner circle. Your homeboys don't have as much to lose as you do by getting in fights and shoot-outs and smoking weed. So why should you stay in that social circle? Wake your ass up! You're not the young man *wishing* for the dream; you now *own* the dream. The key is to not screw it up. Do NOT let someone else screw it up for you!

When I came into the league I thought I was rich. My signing bonus was $450,000 and I got a check for $268,000 after Uncle Sam took his cut. Plus, I was making about $130,000 in salary. I thought I'd won Powerball. But soon I learned that when you've had very little and get showered with a whole lot of dough, it's easy to go crazy.

Few of us have had any training in financial manage-

ment. We spend money on the dumbest things, especially early in our careers, because guys put pressure on themselves to impress. They feel like they need to keep up with their new teammates. I wonder if the owners ever look at the stuff we show up with and shake their heads.

"I cannot believe he's wasting his/*our* money on *that*!"

Some players have the attitude, "I'm going to live it up while I can and when it's over I'll go back and live life like I used to." I don't understand that. That's not what you beat your body up for. You beat it up so you can retire on a higher level and not go back to where you used to be. How many people can end their working career at age thirty-five? You have the rest of your life ahead of you to live on a higher financial level. But that means you have to save—so save, young men, save.

I tell young guys all the time, "Don't try to keep up with the (Pacman) Joneses." Don't go out and immediately buy a Bentley or a Benz. Don't buy every diamond chain and watch in the store. Save your money. Nowadays, the NFL actually holds financial meetings for players. We have 401(k) meetings and meetings to alert us about what scams to watch out for. Most players come right out of college. For the most part, we have more experience playing football than counting bills. The last thing you want is to get cut, bounce around and have your stuff repossessed. It happens a lot because we all like to act as if we're rich.

Perhaps the biggest misconception is that all NFL football players are millionaires. Actually, it's one of the greatest misconceptions in sports, period. We've got a pecking order just like any other corporate entity. Not everyone in any company or corporation makes the same amount of money or is as loaded. Why should the NFL be any different? It's true we

are better off financially than most in the real world, but not all of us have money to burn.

Since it isn't generally known that we have a pecking order on pro teams, the vultures think we all have lots of money. They see us as targets, easy money in their get-rich-quick schemes. A lot of players fall prey to bad business deals because they want to have something going on outside of football, but they don't have the knowledge or time to make the side business successful. This causes them to trust and depend on other people that they may not really know. It's a classic recipe for disaster.

I've been approached with a million ideas all guaranteed to make me rich. One friend asked me to invest in a company that was "gonna blow up and be bigger than eBay." Yeah, sure. Another wanted me to invest in a strawberry-picking patch. I would have cleaned up on that one. I've been approached about llama farms, ostrich farms, racehorses, music labels, too many bars and restaurants to remember, car dealerships, movie scripts, clothing, time shares, land deals.

One friend once told me when I was considering a car dealership, "You know how you make a small fortune dealing cars? Start with a large one." Enough said. Not every deal is a bad deal, but there are a hundred bad deals for every good one.

The NFL does a pretty good job of providing us with warnings each year. They'll explain what scams players have been caught up in. They'll even warn you about specific sleazy instances.

Legend has it that a player once met a girl in a club and she acted like she was all into him. She brought him home and while they were getting cozy, she slipped something in his drink. After being drugged, the player was stripped naked and put into a bed with, get this, ANOTHER NAKED

DUDE!!! The girl took all these naked photos of the player and what appeared to be his gay lover. Of course, they blackmailed this poor guy, but luckily he was smart enough to report it.

We have so many con artists approach us, the NFL provides us with NFL Security, a service that consists of ex-lawmen and investigators who we can call to check out anybody we need investigated.

They procure background checks, run a guy's history, check out a company, and even check up on your nanny. They provide us with credit checks for people asking for business loans. We're warned of pyramid and Ponzi schemes. Schemes involving oil or diamonds out of Africa, schemes involving natural gas and land in obscure regions. It's a great tool that some guys probably don't take full advantage of.

Believe it or not, the most pressure doesn't come from these vultures. The business sharks aren't what get us so unnerved. It's the people we know or who we're close to that often make us the most vulnerable. Family and friends make our wealth miserable sometimes. Newfound riches have a funny way of bringing out the worst in people you are most emotionally reliant upon.

A player's parents can demand money, claiming, "We raised you, now it's time to pay us back." It happens more than you know.

Family members and relatives come out of the woodwork. "I need this and I need that." Just as we aren't fully prepared to handle the rigors of sudden fame and fortune, our family and friends often fail to recognize the proper sensitivity as well.

Oftentimes a player's family feels pressure to impress their friends. The other ladies in their neighborhood will complain to them about how awful it is that their newly rich son hasn't gotten them a big enough luxury car or a lavish enough home.

It's extremely difficult to turn down a parent or a sibling or a best friend. They'll constantly ask for things that will "finally put them over the hump." It sounds cold but you must learn to cut the cord because if you don't, you will eventually end up broke.

If you are the one who takes care of everyone and something happens to you, then who is going to take care of you? The same people who helped you spend the money will say, "What a failure he is for blowing all of his money."

There are players who have to sell their Super Bowl rings so they can survive, and that's tough because they put so much into earning them. I once had a player ask me for $75,000 so he could make it through the off-season, yet he drove a brand-new Mercedes and Range Rover. That's a shame.

When I first came into the league, players drove nice but unspectacular cars. Today's player is the complete opposite. They want to be big shots and spend, spend, spend even before they sign their rookie deals. They want to drive the biggest and best car before they even own a house. Some go and buy a car before they sign their first deal!

The one thing that's hard to understand is how guys like Nate Newton and Jamal Lewis got involved with drug trafficking. There is so much money involved in the sports world, we've already taken a shortcut, so why cut even more corners? Patience is key, but some guys want instant gratification and make stupid, adolescent, costly mistakes.

Look at big Nate. The former Cowboys Pro Bowl guard had a great future ahead of him. He was the most likable man in the NFL at one point. He's hilarious and a very caring type of guy. But I guess he couldn't find ways to cash his personality in for more money after the game. Instead, he decided to become a drug dealer, and a really bad one at that.

He got busted twice with a car full of weed. What kind of drug dealer cruises around with his own big stash? His poor choices put him behind bars, killed his reputation forever. Had he stayed on the right path and worked at it, he'd have a nice little gig right about now. Instead, the most affable guy I've ever come across in this league is a convicted felon.

The great Falcons perennial Pro Bowl running back Warrick Dunn had raised his siblings after his mother, Betty, a police officer, was murdered in 1993 during a robbery while she was at her second job. Warrick still went to college yet helped raise his siblings. When he got into the pros, he continued to raise them. The problem was, as adults, they continued to rely on Warrick for support. They never made a life of their own.

Warrick was suffocating until at one point he cut the cord. He went to a psychiatrist to deal with the guilt and pain. Warrick eventually found the best word a professional athlete can have in his vocabulary: "No." So simple but so powerful, and at times a player's best friend.

Finally, there are those people who break guys' bank accounts along with their hearts.

Women.

Isn't it amazing how good-looking we suddenly become when our paychecks get a couple of zeroes added to the end? The more commas, the more handsome we grow. It wasn't too long ago I was just another knucklehead with dental problems. Now I'm a handsome hound dog with a distinguished, recognizable smile. Trust me, I don't look anything different from the way I did when I drove a Ford Festiva back in my college days.

Guys go back to their college or hometown and the women come out of the woodwork. They'll figure out some excuse why they blew us off in the past. That same girl who

wouldn't have anything to do with you . . . all of a sudden you're full of wit and charm.

You get a feel for which women are looking for a "baller." There are certain spots in each city where players regularly hang out. It's not hard to find those places and the groupies that come with it. They're hoping a player will fall in love, marry them, and have some babies. Even the ones we date for a while. They want to be part of a world filled with what they think is the easy road to glamour, success, fame, fortune and status. Often the same girl will date and sleep with multiple players.

Status is everything. Who always gets the girls? People with status. As a result, the girls are plentiful. If you wanted, you could score pretty much any night you feel like it, but these girls view us with dollar signs in their eyes.

Women can sure take a guy to the cleaners. Why do you think I started this chapter sitting in my lawyer's office? My ex-wife absolutely loved the lifestyle. Before we were together, she was living in the most lavish apartment I'd ever seen, an apartment that even after I made millions I don't think I could afford.

But here I was, a young guy from Germany and Texas who got caught up in dating someone who passed herself off as a successful Oxford University–educated fashion model. The reality? She was a clerk at a retail store yet always lived the good life. What did I know? I was dumb and in love.

Although sometimes I do think she loved me, I realize she loved the money and status more. A major incident that makes this clear is one I didn't know about until after we were divorced.

Before I was in the NFL, I told my parents that if I ever made it, I would buy them a house. Ten years later, when I wanted to fulfill my promise, I didn't put a price limit on

finding their dream house. My parents didn't have an extravagant lifestyle, but I also didn't expect it to be under $500,000.

I was in training camp in the middle of two-a-day workouts at the time, so I asked Jean to help get the house they picked out. My parents had found a place for $160,000. Talk about modest; they certainly could have gone the extra distance, but they held back.

According to my parents' knowledge, Jean balked at this price and told them it was out of the budget and to find another house. There was no budget, yet Jean made them find another house. My parents found another place for $147,000, which was acceptable to Jean. She told them they couldn't have their dream home for an extra measly $13,000. I shouldn't have been surprised by this, judging by the way she treated my family overall. I wish I had figured this out sooner.

Now because of this woman, I'm sitting in my lawyer's office counting my last dollar, keeping track of every penny. But I don't mind sorting through the money, the ledgers and the receipts if it gets me closer to fixing my marital mistakes. I don't hate the woman, but I do hate what I didn't know then and what I know now.

It's okay, though; you take your lumps and learn your lessons. Despite Jean fighting me over the money, I'll never have to cram my oversize body in a tiny little Ford Festiva ever again.

CHAPTER EIGHTEEN

Living a Private Life in the Public Eye

"**Y**o, Strahan, Favre took a dive, you know it's still Gastineau's record!" an oh-so-endearing fan screamed at me as I walked into a restaurant with my friend's sister. "You suck, Strahan! J-E-T-S, JETS, JETS, JETS!"

If I go out to dinner a hundred nights a year, a majority of those times, people feel compelled to challenge my manhood, insult me or whisper while staring and pointing like I'm some circus freak.

That's what I risk every time I leave the security of my own home. I know, I know, you're thinking boo-hoo-hoo, big millionaire star has to deal with a few insults from the big bad public. Suck it up and shut up, Strahan! Right?

I agree. But one of the most difficult things a professional football player has to deal with is learning how to lower his boiling point in public. It's harder than you think. Some of the same people yelling for me to become an enraged violent

New York Giant on Sundays expect me to be the nicest, most genteel Giant Sunday night through Saturday evening.

There is no course in the NFL to teach players how to cope with hecklers, drunks, autograph seekers and paparazzi. Some fans carry over their Sunday routines into the week when they see a player. It doesn't happen now and then. It happens nearly every day I'm out and about. For example, I was standing in line the other day waiting for my frappuccino when one of the guys who worked behind the counter says, completely out of the blue, "Strahan, my buddy who works here thinks he can take you out."

Huh? Why would anybody want to take me out on a Monday morning while I'm standing in line for coffee?

"That's great and thanks for the offer, but I'm not looking to fight anybody. I just want my frappuccino and I'll be on my way."

Many times I get the "You're not as big as I thought you were" line. I also get challenged to fights on the train, at amusement parks, at restaurants, walking the streets of New York City and at the grocery store. Men love to challenge somebody bigger than them.

Sports provides escapism. We shouldn't have that much effect on people's moods and emotions. We're football players! How can some fans get so angry that they feel obliged to scream threats at us, tell us how much we suck, pelt us with insults and even, at times, barrage our children, wives and girlfriends with insults? I can't understand it.

What if everyone's life were as public as mine? What if people screamed out at a neighbor, "Hey, Joe Schmoe, your kid got a C-minus in math, what a little dummy!" Or "Hey, Joe, you suck! Your wife is gonna drop your ass for the pool boy!" "Hey Joe, you got your ass kicked in the stock market this week, hah, hah, hah, you jerk." What if they yelled at

their neighbors' kids and told them how much of a moron their daddy is?

Why, when some people see a professional athlete, do they feel compelled to say what they'd never say to another stranger? Luckily, it's not the majority. Most fans are respectable and intelligent people. But the other few make it difficult.

I had a guy at the Super Bowl in 2007 who wanted to fight me because I declined to take a picture with him. I told him as politely as possible. I was trying to get to an event and I would have been held up in Miami's South Beach taking a bunch of pictures. Literally dozens of people stop you for photo ops on cell phones and cameras.

"I can't take a picture right now, I'll never get to where I'm going."

But that wasn't good enough for Mr. Joe Cool Fan. "Oh, come on, man, just one."

I offered to shake the guy's hand but he kept pressing the issue and rudely responded with, "Come on, man, don't be an asshole."

"That's why I'm not stopping," I snapped back. Pretty soon he was yelling insults about how I sucked and that I'm washed up. He threw in a Favre reference and I jawed back, which I shouldn't have done. He kept yapping and the next thing you know, here I am with some knucklehead I don't even know, trading insults from across the street on Super Bowl week. Stupid, stupid, stupid.

I've had fans yell things at me about my divorce. "Hey, Strahan, need a loan?" Of course, that's a cheap-shot reference to my ex-wife, Jean. Living in the public eye brings out people who love to pile on.

Some fans feel obligated to pontificate about my teammates. "Eli sucks!" "Shockey's an idiot!" Why do fans say

something nasty about a man they don't even know? What kind of reaction are they looking for?

It comes with the job, because without the fans, I'd be broke. I owe fans a lot of what I've become off the field.

I've often thought of screaming back or responding physically, but only once in my career did somebody push my buttons and I actually got physical. You must never go that route. There's way too much at stake and many times the aggressive fan is only trying to score a payday.

The guy who yelled at me that Favre took a dive and that it was still Gastineau's record really pissed me off. I made the mistake of getting aggressive because he crossed the line. I sent the woman I was at dinner with to our table, then walked back over to his group, and the moment he opened his mouth to yell another "Strahan sucks" remark, I palmed the man's jaw and started squeezing his mouth and lips shut. His eyes bulging wide in shock, I told him that if he said one more thing to me, I would knock him out.

Yup, not one of my brighter moments. The real insult would have been if the idiot sued me for my hard-earned money. Really stupid, but, man, did it feel great at the time. One moment of short-term pleasure could have led to long-term grief.

I was in a terrible mood to begin with and was in the company of a young woman who was a friend's sister from out of town and who did not know me. Plus, he was so offensive that about twenty minutes later, he tried to crash my dinner and interrupt my meal. All I could say was, "Come on, man, just leave me alone!"

It turned out the guy was drunk. Drunk or sober, there was no excuse for getting aggressive with insults with somebody he doesn't know. It was a lousy combination of alcohol, testosterone and a guy wanting to show off for his friends.

Guys like him make it harder for us to open up to real fans when we are out. He makes it harder for everyone else.

Sometimes I'll have a private dinner meeting or a date and some stranger will come and sit down at the table without saying a word and just barge in on the conversation. Wow!

During my rookie year, when people approached LT, he was sometimes unbelievably rude about it. You'd get rejection plus a handful of expletives. I vowed back then, "I won't be like that." Years later, I understand his demeanor. You get pushed and you want people to respect your personal space. I sometimes forget that it's all part of the job. Hey, you want to be famous? This is part of the deal.

Ironically, it takes one second to be nice to someone and usually that person excitedly tells ten others about your sweet disposition. Conversely, it takes one second to be a jerk and those stories reach a hundred or more.

The more polite the other person is, the more polite I'm likely to be. Life is a catch-22. I've got to make sure I set the proper boundaries with fans. If I don't, I'll drive my friends crazy. I need to give my friends my attention, but at the same time I don't want to insult any of our fans. Still, in setting these boundaries, people get offended and often take it the wrong way.

Everybody is human. We all have moods. I apologize to all those fans I may have ticked off. But try for a moment to put yourself in my shoes. What if you were an accountant and every time you went out to dinner or out on the street, you were *constantly* hit up by strangers about their personal tax returns? You'd probably tear your hair out.

Since most everyone talks sports all day long, they forget it's a business for me and I don't want to talk about it all the time.

One thing that makes pro athletes bitter is how sleazy the memorabilia business has become. Autographs are great for kids. Who wouldn't want to sign one for genuine fans? Today fans are outnumbered by profiteers who use autographs as a business. It ruins the whole experience because it takes away from giving a genuine fan your autograph. The autograph business has made it all seem so impersonal now.

I know firsthand how great it feels to get an autograph, especially as a kid. When I was thirteen, I shyly asked Herschel Walker for his autograph. (How crazy is it that he would later become my teammate when the Giants signed him as a free agent in the mid-1990s?) It made me feel like the coolest kid, and I'd asked out of the purest of motives.

Nowadays I'll see the same guys every day asking for autographs at training camp. They have pictures, helmets, jerseys, balls, hats and bags of stuff, and often they have two or three people working with them. Some of these guys hire children to act like fans asking for your autograph. It's a sham. Then when you decline an autograph to these people, they tell other people what a jerk you are.

I've been asked to sign just about every body part, but the craziest thing is that some people ask if I'll sign their baby. Folks, don't ask me to sign an infant! Who in their right mind would ask me to put ink on a little baby? It's ridiculous, but it happens.

These are examples of some of the extreme fans. But there are also great ones. Two fans named Scott and Ron Wolf used to come to Giants road games during my rookie season and very politely struck up a conversation with me. They were cool and weren't overbearing. The Wolf cousins are funny guys and recognize the boundaries. They'd see me at the team hotel and wait until I was finished with my other

guests. I'd end up sitting downstairs with them schmoozing until I had either meetings or curfew.

We became friends and for the next nine years, I had an annual dinner with them in New York City to talk Giants football. Another super fan is Sam Hazen, the head chef at restaurant Tao in New York City and Vegas. I love his passion so much I've actually gotten him field passes to watch games from our sidelines. It's great when you can get close to fans who have the passion these guys do.

I love that my career makes people excited for me to sign my name for them. I thank G-d every day that I command such love and respect from people. I once met a fan at IHOP who had a Giants helmet tattooed on his arm. He rolled up his sleeve and asked, "Would you sign my arm on top of the helmet?"

A few weeks later I ran into him again after a game. He reminded me that I had signed his arm above his tattoo. Then he rolled his sleeve up again. The helmet was now accompanied by a tattoo of my autograph! He had gone straight to the tattoo parlor and had them permanently ink it in. I was flattered and speechless.

As a high-profile player in the NFL, after my divorce, I became a favorite of the paparazzi for a while. My ex-wife loves the paparazzi; she *wants* to be known. She got caught up wanting to be famous, but the only thing she's famous for is marrying someone famous. If she sics the paparazzi on me, then that keeps her in the public eye.

I try to spin it in a positive way. If the paparazzi follow me, I really must have done something right. But I don't like when they camp out in front of your apartment and invade your routine. Besides, I have young kids and I really don't want some crazy knowing where we live.

I don't know how these huge celebrities deal with it every hour of their lives. I don't know if it's ever worth it to become THAT famous so they're following your kids. Man, that's got to be rough.

During the height of the mudslinging of my divorce, I was jogging to the gym in the city with my buddy. All of a sudden this guy steps from behind a van and snaps pictures. Then I see more cameras, and more and more and more. They're snapping pictures through the windows, behind cars and even running out in front of us.

Then they waited outside the gym and started snapping photos through the window while yelling at me about my split-up. One person paid for a day membership to come in and talk about the divorce while I was in the middle of a set. He acted like he was there to work out, but he was really snooping.

The one good thing about that day? When you have all these cameras taking pictures, it gives you an adrenaline boost. We picked up the pace faster than normal. Shoot, I'm not going to look slow for the cameras. I'll give one guy credit; while we were running at a really good clip, one photographer was ahead of us running backward with all that equipment and snapping pictures the whole way, and not for a short distance. I don't know who you are, sir, but you deserve those pictures. Your endurance is phenomenal.

Now that the paparazzi have entered the picture (pardon the pun), I've got to be more careful. I can't let them take photos of me squeezing a man's jaw shut at a restaurant, now can I?

In the grand scheme of it all, I still feel blessed. If I had to do it all over again, I'd sacrifice my privacy for the love and admiration. While it may annoy me sometimes, I'd gladly take a thousand fans barging in on my dinner and a million

autograph seekers if it meant just one year in the NFL. I'm sure ten years down the road, I'll wish I could spill my blood all over again, just to hear those fans scream my name in unison one more time.

And while it takes a boatload of money and medicine to keep me afloat, there's one dangerous line I'll never cross.

CHAPTER NINETEEN

Steroids and Other Cheaters' Delights

Four games and a lifetime of damage!

This is the price Chargers pass-rushing linebacker Shawne Merriman paid when he was suspended by the NFL for four weeks after testing positive for a steroid known as nandrolone.

It's a shame because I really like him. He busts his butt on the field and of all the pass rushers currently playing, that's the one guy I'd bet has a legitimate shot at one day breaking my single-season sack record. I'm confident he'll break it, set a new record, and perhaps then break that one as well. I have no questions about him as an individual, but from now on, since he tested positive for steroids, the rest of the league—and I—will question him as a player.

In the eyes of the players, the worst crime you could possibly commit in today's NFL is to get busted for steroids. That makes you a cheater and there's nothing worse than a cheater. I say if you cheat, you should have your butt kicked out of our league. If you need to cheat, obviously this isn't the right profession for you. Maybe you should go be a nightclub bouncer. If you cannot play this sport without having to cheat, I don't want you on my team and I don't want you in our league.

We as players are *that* adamant about the issue. We'd rather you get busted with ten bags of coke and a joint hanging from your lips than get busted for 'roids. You know what our logic is? With street drugs, you're cheating yourself. With 'roids, you're cheating yourself *and* you're cheating the rest of us.

Merriman finished 2006 leading the league with seventeen sacks, but we all looked at it as if Jason Taylor really led the league. Every year Merriman leads the league in sacks, we'll look at his accomplishments with a mental asterisk. I'm not the only one thinking this; it's the general thought among players inside the league. Other stars like Jason Taylor and Champ Bailey have talked out about it. Guys speak out because we feel gypped.

From this point on, guys will always look at a player like Shawn as if he has just found another way around the drug tests, to keep himself bigger and stronger than the rest of us. Even if he is clean, we may never believe it. Once you get tagged with steroids, I don't know how you can do enough to repair the damage to your reputation.

Players aren't very forgiving. Here's why: If one guy juices, then how do we all keep up? Does that mean in order to keep pace with the Joneses, we've got to juice, too? The guys blocking Merriman suddenly feel like they need artificial help to protect their jobs. Where does that leave us—Merriman's fellow defensive ends and pass rushers? Do we need to juice up to keep up not only with Merriman but with all the other blockers who want to keep up as well? This vi-

cious cycle is exactly why the NFL cracks down harder on steroid cheaters than they do on cokeheads.

One of the biggest misconceptions about the NFL is that steroids are commonplace in every locker room. Nothing could be further from the truth. I can honestly say that in my fourteen years in the NFL, I have never seen a guy do steroids or even have a guy admit to me that he juices. Not a single one! I know sportswriters who love to glorify that we're all a bunch of juiceheads, but I've honestly never seen it. I don't think I've ever seen a vial of the stuff in my life.

The NFL averages merely two to three failed pee tests a year for steroids, and that doesn't include the guys that test positive for the weight-loss crap. It's not because we all know how to beat the system; it really is not as prevalent as fans think it is. The hardcore stuff that guys took in the 1970s and 1980s and early part of the 1990s has run its course. The level of steroids in our locker rooms has decreased over the years.

Of all the guys I've ever played with, I was sure about one guy because he got busted for distributing the stuff. That was my rookie year and he was a former high-round pick and honestly, he had the worst body on the team. His body was so bad that every time he walked around with his shirt off, our former running back Dave Meggett would let out, "Ewwwww."

Don't get me wrong, I'm not so naive to believe that our locker rooms are completely clean. Steroid use is not done publicly and isn't discussed. We have our own suspicions about guys, but in all honesty, I don't think there's much of a problem inside our locker rooms anymore. You don't need to do it anymore because of how sophisticated the supplements have become. Steroid use is nowhere near where it was when I came into the league. You'd see guys coming out of the draft and they already looked like grown-ass, chemically enhanced

men. Today many more guys come in with baby fat and bodies that don't suggest anything illegal. We've replaced steroid bodies with creatine bodies. Tons of guys are on creatine and other supplements.

Early in my career you could tell who was using stuff, but as the supplements business grew, more sophisticated guys stopped using illegal stuff. Why in the heck would you risk your reputation and four games of salary when you can achieve nearly the same results with an aggressive supplements program? Think about it: Is it worth a four-game suspension's worth of pay and a permanent asterisk on your name in exchange for a few percentage points more of muscle mass than what supplements can provide you?

The risk isn't worth it anymore because there are now risk-free rewards. They're risk-free as long as you use the supplements authorized by the NFL. But even with safe stuff we still run into problems with the "supps."

One of the biggest problems we face as players is that as responsible as we are for what goes into our bodies, we're getting absolutely zero help from the Food and Drug Administration (FDA). Why would the government refuse to regulate what companies put into their supplements? It's big business, but also a dangerous business. There's nothing to stop a company from putting steroids into their products and have some guys in our league test positive as a result.

One of my former Giants teammates, running back Mike Cloud, fell victim to this problem. He drank a basic chocolate protein shake that you'd find at any nutrition or vitamin store. It was the same protein shake many high school kids love to drink as they build their bodies through their formative years. (As a parent, you should be petrified about what is *really* going into your sons' and daughters' bodies.)

Much to his shock, Mike tested positive for nandrolone,

the same stuff as Shawne Merriman. He brought the powder to the NFL to have them test it to see if, in fact, it was tainted. Sure enough, that chocolate powder came back with a positive test for nandrolone, and even with this evidence, the NFL still suspended him. Zero tolerance policy!

The NFL tells us at the start of the league year that each player is responsible for what goes into his body. We are provided with a list of league-cleared supplement products. If we choose to go outside the supplements that are okayed by the NFL, then we're basically left to hope and pray that nobody in the supplement's lab tainted the product. Not only was Cloud still suspended the four weeks, it happened when he was a free agent so he had to inform every single team interested in him that he was hit with a four-game steroid suspension. It absolutely destroyed the marketability he may have had.

Merriman claimed he was a victim of the same thing but couldn't prove it the way Cloud could. But if he is innocent and got implicated by a tainted bottle, it's a shame, because nobody believed him.

The other problem? Out of one hundred bottles of a certain supplements product, ninety could be completely clean but ten are dirty and would provide a dirty test. We have the responsibility of bringing a supplement to the team to have it tested by the league to make sure it's clean *before* we use it. The problem here is that one of the bottles we bring in could be fine but then the fifth bottle be tainted. Sorry, Player X, four game checks and a tainted rep for you!

Your only hope is to have that bottle tested by the NFL and hope they show leniency with their zero tolerance policy. At the same time you have to hope the test that came back dirty wasn't taken when you were at the end of the bottle. If you threw it out and no longer have even a semblance

of proof that you were bamboozled, it's four game checks and a bad rep for the rest of your career.

The NFL does not joke around when it comes to this testing. They can't, because every single guy who tests positive has an excuse. Nobody in the NFL ever said, "Damn, you caught me. I thought I was going to get away with it."

One guy claimed his pee test was tainted and demanded that the NFL pay for a DNA test to clear his name. After much squabbling, they conducted the DNA test. Not only was the sample his, it was dirty with 'roids! Everyone has an excuse.

That's why the league makes the testing process as thorough and utterly degrading as possible. The process, first off, is completely random and a total surprise when you come to work. We'll have two "pee men," as we affectionately call them, waiting for us by the door as we arrive at work. There is no heads-up, no warning. All you get is, "You're up today."

You must pee before practice. You can't go out to the field unless you've taken the test, so most guys go to meetings and drink tons of water so they can pee enough for the pee men. When you're ready, you have to go to another locker room. For us it's the locker room that the referee and officials use on Sundays.

When we get in there, we've got to take our shirts off and drop our pants down to our ankles. We get a complete strip search because of Onterrio Smith, that dumb ass running back for the Vikings, who was busted with an artificial penis known as the Whizzinator. It's a fake ding-dong with a freeze-dried sample. Just add water and, presto, you have a clean test.

So thanks to Mr. Dumb Ass Whizzinator, we're given the Rahway Prison treatment. Not only do you strip, but the pee man or both of them have to watch you pee to make sure it's really your schlong. Gee, thanks so much, Onterrio.

After that, we pour the sample into two compartments in a cup and seal it with a sticker with a serial number on it. But you also have to have some left over for the pee man to test on the spot with a little stick. I think he's checking to make sure it's actually a man's urine. In the past, one guy supposedly tested positive for being a female and another guy's piss turned out to be a sports drink.

If Capitol Hill knew how deep the NFL got with their testing on steroids, we'd never get lumped in with baseball in those steroid hearings. Baseball looked like it was trying to hide their problem. The NFL chose to weed out their problem and give guys an alternative. The NFL *wants* to bust guys. They were trying to lower the boom and this year the NFL will go even further by using a more advanced test and administering more random tests. So for the guys who are hiding it, they'll start catching even more cheaters.

Even with this testing, I think the only ones getting past it are the ones who have incredibly advanced knowledge of how to cheat. There are masking agents but some of those get tested as well. Even if a guy's pee is too diluted by water, they start to get leery of you.

We'll never catch everyone. Some jerks will always find a way to cheat. The steroid makers are three years ahead of the steroid chasers. There are makeshift laboratories throughout the country where they make new steroids that cannot be detected.

The only way to test for any given steroid is to have the drug in the first place. If the authorities don't know a new steroid is being produced and don't have its exact chemical makeup, they can't find an accurate way to test for it. There will always be new things that allow guys to cheat. It's an epidemic in America.

The only thing that could stop it is for us to start self-policing. There's too much money to be made today for guys ever to do that. People outside of football would probably do much dumber things than steroids if someone promised them a $20 million windfall. Much, much worse things.

I don't know if they'll ever be able to catch HGH, or human growth hormone. There is a test that exists but it has very low accuracy. Plus, it comes from a blood test and the lab is in Europe. You can't suspend a guy for HGH based on a blood test sent across the Atlantic.

HGH is all the rage—not just in the NFL but across America. You can kind of tell some guys who are overdoing HGH because they may go home for an off-season and come back huge . . . all over. Not only have they leaned up while their muscle mass has exploded, but their skulls have clearly grown as well. I was told about one star who came back one off-season and his helmet size increased by three sizes!

The problem here is that when guys get that big that quickly, they often start pulling or popping muscles. Maybe you can get that big for the beach but not for suddenly racing your body down the field play after play after play.

I've also heard that some doctors will go to a team hotel on the road at times, go from room to room and shoot players. I'm not one of those players so I cannot say who or how or how often or how many guys. I don't even know if there are guys on my team who do this. I did, however, hear about the practice.

There is another guy who was brought into the team hotel to shoot injured guys with some miraculous mineral compound. I have no idea what it was but I know that guys like

this are, at times, set up through a player's agent or directly by the player.

I love that the NFL goes after the cheaters as hard as they do. Even if the guy is playing right next to me, if he's cheating, he should be weeded out. It is a little crazy that steroids piss me off more than when guys do other stupid stuff off the field. A guy associated with a heinous crime won't be ostracized as badly as a 'roider!

Marijuana is probably the choice drug of most players. We get tested once for marijuana and when we're clean, we don't get tested again for a year, so guys smoke to their heart's delight. As long as he doesn't get caught, we really don't care if a guy is smoking, just as we don't care about his drinking a few beers. I have personally never even tried a joint in my life, wouldn't even know how to smoke the thing.

I've played with guys who smoked weed on a very regular basis. Some every single day. We all know the weedheads, but we can care less about it. Juice? That, we care about. The big difference between the two—weed guys don't bother hiding from anyone other than the league. Juice, they try to hide from the league as well as their teammates.

If there's a way to cheat, some guys will simply find the path. They'll push anywhere they can to get an edge over the rest of us. But the one thing we're cool with, the only way for any of these guys to really clear their names is to admit it. Just come clean and own up to it; deal with the immediate consequences and move on.

When the New York Yankees slugger Jason Giambi in effect admitted steroid use, he went into a slump and got absolutely destroyed for a while. But he admitted his wrongdoing, fought his way out of the slump and eventually all was forgiven. He owned up to doing something stupid, plain and

simple. Barry Bonds should have taken the approach of Giambi, because people want to forgive you if you are truthful about it. When a guy lies and won't admit it, you got a problem. Think about it: When somebody has a drug problem, you want to help them. You root for a man to recover. But for those who refuse to admit a problem and just ruin themselves, you shake your head and move on.

We as players want to help guys if they want help. If they don't bother, then we have enough other people who want our help and we move on.

But I honestly do not know who needs to step forward. Can we guess sometimes? Sure, and nowadays a locker room is so open, guys will blurt out, "You're on that stuff, huh?" Or "When you start hitting the needle, bro?" Still, nobody ever admits it outright and I think with the science of all the specialists and supplements, many of the guys we suspect aren't even on it.

Whenever a guy shows up much bigger after an off-season of working out, we half jokingly accuse him of hitting the needle. One year Tiki came back from an off-season of working out with Ronde and some people started privately questioning if he was hitting the needle. Did I think he was? Hell, no, he's too clean for that. Ronde got huge, too, but go watch those two work out at their gym in Jersey and it immediately becomes clear why they grew so much.

But that's what we do. If anybody does anything to improve himself, we accuse him of juicing. Or when a fat guy comes back in shape, we accuse him of getting a stomach bypass. Jonas Seawright, one of our young defensive tackles, came back this off-season down thirty pounds and even the coaches were jokingly accusing him of getting his stomach stapled. We knew he didn't but we couldn't pass up that joke.

Usually the fat guys just take diet pills, some of which are legal and some of which aren't. Actually, I believe these pills are used by guys in our locker rooms more than steroids.

Remember, we get fined if we are overweight. Our weight gets checked every week and the stress of the season causes guys to give up any sort of diet. In many cases guys fight stress by finding a vice like food.

The problem with the diet pills is that if you get busted, it's reported that you have been suspended for four games under the NFL's Anabolic Steroids and Related Substances Policy. Anabolic steroids is suddenly associated with your name, even if your body looks like utter crap.

We have more forgiveness for those guys than the juiceheads. If a guy is using a weight-loss drug and his body is bad, we'll just rag on the guy for a while for getting ripped off. "I don't know what you paid for that stuff, but do they give refunds?"

Diet pills are a big deal with the NFL because many of them are used as a replacement for speed. Finding something extra to push us through practice and geek us up on game day is a huge part of our game.

Yet as we stand on that sideline listening to the national anthem, awaiting that majestic flyover, why in the world would we need any extra boost coursing through our veins? But I do, as do the guys I'm hitting the trenches with and my opponents trying to run my butt over. What we take to give us that boost has changed over the years. Right now it's diet pills and many of them are legal. But if that Colts-Giants game were played back in 1993, my first year in the NFL, guys on both sidelines would be geeked beyond belief on some sort of speed, amphetamines, reds or greenies.

During my rookie year, we were in a play-off game against

the 49ers and one of our defensive linemen ran out of speed. He relied on the boost so much he was actually licking the empty bag for residue! Those days, I assure you, are long gone.

Today's NFL is far from the old *North Dallas Forty* movie where they were handing out speed left and right and smoking cigarettes at halftime. That was the late 1970s, and it was done by players generations before me. Could you imagine walking into a halftime locker room of the greatest athletes in the world and see guys sitting on their bench puffing cigarettes?

But think how much our game day locker rooms have changed in just ten years when it comes to how we jack ourselves up. Speed was prevalent for years and then suddenly it vanished, almost overnight, when the ephedra drinks came around.

As the energy drinks came into fashion, the pills began to disappear. There are so many energy drinks out there now that do the same things as those old-fashioned greenies, the pills are no longer necessary. The only pills you really see are Ritalin and other ADD drugs that act as amphetamines. Although some guys try to land these for help, most are prescribed by a physician and monitored by the team.

A few years ago ephedra took the NFL by storm and we were all on that. Hell, you'd look over on the sidelines and see a coach drinking that stuff to get jazzed up.

Some guys would down a couple for pregame warm-ups, go to the bathroom, and then drink another for the first half, then another for the second half. They were still going nuts after the game and then they'd rely on an entirely different pillbox to bring them down. That is when Ambien and other sleep aids started to seep in as well. They needed something just as powerful to counteract the speed of the ephedra

drinks. If they didn't bring themselves down, they'd stay awake all night long, then crash at work the next day. A lot of guys gathered in the fenced-off Player's Only parking lot after a game and pounded beers to take the edge off after a game.

Once guys like the Vikings Pro Bowl tackle Korey Stringer and an unfortunate number of high school players died, we were forced to change what we put into our bodies again. Not only did the NFL ban ephedra, but the government followed suit. We're lucky for that because, as a player, you always believe "it won't happen to me." Even if a few of your own teammates have died from it, I guarantee you'll still have a whole slew of guys willing to use the stuff, saying, "It won't happen to me." Our search for an edge on game day makes us ignorant. Don't ask about the dangers and hopefully we won't find out.

Once the ephedra got banned, companies started coming out with ephedra-free stuff that does the same thing but without as much danger. Some guys still use some of those drinks, but at this point, we've figured out something else.

Believe it or not, now it's pretty much coffee and Red Bulls. You know what I've realized after all these years? Red Bull does pretty much the same thing as the old speed pills or the ephedra. It gives you the same peppy feeling and you can drink it in the locker room knowing that (a) you won't die and (b) you won't get popped for four games.

But how about this? In the span of twelve years, we went from speed pills to Starbucks and Red Bull. The only thing we complement that with is a couple of ammonia caps, or smelling salts. The smelling salts clear our heads right before we take the field. Because our adrenaline is rushing so fast, we sometimes have to take a few deep whiffs to get the desired effect.

Who would ever have thought that a man readying for gladiator-type battle has to throw down a couple of heavily

caffeinated lattes or espressos before he tries to tear some-
one's head off? Maximus would be so ashamed.

But not as ashamed as I was when my boy Merriman got
busted. Man, he's just too good for that. He's too good a guy
and too good a player, but he will forever be tarnished and
questioned.

Four games of pay is a tough pill to swallow. But having
to play the game under a cloud, trying to prove his innocence
to his peers, is tougher. Why couldn't he just have gotten
busted smoking weed? All would have been forgiven.

CHAPTER TWENTY

Super Bowl Shuffle

I'm watching the Bears take the field against the Colts from a house in Miami and my palms begin to sweat. I know exactly how each player on the Bears and Colts feels because I've been there. I played on the biggest stage in the world of sports just six years before, January 2001. When I watch a Super Bowl I'm not playing in, I get nervous for the guys playing and my body reacts. I sweat.

I was in Miami for the festivities of Super Bowl week. When it comes to the Super Bowl itself, I'm a big-time hater. I have no interest in attending the game. I get tickets every year and give them away with no interest in watching somebody else play on a field *I* should be playing on.

I love watching the "24/7 football guys." They hate this day, too! I was cracking up watching my man Brian Urlacher during his media day. You could tell that about ten minutes into the hour session, he was done. It was hilarious watching him slowly lose patience. He had had enough and just wanted to hit somebody. Some guys aren't too comfortable with the media. That's Urlacher to a tee. The more repetitive the questions got, the shorter his answers got. I think if he could have laced it up and played the game that afternoon, he would have.

Urlacher, Peyton Manning, Marvin Harrison, Lance Briggs. They're introduced and I'm a jealous fool. It stings me that I'm not out there on the Super Bowl field—forced again to live vicariously through others. What did I do wrong? Why was I not there? Did I do something bad in a previous life and this is my form of punishment? A ringless existence?

I do play the game for the money and camaraderie. But the ultimate reason I've taken all those stupid injections and beaten up my body is for that ring. In 2001, my Giants teammates and I talked about the Super Bowl in Tampa on the sideline of the NFC Championship Game after we blew out Minnesota 41–0. We talked about how incredible it is to work your whole career toward one goal, never knowing if you'll ever really accomplish it.

The feeling of relief was overwhelming. It's like we climbed all the way up a mountain and took in the beautiful view in solitude. Multiply that feeling times 100 and that's how we felt coming off the field following the thrashing we gave the Minnesota Vikings. It strikes you so hard, you feel like you want to cry. My soul and spirit felt unbreakable. I was living football's equivalent to heaven on Earth. Every worry, ache and pain, real-world problems, all gone.

The thing that brought me back to reality was my cell phone. After the Vikings game, by the time I got back inside our locker room for the postgame celebration and media session, my cell phone's mailbox was filled with ticket requests. I could no longer accept new messages. I had family members I never knew I had and "friends" I hadn't talked to in

years, all asking if I could get them a ticket to the Super Bowl. It was amazing how many people were suddenly related to me. I had acquaintances who somehow believed they were not only entitled to tickets but were special enough for me to get them into parties as well. I have no idea how many of my *true* family and friends called that night after the hangers-on filled up the message box. It was ridiculous.

The feeling I had when we gathered at the stadium to embark on the plane ride down to Super Bowl week was like a twenty-fifth high school reunion. Every time somebody pulled up and joined the group, we greeted him with hugs and laughs, like long-lost friends. Every teammate, whether you liked him or not, was suddenly your best friend. I had fifty-two best friends that day. It was total euphoria. It was surreal. The whole time, I was waiting to wake up from the dream. Finally it smacked us between the eyes. This was, in fact, no dream.

The plane ride down to Tampa was exhilarating. It made the whole ordeal a reality. We were told to bring video cameras and catch everything we do on tape. This may never happen again, so tape every little thing. Players roamed the plane interviewing other players, roasting guys, busting on one another.

As we began our descent into Tampa, the vibe inside our plane immediately shifted. The party came to a screeching halt. As we landed, guys started to tighten up as most of us tried to hide our giddiness. Then the plane doors flew open and the cameras began to roll.

I didn't want to be caught on camera with the wrong expression, because this week every little thing is broken down. Every word, every expression, every step is dissected, discussed and analyzed by every "expert" in America. I walked out of the plane and asked G-d, "Please help me look like I

belong here." I didn't want to seem too happy because people might say I wasn't focused. I didn't want to seem too focused because then the media might claim I was too tight.

The most difficult task was trying to convince myself this game was "just another game." The Big Lie. Of course it's different! There's nothing like it, but in every interview you lie and try to explain how you're simply playing a football game, just like we've done hundreds of times before. What a crock that is!

That first night, I stayed at the hotel by myself. I didn't feel the need to party. I didn't feel the urge to enjoy the sideshow part of Super Bowl week. I'd worked too damn hard to screw this thing up by trying to party with the masses. We were the elite. We'd already defied the odds by getting there; why screw it up now?

My teammates didn't go crazy that week, either. It would have ticked me off if guys were out partying late. This was the one week of the year that players really tried to police each other. I understood that players were excited about being there, but I figured these parties are the same every year. They'll be here next year, too. The ladies will be around. Hell, if we win, the number of women throwing themselves at us *after* the game will triple.

Bottom line: Don't screw up *my* chances of winning. I need you guys now more than ever before. Come on, brothers, give us one more week of total focus. Let the nightclubs go untouched for one week. That's all I ask.

At 2007's Super Bowl I saw a pretty big name out on Ocean Avenue on South Beach about twenty minutes before curfew. I pulled him aside. "What are you doing? You better get your ass back to your hotel. I don't think you realize this, but you may never get back here. This is your one chance.

You've got fifty-one other weeks to party. Come on, young buck, don't be stupid."

The player got upset with me. He's a damn good player, too, but he was selfish. What if it got reported that he was seen drinking well past curfew? He'd become a goat forever. As his teammate, I'd beat his ass if he became a distraction, especially if we lost the game. Seeing that guy not wanting it bad enough ticked me off. I would have given anything to be in his shoes, to have another chance to play for a ring. To any other young player who reads this book, get that through your damn skull!

IT'S NOT JUST ANOTHER WEEK TO PARTY!

If you don't want it bad enough for yourself, at least do it for the NFL brothers you fought in the trenches with all year long. Go down there to win. Nothing else.

Remember I said you have to act like it's just another game? The first night we met with the media, it was nuts. The Sunday night we arrived at the hotel was a media frenzy unlike no other. And this would be the lightest day of the week for interviews. Lightest day? There were at least fifty times more media at the first session than any play-off game I had ever been involved with.

We confronted the press throngs every day, one of which was at the Super Bowl stadium, two of which required us to wake up at 6:30 A.M. for a session with hundreds of cameras and thousands of media members. Then you answer the same questions over and over and over again. The first night of interviews was pretty cool because you're finally doing what you've watched so many championship players do before. But after you field the same question a hundred times, for four more days, it gets taxing.

Jim Fassel, our coach at the time, said, "Don't give the

Ravens any ammo, don't say anything bad about them. Don't say anything that can go on their bulletin board."

Looking back, I shouldn't have been so afraid to speak my mind. What were they going to do? Play harder because of something I said? Would they suddenly get more talented? It's the freakin' Super Bowl! If you aren't already more jazzed up for this game than any other, then you should be down in Tijuana getting drunk. I was very vanilla that week—and that's one thing I am not! I wish I had been my usual ebullient self.

The wildest part of the week was the famous Media Day, where we were perched atop podiums at the stadium taking questions from the wildest group of questioners you'll ever see. Somebody hired the two kids who were kicked off that year's *American Idol*: the one Simon likened to a bug-eyed bush monkey, and his portly friend who got laughed off the show. The duo asked players to sing the national anthem with them on camera. Famous comedians asked stupid questions and Nickelodeon hired a guy to dress up as a nerdy Superhero to pelt us with ridiculous queries. I met reporters from every newspaper and magazine in America, TV and radio hosts of reality shows, and network news and entertainment shows.

You try to have fun with it since it's your only chance to shine, aside from the game itself. I got every type of question you could imagine. Questions about the gap in my teeth, growing up in Germany, going to a black college, old coaches, what my breakfast routine was and what my favorite cereal was. Questions about game plan, questions about the Ravens, questions about other teams, questions about questions asked of my teammates. It got maddening.

The part of the week I enjoyed most was the part I hated

most during the year—practice. Practice was my lone escape from the hysteria. We were off-limits to the press. Practices were shorter and guys were more jovial because we saw light at the end of the tunnel. You realize this will be your last week playing with some of these guys and your appreciation for the man standing next to you grows.

When I was out on that practice field, I didn't have to worry about tickets to the game or who wanted to eat where or which guest I needed to take care of. Here, I didn't have to bother with anything other than the game.

During the season, practice felt more pressurized, a lot more intense. Guys were playing angry and the monotony of the season caused frustration. You're so sick of looking at the same damn faces across from you every single day. All those players who use anger as motivation, it's all out the window during Super Bowl week. It's a time to be one of the fellas, with the fellas.

We practiced at the Tampa Bay Bucs facility, the worst place in the NFL. It was a joke. Their rusty-ass weights must have come from a prison yard. I couldn't believe an NFL team actually called this place home. It's Super Bowl week; why would they put us in the Bates Motel of practice facilities? Shouldn't they find us the Ritz-Carlton of practice facilities?

The Bucs players' lockers become our lockers for the week. I had Warren Sapp's locker, which gave me carte blanche to try to upset my portly Pro Bowl friend. He left his Lineman Challenge trophy in it to show people that if you worked as hard as he had, maybe you, too, could be a Warren Sapp someday. I took a piece of tape and wrote "Michael Strahan, the Real Champ" and taped it to his trophy. I heard that didn't sit too well with him. I just wanted to bust his ass. Mission accomplished!

Every time I left practice, it was back to a never-ending stream of requests. Come on, people, gimme a break! Let me focus on the biggest week of my life. Don't make this about you and your quest to be part of it. Isn't this week supposed to be about me and not about whether I can get you into a party?

I wanted to immerse myself in meetings. As I've said, normally, I hate the monotony of meetings. Scratch that, I *despise* the monotony of meetings. But this week those meetings were different. I craved information—any additional scouting reports, film work or any tidbit I could get on my opponent. That made prep week special. Nobody was falling asleep. Nobody needed a single cup of coffee to stay awake. This week guys voluntarily stayed in the hotel and went downstairs to watch film together. Guys sat up late at night and studied harder than they ever had.

We were bused to and from practice. Our elevators were separated from the lobby by an enormous curtain. It was like the New York Giants were trying to hide from the surreal scene going on outside the curtain. When I peeked around the other side, I saw merchandise being sold and hundreds and hundreds of fans. It was like a crazy flea market of sports fanatics around the clock who never slept.

Just like every other game, right? Every time we said that, we lied through our teeth. In my case, I was lying through my gap.

It's funny. While I enjoyed the week, I expected more. From a pure playing perspective, the highlight of the year was still the NFC Championship Game. I wasn't living my normal NFL life inside the helmet. I was in the hotel by eight o'clock every night. I never partied, I didn't hit the streets. I put myself on a very strict curfew.

No, it wasn't a fun week for me. It seemed like a long week but went by so fast. All I wanted to do was put on the pads and get the game started. Since I've voluntarily missed the parties and outside fun let's start the damn game already.

CHAPTER TWENTY-ONE

Super and Not So Super Saturday and Sunday

As difficult as Super Mondays through Fridays are, Super Saturdays and Sundays are much more brutal. The night before the big game I lay in bed and watched all those TV shows that break down the matchups and then break down the breakdowns. It's a constant loop and I found myself watching the same shows over and over again. I tried to turn my mind off at eleven o'clock, but my brain told me to stop my whining and turn the damn TV back on.

I turned back to the matchup shows, looking to see if maybe somehow I missed something. Did they have any information on my matchup with Ravens right tackle Harry Swayne that I may have missed? Midnight came and went. I tossed and turned. I stretched out a bit, trying to tire myself out some more. One o'clock came and went. Then two o'clock came and I really began to worry that I wouldn't sleep at all, that I would have to drag my tired ass in front of the world for all to see.

You know what it's like. You have a big meeting the next day, you're excited and you can't sleep. So you start watching the clock and worrying. You get jittery, nervous. The more you clock-watch, the more desperate and frustrated you grow, until you finally doze off a few short hours before it's time to get up. Eventually my body just gave out on me. I fell asleep around three o'clock.

When I woke up Super Bowl Sunday morning, I turned on the same TV shows I fell asleep to. Yup, I watched them all over again. I also awoke with this feeling of invincibility. There was no possible way we wouldn't win. We had studied the Ravens for two weeks. The only problem, the guys on the other team were probably waking up to the same feeling. We both can't be right. The entire day I felt like it was my destiny to get that ring. I couldn't wait to take what I honestly believed was mine.

The biggest challenge of Super Bowl Sunday is containing your excitement. It was the longest day of my career. I started clock-watching again and did things I hoped would eat up large amounts of time. But the day crawled and the wait was torturous. The closer it got to departure time, the more nervous I got. The longer the wait, the more my body tightened. Midway through that day, I was transformed from my jovial self to "Game-Day Stray." GDS isn't the nicest fellow. I don't like to talk to or make eye contact with anyone else. I get very ornery and any little thing that takes away from my focus aggravates me. Even a "Hi, Michael" agitates me on game day. Phone calls infuriate me. It's not that I'm trying to be nasty, but it just comes out on game day. I didn't want to hear from family, friends or acquaintances. I was trying to find my inner wrath. Don't get in the way of that.

On the ride over, one thing lightened me up a bit. Traveling through the streets of Tampa I saw people wearing No. 92

jerseys. I felt like I was in some fairy tale. I don't have words for it. Was this really happening to me? I was this knuckle-head who grew up in Germany, the youngest kid in his family, playing in a game I've always idolized, and now fans were wearing my family name on their backs.

An incredible euphoria surged through my body. I welled up with tears as I thought about all the people in my life who I knew were proud of me that day. People who have passed on, people I grew up with, old teachers, girls who blew me off as a kid or teenager, old coaches and childhood friends I thought would remain my best friends forever but haven't talked to in ages.

When we arrived at the stadium, we were presented with the only thing that made this week resemble every other week: We went into the locker room and went through our same weekly game-day routine. It took six days to find something that felt like "it was just another game." All of our superstitions, all of our little nuances and routines popped up again. We taped up and laced up just like in any other road game. But that's where the commonality ended. I didn't want to leave the confines of the locker room because for the first time all week, I enjoyed the familiarity. But that comfort soon ended. What lay behind those steel doors was something completely different from anything I'd ever experienced.

I went from the dark to the light. I ran through that tunnel for warm-ups, shooting out of the darkness to the flash of cameras everywhere. There were more TV cameras than at any game I'd ever played.

Once I flew out of that tunnel, my engine revved on over-drive, bursting through the red zone when suddenly I was smacked with a disappointing reality. It was half as loud as a normal game because, usually, an entire stadium is packed with crazed supporters of one team or the other, and their collective cheers and boos can be deafening. It took half a second to adjust to how relatively quiet the place was. An impartial crowd? Something wasn't right.

Regardless of the lack of crowd noise, when I saw my teammates, I realized I was one step closer toward winning the Lombardi Trophy. At that point my blood started to boil. I didn't need crowd noise. The place might as well have been empty. We were sooooo jacked up for warm-ups, our coaches told us to calm down because they didn't want us to burn out hours before game time. My heart raced as if I'd just run eight 100-yard sprints in a row.

We were flying around, jumping up and down and slapping our guys. I told myself every couple of minutes to slow down. I was out of breath before the halfway point in warmups. If you had hooked me up to a heart monitor stress test, a doctor probably would have told me to get off the treadmill.

Of all the luminaries lining both sidelines and each end zone, I didn't recognize anybody. I've since read about celebrities like Britney Spears and Justin Timberlake being there and legendary football players lining the field, but the only person my eyes stopped on was Mr. Charles. Ray Charles! I couldn't believe it. He was there to see me, to see us! (Yeah, I know, he couldn't actually see us since he's blind.) I kept thinking, "Okay, this thing just got a whole lot more insane."

By the time we finished our normal stretching routine, I was completely drained. I'd become exhausted as if I'd already played three quarters. Back in the locker room, even resting became exhausting.

We had to wait nearly an hour between the time we left the field for warm-ups to the time all the pageantry was done. Let's start this damn game already! Your body knows what time it has to be ready. On Wednesday and Thursday my body knows it's okay if I can't walk. It starts loosening up on

Friday and by Saturday I step it up even more. On Sunday your body gets used to a certain rhythm. That's why so many Super Bowls start off sloppy. We're all out of the rhythm on a day when tensions run so much higher than normal.

A professional athlete's life is all about following routine and structure. Our minds and our bodies adjust to it, but this game went against everything we were trained to do.

I'm used to a quick time frame and a set amount of time between warm-ups and introductions, then usually a ten-minute break for last-minute touches and the coach's speech. But this game had three times the wait. The anxiety started to get guys tight again. Our muscles went cold. Guys were strewn about the locker room trying to keep their muscles loose and warm.

It's about this time I noticed the men looking around at other guys to see how each of us were reacting. I remember thinking to myself, "This game is huge, but you better fake it and put on a good act like it's no big deal." I had to set an example.

I now see why New England won all those Super Bowls in their recent run. When you know what to expect and how to remain calm, that's a huge advantage over those of us who don't know any better than to burn ourselves out.

Former Steelers running back Jerome Bettis told me that before the Steelers Super Bowl, Patriots head coach Bill Belichick, who was working the game for ABC, told him in pregame to calm down and take it real easy in the warm-ups and start firing when he came out on the field for introductions. Great advice. Gee, where were you when I needed you, Bill?

As we left the locker room one last time, we walked through the tunnel and I was too juiced up at this point to hear anything except the loud thunder of my own heart pounding. I felt the pulsating surge in different pressure points throughout my body. They all banged the drum together, in unison, in conjunction with the crowd's chants outside. It was so loud I wondered if my other teammates could hear it, too. My mouth grew dry to the point where I felt I was going to choke.

I didn't feel an ounce of pain. I felt unstoppable, like I could outlift every one of those guys on an ESPN strongman contest. "I am one invincible ass-kicking machine!" I felt like ten guys could try to stop me and I'd still get to Trent Dilfer all night long.

As I ran out of the tunnel for my grand introduction, I wish I could tell you I had some amazing premonition or the most euphoric feeling of my life. But my thoughts weren't even close to that. You know what was coursing through my mind? "Please don't trip, whatever you do, don't trip running out onto that field in front of the world. Do not make a fool of yourself." I thought that during my first NFL game, too, but no other time before or since.

When I got to the rest of my team without tripping and making a fool of myself, we were jumping around. I don't know how the human body can exert this much energy twice in one hour and still be fresh for a three-plus-hour battle. But we were.

After Ray Charles finished his rendition of "America the Beautiful" and the national anthem was proudly sung, somebody standing next to me nudged me to look up at the Jumbo-Tron and a black dot in the distance. The dot grew closer and closer, larger and larger, until finally a Stealth bomber silently hovered over our stadium. It was the most massive machine I've ever seen, yet it flew under cover of complete silence. The crowd went wild and every single piece of hair on my body fired to attention. My goose bumps had goose bumps. It was the most majestic thing I have ever seen in my

life. Those tax dollars were well spent. To grow up an army brat and then see a military machine like that left me breathless.

As the game grew closer, it was time for the coin toss. The former Giants/Jets/Patriots/Cowboys head coach, Bill Parcells, and the former Giants great O. J. Anderson were part of the coin toss. I'll always remember Parcells giving us a look like, "Now's the time to pull your nuts up. This is it, let's freaking go!"

I looked at Jessie Armstead and he was in all his glory, but then I turned and looked at our quarterback, Kerry Collins, and I said to myself, "Please, please don't be as nervous as you look." He looked as scared as I've ever seen the man and, boy, was I hoping he would snap out of it.

I honestly couldn't tell you if he did or didn't, because that was the last thing I remember from my grand Super Bowl experience.

When I walked off the field after the coin toss, my entire memory grew hazy. I stepped onto the sideline as we prepared for the opening kickoff and my memories pretty much end there. I don't recall the kickoff. I have no idea who even kicked off. It all stopped there for me.

How much does that stink?

I remember three things from the actual game, two of them from the same play. I pressured Dilfer into unloading too soon and he was picked off by Armstead for what would have been an interception returned for a touchdown. The officials screwed up and called it back. It was the worst call in Super Bowl history. (But that's for another day.) I remember Jessie's run, watching him from the ground and I remember laying there looking at Dilfer's face because I think I hurt him on the play.

I don't actually remember hitting Dilfer, just the expression on his face when we were on the ground. I don't remember Jessie grabbing the pick, only what he looked like running for the end zone.

The other thing I remember was pretty funny. Our middle linebacker Micheal Barrow and their star running back Jamal Lewis were literally trying to kill each other the whole night. I've never seen two guys try to hurt each other like these two guys on every single play of a game. At one point there was a pile and Barrow lost his mind and began choking the Ravens runner.

A bunch of us jumped on Barrow to release the man's throat. "Let him go, Micheal. Let him go. Don't get kicked out of this one!" Barrow is actually a very religious man. When we pulled him off Lewis and yelled at him to calm down, Barrow barked back, "He cursed at me and I'm going to choke the devil out of that man." He yelled in a way that would made any evangelical preacher proud.

A Super Bowl becomes so surreal, it's like you're two different selves playing. One self, the physical part, is out there going through the motions and moves you've been trained to make. Your other self, the mental half, stands on the sideline watching the physical part play. It was the weirdest feeling of my career.

I've heard other players say it becomes just another game after the first series or after the first quarter. But for me, it never became a regular game. I can remember damn near every play of my career. You tell me about a play and I'll remember it. You can show me any play of my career on film and I'll remember the call, the situation and anything funny or odd that happened on the play. This game? I don't remember a single play, only a couple of aftermaths of plays. I was in the Super Bowl Twilight Zone.

I've even gone back to watch it on video and it still

doesn't ring much of a bell. I've grown to resent it to the point that over the years I get angrier and angrier that my own psyche robbed me of a whole game that should have been a memory for the ages. Instead, it's all a big, blank hole in an exhausting day.

After the game, I felt relief more than any other emotion. Anger over losing didn't creep in until a couple of weeks later. That night, I was spent. I walked out to the team bus and did something I'd never done in my life—I lit up a cigar. I had never smoked one before that night, but I stood there and I just looked at my guys and how proud I was to have made it this far with my family of gladiators. It was the most relaxed I had been all year. It was finally over even if the results weren't what I wanted.

As Super Sunday 2007 rolled to a close, I began thinking about Urlacher and Peyton and all the players. How many of those guys won't remember a thing about today's battle? I wonder if it's happened to anybody else. I'll probably never ask.

I have tried to dig deep to uncover what caused this mental block. I've never discussed it before writing this, because it's caused me much bitterness. Nothing jogs my memory. I don't think I've blocked it out because we lost, because during the game, I couldn't have foreseen the outcome. I don't think it overwhelmed me, either, because early on I felt the same feelings I feel in other games. Ready to win.

But this game was definitely different. This game short-circuited my memory bank and stripped me. How could I have taken all those injections, sat through all those meetings, endured all those injuries and dealt with all the crap if I couldn't even remember arriving at my lifelong goal?

Fourteen years since I first stepped onto that field, I've endured injuries, fights, wives, money scammers, head coach

after head coach after head coach, injections, pills and too many teammates to remember. All for the chance to get to that big game.

I've laid down so much blood out there, I can't bend down and touch my toes four of the seven days in the week. All I ask is the chance at a memory or two from the game of games. I'd give back the ring, I'd spit-shine the trophy every single day if I could have walked away from it all with a title and memories from that one day.

Unless our team finds destiny somehow in 2007, it won't happen for me again. Was it all worth it? Is a lifetime of pain worth it? Is a lifetime of internal scars that I fear will cause lifelong pain worth it?

I've had a record-breaking quarterback sack of Brett Favre that the world viewed as a farce, three head coaches, a lot of injuries and a heck of a lot of days when I made a quarterback's life an absolute misery.

I'll forever cherish the relationships I've made over the last fourteen years. I'll love my memories of the practical jokes, the fights, the hazing and the locker rooms where I have lived, eaten, breathed and hurt.

If somebody came to me fifteen years ago and said, "I'm going to make you a star player, but in ten years you won't be able to get out of bed pain-free, your fingers will dislocate on a weekly basis and in about twenty-five years you may walk with a permanent limp," would I still do it?

I ask myself that question all the time. Was it all worth it?

Are you crazy? You're damn right it was!

Acknowledgments

I would like to thank all the players and all the coaches that I've come into contact with over my career. Without your dedication, craziness and camaraderie this book would never have happened. Thanks to all the fans for both the cheers and the boos, the thumbs-up and the middle fingers. You have truly inspired me to always play my best and to never disappoint you. This book was written for you.

I would like to thank Scott Waxman and and Byrd Leavell at the Waxman Agency and Bill Shinker, Brett Valley and Patrick Mulligan at Gotham Books. Thanks to Keith and Ken Zimmerman for their work on the book. I would like to thank Maury Gosfrand and my friend Jay Glazer. Without you, Jay, this wouldn't even have been a possibility.

Thanks to my brothers and sisters: Sandra Strahan, Debra Strahan, Gene Jr., Chris Strahan and Victor Strahan. Thanks to my agents Tony Agnone, Rich Rosa and Eddie Johnson. Thanks to my brothers-from-another-mother Ian and Dana

Smith. Thanks to Rich Salgado and John Laffel for helping make this happen. Thanks to Gene Wolfson, Harvey Sanders, Kenneth Cole and Peter Hochfelder and to all my friends that have inspired me to be my best on and off the field.
—Michael Strahan

I'd love to acknowledge a small special group. I've got a horrible case of ADD, in fact I've already forgotten what I'm doing. . . . Oh yeah, thanking people. My mom Irene, Dad Ed, and brother Tg and his lovely wife and kids Julie, Max and Nathan for always reminding me of something that I forgot because of the ADD. To Michelle and Samuel for laughing at Michael and me fighting worse than most enemies and appreciating the entertainment value of two idiots and the things they say. To my friends who let me bounce all my ideas off of them, such as Rick Jaffe, George Greenberg, Alex Marvez, John Mullin, Scott Smith, and of course my most trusted advisor, agent and friend, Maury Gostfrand. To my main man at Fox Sports Radio Andrew Ashwood, who while I was worrying about titles for chapters was trying to kick the living crap out of cancer. "Yeah, babe!" To all the people at Gotham and Byrd and Scott who helped from the start. To all my friends in the NFL who provided stories for this book and confirmed some of the funnier ones that make this book what it is. Finally, to my big gap-toothed friend Michael who I've lived through so much with.

I want to thank my loving and wonderful wife Michelle, and my son Samuel, the best son in the world. I want to thank my best friend Adonai for never letting me feel alone. Jay Leno said it best: "With hurricanes, tornados, fires out of control, mud slides, flooding, severe thunderstorms tearing up the country from one end to another, and with the threat of bird flu and terrorist attacks, are we sure this is a good time to take God out of the Pledge of Allegiance?" Thank you God for making me feel like you created the world just for me, yet at the same time granting me the wisdom to appreciate I am nothing more than dust and bones.

 —Jay Glazer

Index

Note: Search for team names under their cities or states.

Warner, Kurt, 70, 138
Washington Redskins, 52, 81, 95–97,
    159–74
Way, Charles, 66
Westbrook, Brian, 91–92, 101, 214
Wheatley, Tyrone, 142
wideouts, 154
Williams, Brian, 152
Williams, Darrent, 81
Williams, Erik, 117, 155, 156, 163
Williams, Roy, 94
Williams, Shaun "Left Jab," 42–43
windpipe, punches to, 156
winning, 100–101, 130, 159
Wisniewski, Steve, 155, 163
wives of players, 79. *See also* Strahan,
    Jean

Wolf cousins, 256–57
women, 95, 96, 248–50
workouts, 191
work week, 189–212
    Monday, 191–94
    Wednesday, 195–208
    Thursday, 208–9
    Friday, 211
    Saturday, 87–88, 140–42, 211, 285–
        86
    See also meetings *and other
        specific tasks*
wrist injuries, 121

Yeganek, Al, 48
Young, Bryant, 123
Young, Vince, 127, 145